The Strike
in the
American Novel

by

FAY M. BLAKE

The Scarecrow Press, Inc.
Metuchen, N.J.   1972

Library of Congress Cataloging in Publication Data

Blake, Fay M   1920-
    The strike in the American novel.

    Bibliography: p.
    1. American fiction--History and criticism.
2. Strikes and lockouts in literature. 3. Labor and
laboring classes--U. S. I. Title.
PS374.S8B6   813'.03   72-623
ISBN 0-8108-0481-6

CONTENTS

INTRODUCTION

This book is an attempt to trace chronologically the use American novelists have made of the strike. I have used a rather limited definition of the strike: a work stoppage resulting from disagreement between employer and employees. Farmers' strikes, student strikes, purely political strikes in American novels have not been considered, but the strikes of sharecroppers, dispossessed landless farmers and migrant farm laborers are included, since the relationship of a landless farmer to the owner of the land is directly analogous to that of the factory worker and the owner of the factory. The worker and the farmer without land of his own both have only their labor with which to bargain and both withhold that labor when they strike.

The strikes in these novels are often based on actual events so without any illusions about being a historian, I found it necessary to pay some attention to what happened in a few of the more dramatic and significant strikes American workers have fought. The historical background became even more important when I tried to discover why some periods produced so many more novels that included strikes than others. It was evident that none of the novels could be completely divorced from the contemporary economic scene within which it was created. When great strikes were actually being waged, when economic issues were exorcising masses of the population, more novelists were writing about strikes. In calmer, transitional periods the

1

number of strikes in the novels tapered off.   For each period I have tried at least to indicate what was happening on
the labor scene.

How the novelist handled the strike depended in part
on how contemporary society regarded the strike and in part
on his own insight and skill.   The better the novelist the
less influenced he was by the attitudes of most of his contemporaries.   But most of the novelists who used strikes in
their novels were amateurs or hacks or apprentices in their
trade, and it is easy to trace the effect of their particular
historical period on most of the novelists considered in this
book.

The strike itself is often the least revealing aspect
of the novel.   I was not especially concerned with how accurately the novelist described a strike, although I was interested in the attitudes which his inaccuracies revealed.
When the novelist uses a strike, he is often getting out of
his system his attitudes towards workers, towards poverty,
towards individualism, towards collectivism, towards minority groups.   Sometimes he just wants to get off his chest
some purely personal prejudices, and many of the strikes
in these novels are purely vehicles for a great deal of down-
right malice and spite.   Many of the novelists who use
strikes are not even up to this low level of intellectual en-
deavor.   They sat down to write a novel, they needed a
device to show off the hero's courage, so they set him in
the midst of a strike, on one side or the other, and let him
fight his way out.   Not every novelist who uses a strike
gives a damn about strikes.   But American attitudes toward
workers, poverty and individualism have changed significantly
over the past century or so, and it was these changes that
I tried to track down in the novels.

Before the Civil War it is hard to find any novels at all that deal with working class life. A few take a passing look at life in the city; a few portray the life of the poor (the dregs of society in preference to honest-to-goodness workers); a few deal with New England mill towns, but without finding it necessary to picture life within the mills. Beginning about 1870 a number of novels include strikes as part of the plot. The novelists are not at all interested in either accuracy or authenticity. They need a violent clash between two contending forces. Never mind that all but a handful of real strikes were settled amicably. All the fictional strikes are violent. Never mind that most of the real strikes were won. All the fictional strikes are lost.

It was not until almost the turn of the century that a few professional novelists began to write about strikes both seriously and skillfully. Most of them still looked at workers through middle class eyes but they were beginning to move away from the earlier conviction that poverty was a divine punishment and that workers had only themselves to blame for their downtrodden lot. World War I shattered a great many illusions. Postwar novels began to reflect a growing cynicism and doubt, and novels began to use the strike as a symbol not of the workers' failure to rise but of American society's failure to give everyone an equal opportunity to rise. The unprecedented Depression of the 1930's put the finishing touches to the downfall of the American Dream. Strikes become not only frequent in the novels of the Thirties, but endemic. And most of the strikes are examples to prove that American society has broken down and that a thorough, cleansing revolution is just around the corner. There even develops a new genre, the "strike novel," in which the strike is not a part of the novel--it is the novel, and it foreshadows a new and better world in the making.

Chapter 1

WORKERS AND THE POOR: BEFORE 1870

The American novelist before the Civil War saw his
country as a rural or small town society in which most
people worked as self-employed, relatively independent
farmers or shopkeepers or professionals.   He was right.
Most people did.   But the novelist was overlooking some
important changes.   The factories of New England and the
mines of Pennsylvania were slowly but inexorably beginning
to absorb thousands of Americans, and the city was beginning to swallow the villages and small towns of America.
Thousands of Americans, forced into mills from unproductive
farms, found their lives, for the first time, governed not
by the seasonal rhythms of rural life but by factory bells.
Native Americans made their first, often abrasive, contacts
with immigrants driven by hunger from their own countries
into the mines and mills of America.   The independent
farmer or merchant was becoming a "hand," working for
a wage and owning nothing.   Factory life brought new kinds
of discontent, and industrial strikes soon appeared.   (The
earliest recorded strike broke out in 1775 when New York
City printers struck for a higher wage and won).

The theories of Fourier, Saint Simon and Owens began to filter into America early in the nineteenth century,
and experiments like Brook Farm and New Harmony re-
flected a growing concern with the effects of industrialization and with socialist ideas.   To the novelists, however,

4

these new social and economic developments were of distant
concern.   For almost a century after the first strike, they
made no literary use of the strike.   Even the urban industrial setting was generally ignored in the American novel
before 1870.

Beginning in the 1840's, however, a small group of
novelists found the city--especially turbulent, restless New
York--an exciting new background for their novels.   The
quickening interest in urban life was, more or less, con-
centrated on the poverty to be found in the city.   Poverty
was, of course, nothing new.   There had always been plenty
of poor people in America, both in the cities and in the
countryside, but the theme of poverty was a new one for
the American novelist.   The appalling economic crisis of
1837 probably helped to reveal more nakedly the human
effects of poverty, but the relatively few and minor novelists
who were beginning to exploit urban poverty had other purposes in mind.   They were looking to the cash value of
either the sentimental or the sensational aspects of poverty,
and urban poverty, they found, could be described more
dramatically and more picturesquely than the humdrum deprivations in the villages or on the farms.   The novelists
were intent on either wringing every last sentimental tear
out of their readers or terrifying and shocking them with
sensation piled on sensation as they burrowed their way in
and out of the hovels, alleys and ginmills of New York's
notorious Five Points.

Without exception, the plots of Augustine Duzanne's
The Tenant-House (1860), George Lippard's New York: Its
Upper Ten and Lower Million (1854) and Elizabeth Smith's
The Newsboy (1854) are melodramatic and sensational.   Kid-
napings, murders, long-lost children and long-kept secrets,

suicides and tearful death-bed scenes abound.   Working-class
life is really not explored in most of these urban novels.
The authors tend to deal more lovingly with the criminal or
"lumpen" element than with people who work for a living.
Fallen women, forgers, hopeless drunkards, bankrupt ex-
gentlemen--not factory hands or draymen or carpenters--
throng their closely printed pages.   The reason is clear.
It is, of course, much more difficult to sustain readers'
interest in a factory hand drudging away at dull routine
tasks for twelve or fourteen hours a day than in the high
jinks of forgers or kidnappers or even in the stinking and
picturesque rags of beggars, rag-pickers, chimney sweeps
or crossing-sweepers who flit through several of these novels.
The closest we ever approach the actual world of work is
through flickering glimpses of New York's colorful street-
huckster population: newsboys shouting an extra or a new
installment of a popular serial, apple and chestnut vendors,
matchsellers, the yeast-girl, the ice-man, the milk-man--
all cry their wares through the streets or in the market-
place.

          The one actual working type most of the novelists of
poverty do depict is the seamstress--underpaid, underfed and
overworked.   Underpaid she certainly was.   During the 1820's
the War Department was paying twelve and a half cents a
shirt, which meant in those pre-machine days a weekly wage
just about equal to what the Provident Society gave its clients
as charity.   Some of the novelists imply, without ever saying so, that seamstresses eked out a living as part-time
prostitutes, and they probably reflect what was a reality.
Many of the fictional seamstresses die young of tuberculosis--
also a reality.   Occasionally, the novelist shows his seamstress working with sister-drudges in a shop, but more

usually in this period of cottage industry she picks up the
garments, sews through a fourteen- or fifteen-hour day,
then returns the finished articles only to be cheated ruth-
lessly by her storekeeper employer.

In the 1850's a new type of novel makes its first
appearance. The novelist is concerned with people who
work for a living and occasionally shows them at work.
Novels like Sylvester Judd's Richard Edney and the Governor's Family (1850), Day Kellogg Lee's The Master Builder;
or, Life at a Trade (1853) and Rebecca Harding Davis's
Margret Howth. A Story of Today (1862) actually attempt
to show the lives of those who work with their hands. Judd's
worker-hero, Richard Edney, begins his adventures as a
sawmill operator working nine hours a night. His munifi-
cent pay is eighteen dollars a month. Richard is both valiant
and pious. He attends church, teaches Sunday School and
resists all temptation to drink. Eventually he rescues the
Governor's daughter when her horse runs off with her sleigh,
and he ends up as the rich and respected owner of the sawmill and the Governor's son-in-law. Day Kellogg Lee follows his hero, Arthur Sumner, through his apprenticeship as
a carpenter to a successful self-sufficiency as a carpenter,
builder and architect. The novelist follows an old tradition
of the romance, however, in which the hero must not stem
from lowly origins. He cannot have Arthur an authentic
workingman so he contrives to reveal him as the long-lost
son of a well-to-do businessman. Both Judd and Lee have
taken the trouble to find out a little about life in a sawmill
or a carpenter's shop and give us some information about
the techniques, work patterns, clothes, even the special jargon of their heroes' trades. Both novelists also contrast
the sturdy independence and solid worth of their working

heroes with the laziness, foppishness and flippancy of young
men of the merchant and professional classes.   The novelists
are quite frankly doing a missionary job.   They warn young
men away from the fame, quick riches and excitement beginning to become temptingly evident in the world of stock-
manipulation, and urge them instead to seek the solid rewards to be found in an industrious life.

   In Richard Edney we can find one of the first hints
that all is not serene in the relationships between employer
and workmen:

> 'They would put on the screw,' said Mr. Merlew:
> 'they would make nigger-wheels of us, if they could,
> and keep us always at it; they would like to see us
> saw-dust under their feet.'[1]

The author is quick to let us know, however, that Merlew
drinks, so we needn't pay much attention to what he has to
say.   For us, more than a century later, the worker Merlew's words foreshadow the literary future.

   The most somber and unusual work in this small
group of novels depicting factory life is Margret Howth by
Rebecca Harding Davis.   In a story printed anonymously in
The Atlantic Monthly in 1861 the author had already revealed
her deep sympathy for the factory hand.   Her picture, in
"Life in the Iron Mills," of the overworked drudges who
drag out their miserable brief existences in the mills is in
startling contrast to the cheerful, generally optimistic tone
of other contemporary fiction handling the factory theme.
In Margret Howth she sets her scene in an Indiana woolen
mill.   Although her language is rather high-flown and her
characters and incidents overdrawn, she probes the ruthless
ambition of the millowner and the degradation of the millworkers' lives.   Her mill is no bright, sunny beehive of

industry.

> Overhead the ceiling looked like a heavy maze of
> iron cylinders and black swinging bars and wheels,
> all in swift, ponderous motion. It was enough to
> make a brain dizzy with the clanging thunder of the
> engines, the whizzing spindles of red and yellow,
> and the hot daylight glaring over all. The looms
> were watched by women, most of them bold, taw-
> dry girls of fifteen or sixteen, or lean-jawed wom-
> en from the hills, wives of the coal-diggers. There
> was a breathless odour of copperas. [2]

Mrs. Davis' ambiguous attitude toward the working class is
epitomized in Lois Yare, the ugly mulatto girl, a mixture of
black and white, good and evil, nobility and degradation.
Lois remembers the years in the mill with horror, where
from the age of seven she worked, becoming, as she says,
"part o' th' engines, somehow. " The author veers between
sympathy for Lois's cruelly difficult life and revulsion for
the crippled ignorant peddler girl.

There is another small group of novels which deals
specifically with the girls working in the textile mills of
Lowell, Massachusetts. The earliest is Ariel Ivers Cummings' The Factory Girl: or Gardez la Coeur, published in
1847, and followed by Norton: Lights and Shades of a Factory Village: a Tale of Lowell (1849) by the pseudonymous
"Argus, " Day Kellogg Lee's Merrimack: or, Life at the
Loom (1854), Martha W. Tyler's A Book without a Title:
or Thrilling Events in the Life of Mira Dana (1855) and
Madge: or, Night and Morning (1863) by "H. G. H. " (Hannah
Elizabeth Bradbury Godwin Talcott). By the 1850's there
were thirty textile mills around Lowell, employing hundreds
of girls and women. They worked twelve to fourteen hours
a day for one to three dollars a week, and most of them
lived in boarding houses in or near Lowell. Distinguished
visitors to Lowell (Charles Dickens and Harriet Martineau

among them) commented favorably on the mills and paid high
tribute to The Lowell Offering, a periodical written by the
mill girls themselves. Their stories and essays rarely
dwell on the work in the mills. They describe idyllic
scenes in nature, preach pious little sermons or tell whole-
some little stories in which everything ends happily. The
contributors to The Lowell Offering were not professional
writers. The wonder is that after twelve hours in the mills
they could produce the Offering at all. But they were imitating as best they could the professionals of their day, to
whom life inside the mills was of very little interest. Once
in a while the determined cheerfulness of a tale breaks down
and we get a shadowy glimpse of the girls' real lives---the
noise, the hurried tempo, the constant clang of bells and
whirr of machinery, the inadequate food in the boarding-
houses, the crippling accidents, the incessant watchfulness
of the overseers.

Most of the novels about Lowell have many points of
similarity. All of them tell the stories of robust young
country girls who come to Lowell and its textile mills either
to support themselves or to help support their families struggling on some rocky New England farm. All the girls come
to the mill for a temporary stay and confidently await the
time when marriage, improved family fortunes or, in the
case of the heroine of Madge, a teaching job, will release
them from the mill. In none of the stories does the reader
ever get the chance to set foot inside the mill itself. All
the novels stress the advantages to be gained from a few
years' work in the factory. The authors emphasize the physical discipline imposed by the mill, a discipline which will
prepare the girls for their real role as hard-working wives
and mothers. The mill will also serve to teach American

women independence. Not impudence, mind you, or "running
into any senseless fashions or mannish ways," as Day Kellogg
Lee warns, but a taste of the independent and progressive
spirit characteristic of young America.

Not that working in the mills was without its dangers.
The novelists warn that rich seducers lurk about Lowell, intent upon ruining the indolent, the naive and the luxury-mind-
ed. Demon Rum and card-playing can be the first steps on
a road leading straight to perdition. Worst of all, and never
to be talked about except in discreetly veiled language, is the
looming possibility of a sexual adventure followed inevitably
by an early death.

Here and there the author hints dimly that all is not
paradise inside the factory walls. In Mrs. Talcott's novel,
Madge, the heroine's health finally breaks down irretrievably.
Day Kellogg Lee admits, in Merrimack, that wages are very
low, although he insists that suffering has its rewards, too,
even the half-starvation of the Lowell boarding-houses. Mill
operatives have difficulty finding board with respectable families, Mrs. Talcott admits, and Lee concedes that there is
really not much opportunity for the mill worker to develop
her social, intellectual or domestic talents. But, on the
whole, the novels picture a cheerful society of healthy active
girls working hard for three or four years and then leaving
the mill forever for their own prosperous firesides.

In only one novel is there direct evidence of drastic
paycuts and direct counteraction by the mill girls. Mrs.
Martha Tyler's A Book without a Title: or Thrilling Events
in the Life of Mira Dana (1855) is incredibly badly written.
The melodramatic succession of shipwrecks, illnesses and
secret machinations are only pegs on which Mrs. Tyler
hangs some of her pet grievances, especially the tribulations

of neglected wives. Her novel has only one distinction. It is the first--by a decade and a half--to make use of a "turn-out. " Historically, the author lags a whole generation behind reality. The first strike in Lowell took place in 1834, and even before that (in 1828) the millworkers of Dover, New Hampshire, walked off their jobs--or "turned out. " As a literary curiosity, however, Mrs. Tyler's novel is unique. Hers is the earliest novel to describe a strike and hers is the only heroine to lead the "tramping committee" (picket line) of four thousand strikers. Mira Dana obtains legal and religious advice for the girls, braves the paymaster in order to collect money due them, and unites them in a determination never to return to work in the mill.

Mrs. Tyler is not really very much concerned with the sociological implications of her "turn-out. " She has grasped at the strike as a literary device which will reveal the stalwart virtues of her heroine (who is, quite obviously, Mrs. Tyler herself). Instead of telling us that Mira Dana is courageous, spunky, intelligent and likeable, she shows her heroine in action. It is too bad that such an admirable technique goes so badly astray, but Mrs. Tyler's deplorable lack of talent and her crotchety insistence on grinding some personal axes turn A Book without a Title into a novel without merit.

Most of these early novelists use their novels for more than merely telling a story. They want to preach a sermon, teach a moral, instill a lesson. The most insistent drumming is on the temperance theme. Much of the wretched poverty in these novels is attributed to the sodden heads of families who squander on drink what belongs to the neglected wife and starving children. "'Mother, it is all over now, ' said Susan Miller, as she descended from the chamber where

her father had just died of delirium tremens, "[3] begins one
engaging tale in The Lowell Offering. If drink wasn't leading to starvation and ruin, it was leading to seduction and
ruin. Even a sip of wine with a stranger could be the beginning of the end for an unwary or headstrong girl.

When the authors are not thumping the tub for temperance, it is for thrift or chastity or hard work, or for piety
or any of the other Puritan virtues. Young girls are cau-
tioned in heavily veiled phrases to avoid the blandishments
of slick city seducers; young married couples are warned
against buying anything without cash in hand; wives are urged
to submit patiently to their husbands. It is not difficult to
imagine why so much moralizing found its way into the nineteenth century American novel. Many of the authors were
actually clergymen or the wives of clergymen. Their preaching is professional stock-in-trade, so to speak. Those novelists who are not themselves in the business of preaching are
often pious gentlewomen, scribbling to support themselves
genteelly, and, like many of the middle class of the period,
deeply influenced by religion, Calvinist Protestant religion.
Finally, there is a rather more literary (and snobbish) reason for the heavy coating of moral lecturing. Novels in the
pre-Civil War period were still regarded as somewhat infra
dig. In Hannah Talcott's Madge, for example, the young
heroine reads avidly and works feverishly to save enough
money to return to school, but she reads books of theology
or history. She is contemptuous of the frivolous novels her
lighter-minded companions cherish, and her contempt is a
measure of the author's own. When a novelist has decried
her own product, what excuse can she offer for spawning
still another novel? None--except that her story is not just
a story, but an earnest beacon lighting the path to the good

and the right.   Even that excuse is not quite good enough for
a number of these novelists.   Many of them hide behind a
shield of anonymity.

The tiny number of pre-Civil War novels dealing with
urban and factory themes gives only the merest hint of what
was happening to American society.   The strike, used only
once, is hardly on the novelists' horizon although it was already a historical reality in America.   Industrial changes in
American life were only just beginning.   To all of the South
and much of the Middle West industrial life was an alien concern.   The closest most Americans ever came to the factory
system was probably through the reading of an occasional
English novel, for in England the problems of industrialization were already embittering realities, and the English novel had begun to deal with the new economic alignments long
before.   The American novel, in the main, stayed away from
the industrial scene and its problems.

There are good historical reasons for the lag in
American fiction.   Industrialization in America began much
later than in England.   The mother country deliberately hampered industrial development in the Colonies before the Revolution, and until the 1840's American economy remained predominantly agrarian.   The novelist had little occasion to deal
with industrial themes or to experience the effects of industrialization.   His English contemporaries, on the other hand,
could hardly avoid the impact of an industrial economy.   Beginning in the eighteenth century with the Enclosure Acts,
dispossessed farmers began pouring into the slums of London
to find work.   By the middle of the nineteenth century exas-
perated, nearly starving factory hands had engaged in many
bloody strikes which some novelists (Mrs. Gaskell, Mrs.
Trollope, Charles Dickens, for example) had witnessed

personally.

The American literary lag is also related to the Puritan heritage of the young nation. Puritan theology impressed on American minds the conviction that failure was a God-given condition, a punishment for sin. The good man, the only kind who is real material for the hero of a novel in these early days, would either have become a successful entrepreneur or would have sought his fortune at sea or on the western frontier. Those who led lives miserable enough to induce them to strike were hardly suitable novelistic material.

In addition, the long literary tradition of the romance tended generally to limit the American novelist to the use of characters from the lower economic classes as comic figures, and the literary tradition of imitating older European models hampered experimentation among American novelists. In this period they trailed at least a generation behind the novelists of England. American novelists, suffering from an inferiority complex common to all colonials, shied away from imitating the avant garde among their English contemporaries. Well established themes, characters, even moral stances were safer models. They needed both personal experience with industrial society and the confidence to strike out on their own experimentally before they could deal competently with urban industrial problems in their novels.

In very small number and with uniformly dismal lack of skill a few American novelists were making their first tentative experiments in the use of a new milieu. Those who chose the city as their locale were not really interested in the industrial scene. Their concern lay in an almost prurient obsession with urban degradation. They are not trying to explore man and his human response to his daily environ-

ment.   They want to exhibit man sunk to his lowest depths.
The novelists of the poor are striving to elicit that delicious
shudder of horror--and triumph--everyone secretly feels
when he is confident of his own security and superiority, the
same titillation a shocking newspaper headline gives us at
our breakfast-tables.   Essentially underlying the novelists'
explorations into urban poverty is the unspoken conviction
that poverty is a punishment.   Good people are divinely rewarded, if not with wealth, at least with a decent competency.
And they show both their goodness and their gratitude by
their willingness to sympathize with the less fortunate.

Both the novelists of poverty and the smaller number
of novelists who used the factory as a background were influenced by Calvinist theology.   The difference between them
lies in the classes they chose to portray.   The novelists of
the poor guide us through a hell populated by the damned.
The poor cannot possibly be destined for salvation so the
novelists can indulge in explicit scenes of drunken violence,
disease-ravaged deathbeds and the whimpering of starving
children.   The heroines of the Lowell novels, on the other
hand, are good girls who are intended to find their way to
Providence.   They are not factory-workers; they work in
factories only temporarily, and invariably marry into the
middle class.   As members of the elect, born to be saved,
they can voluntarily work and live with the unfortunate for
a brief time before they ascend to their rightful places in
society.   While they work at Lowell, they secure their salvation by good works.   They comfort the poor and the afflict-
ed, and set them on the road to piety.   But the heroines
themselves are never seen actually at work in the mill.
That kind of degradation is not for the elect.   It is worth
noting that none of these Lowell graduates moves up the

social ladder by her unaided efforts alone. A generous doctor or a sympathetic lawyer or a long-lost parent ultimately
frees Cinderella from her bondage, but while she remains
in Lowell, she cannot be shown as sullied by the dirt of the
mill.

None of the novelists in this group is an able enough
craftsman or profound enough thinker to portray recognizable
human beings, but, all unknowingly, these writers are American literary pioneers, the first to deal with a setting new to
American fiction.

Notes

1. Sylvester Judd, Richard Edney and the Governor's Fami-
       ly (Boston: Phillips, Sampson and Co. , 1850), p. 58.

2. Rebecca Harding Davis, Margret Howth. A Story of
       To-Day (Boston: Ticknor and Fields, 1862), p. 116.

3. Mind amongst the Spindles: a Selection from "The Lowell
       Offering" (London: Charles Knight and Co. , 1845), p.
       92.

Chapter 2

BRUTE FORCE: 1870-1895

With the end of the Civil War the victorious industrialists of the North were free to proceed full-blast with the
development of industry, commerce, communication and
transport. During the twenty-five years between 1870 and
1895 they moved ahead rapidly, often brilliantly and, even
more often, corruptly, toward the full exploitation of the
continental resources of the United States. In New England
an intricate industrial complex developed speedily. In the
West the discovery of gold and silver was feverishly exploited. East and West were linked by the first transcontinental
railroad, a saga which included Federal and State grants of
thousands of acres of public land to private interests, wanton
destruction of wildlife and ruthless extermination of the Indian. Frantic railroad stock manipulation, with the active
connivance of Senators, Congressmen and a Vice President,
produced dividends as high as 340%. It also produced major
economic panics and depressions in 1873 and again in 1882.
Such naked greed, corruption and brutality also precipitated
industrial unrest. Between 1880 and 1887 alone, the Commissioner of Labor reported an incredible fifteen thousand
strikes. [1] During the period there were four blockbuster
strikes which shook the country out of any lingering agrarian
nostalgia.

The Railroad Strike of 1877 was the first national
strike in America's history. It began in Martinsburg, West

Virginia, in protest against a series of wage cuts, and
spread quickly to Pennsylvania, New York, Chicago, St.
Louis, and even as far as San Francisco (where the strike
took the ugly form of a race riot against the Chinese). For
the first time in United States labor history the Federal
troops were called out against the strikers.

The 1886 Haymarket affair in Chicago began with a
strike at the McCormick Harvester plant in support of the
growing demand for an eight-hour working day. It ended
with the execution of four anarchists accused of complicity
in a bomb-throwing. The strike culminated in the disintegration of the Knights of Labor, whose president, Terence
Powderly, opposed the eight-hour movement. The newly organized American Federation of Labor, which supported the
demonstrators (but not the anarchists), emerged as the new
spokesman for organized labor.

In 1892 the Carnegie Steel Company locked out strikers at Homestead in an attempt to destroy the Amalgamated
Association of Iron and Steel Workers. During the strike
the company employed three hundred armed Pinkerton agents
to protect strikebreakers. The resulting clash has left an
unsavory reputation for the Pinkertons which still persists in
the ranks of organized labor.

Finally, in 1894 the Pullman strike precipitated violence once more. George Pullman adamantly refused to arbitrate even after President McKinley dispatched his brother
as a mediator. The strike resulted in the disintegration of
the American Railway Union founded by Eugene V. Debs a
year earlier.

The turmoil of the post-Civil War era necessarily left
some indelible impressions on the intellectuals of the country,
impressions and convictions which were eventually mirrored

in many of the novels of the time. The young labor movement was widely regarded with fear and suspicion. The newly
reunited nation, just recovering from a bitter and destructive
civil war, seemed to some to be heading toward still another
"irrepressible conflict, " and organized labor appeared to be
an unsettling agent, stirring up dissension where peace was
so desperately desired. In novels like Abigail Roe's Free,
Yet Forging Their Own Chains (1876), Thomas and Anna
Fitch's Better Days (1891) and Amanda M. Douglas' Hope
Mills (1879), characters comment on the new industrial conflicts as the beginning of another civil war. Apologists for
the ante-bellum South had already frequently drawn the analogy between the chattel slave and the wage slave. They had
persistently argued that even the most inhumane slave owner
at least protected the well-being of his slaves because he
had a cash interest in his property, while the Northern industrialist had callously and cleverly sloughed off any concern for his easily replaced "hands. "

The novels of this period which deal with strikes and
labor unrest were almost invariably written by Northerners.
The South was still absorbed in efforts to recover from the
dislocations and destruction of the war. The Northern novelists are all opposed to slavery but most of them deny any
similarity between the condition of the slave and the factory
worker. The free industrial worker, they maintain, could
attain a decent standard of living or become a factory owner
himself through hard work and perseverance. The malicious
minority who were agitating for union organization were creating conflicts where they really did not exist.

Novelists also reacted to the widespread graft, corruption and chicanery of the time. There are many denunciations of the new industrial oligarchy scattered through the

novels. But sometimes, as if in spite of the author's conscious desires, a respectful admiration for the robber barons
filters into the novels. There is a kind of envy, even if
grudging, for these masterful leaders who command obedience
not only from their workers in the mines, the factories, the
railroads and the mills but also from many who are eminent
in their own right. Corporation lawyers prepare their briefs
and plead their cases in court; literary men praise them in
the most prestigious journals of the day; legislators argue
for laws which serve the interests of financial wizards.
Thomas Denison's John Ophir (transparently based on the
personality of Jay Gould) in An Iron Crown (1879), Henry
Keenan's Aaron Grimstone in The Money-Makers (1885) and
Charles Dudley Warner's Rodney Henderson in A Little Journey in the World (1889) are all forceful men. They manipu-
late, cheat, steal--true--but they dominate the other characters in the novels shrewdly and successfully. The tribute
which the novelists pay to patently greedy, anti-social and
criminal capitalists faithfully reflects the temper of the
times. A philosophical rationale for admiring the bold buc-
caneer is inherent in Social Darwinism and Manchester Utili-
tarianism, new and heady theories rapidly accepted by many
Americans. If the whole world of Nature is a rapacious jungle of competition in which only the fittest survive, so is the
society of man. If the economic market based on the principle of laissez faire will eventually provide riches for some
and destitution for the least fit, then so be it. A financier
who succeeds in gouging millions or a sweatshop owner who
manages to pay his workers three dollars for a ninety-six-
hour work week has only exhibited his superior fitness to
function within the inexorable laws of economics. The im-
mensely popular preacher, Henry Ward Beecher, summed it

all up (and gave it divine sanction) when he said: "God has
intended the great to be great and the little to be little. "
The novelists generally acquiesced in this popular spirit,
but it is perhaps to their credit that several show a dawning uneasiness and hesitation.

By 1890 there was no longer an open frontier in the
United States, and one of the pet stereotypes of the novelist
--the valiant, forceful, self-reliant hero who makes it on his
own in a desperate struggle against Nature's rigors--was
largely an anachronism.   Not that that prevented the novelist
from continuing to use the frontier as a literary device.   On
the contrary, he kept turning almost in desperation to the
lucky gold strike, as in Thomas Denison's An Iron Crown,
the Fitches' Better Days and Mary Hallock Foote's Coeur D'
Alène (1894), or to accounts of the U. S. Cavalry cleaning
out pockets of Apaches in the West, as in Charles King's
Foes in Ambush (1893).   As a matter of fact, many novelists were still clinging nostalgically to a way of life that had
been irretrievably lost before the end of the century.

In the face of the conflicts and the frenetic tempo of
an industrialized society, many of them, even while they
were writing about factory strikes, were recalling longingly
the serenity of rural and village life.   Villages by the hundreds had ceased to exist, swallowed whole by the demand
for "hands" in the growing number of factories and mines,
but the novelists were still describing villages.   In Thomas
Bailey Aldrich's The Stillwater Tragedy (1880), for example,
the iron mills of Stillwater are in the dim background while
Aldrich lovingly describes the bucolic, paternalistic Slocum
Marble Yards.   In several of the novels a strike is crucial
to the plot but much of the action takes place on peaceful
farms or country estates far removed from the industrial

setting (in Frank L. Benedict's Miss Van Kortland, 1870, and
Robert Grant's Face to Face, 1886, for example). Novelists
are still contrasting the serenity of the countryside with the
temptations and dangers of the city. Thomas Stewart Denison's character, Arthur Wilson, in An Iron Crown, makes a
fortune in the city but finds real happiness when he settles
down in a quiet country village, and Edward King contrasts
the hectic deprived life on New York's lower East Side with
a cooperative agricultural colony in rural Connecticut in
Joseph Zalmonah (1893).

If it is not quite feasible any longer to head for the
frontier, the novelists stoutly maintain that any really superior man with drive, energy and good sense, can fight and
overcome the frontier in his own backyard. Anyone who
really wants to can become rich in his own business. "In
this country no man need go hungry or in rags, " "Every
soul of us has the privilege of bettering our condition if we
have the brain and the industry to do it, " "No door is shut
against ability, " "People are poor in this country because
they are thriftless and improvident"--self-made men in the
novels repeat many variations on this theme.

Not all businesses are equally legitimate, however.
Ironically, against the one activity in which it was still actually possible for the commoner to become a millionaire--
stock manipulation--the novelists draw the line. When a
man embarks on the Wall Street route to wealth, he necessarily sacrifices his own integrity and the happiness of those
close to him. Thomas Stewart Denison's An Iron Crown,
George Dowling's The Wreckers (1886), Harold Frederic's
The Lawton Girl (1890), Henry Keenan's The Money-Makers
and Charles Dudley Warner's A Little Journey in the World
all paint financiers as destructive, anti-social men in no un-

certain terms, although with varying degrees of literary com-
petence. Frederic's novel, one of the more interesting in
this group, shows a weak young man duped into a financial
conspiracy by two scoundrels, while Warner's, written with
a good deal of verve and credibility, describes the gradual
degradation of a moral and upright girl through her association with the unscrupulous money-making methods of her husband.

The American novelists' concern for Christianity becomes almost an obsession in the second half of the nineteenth century. Understandably so. The easy faith in virtue
rewarded and vice punished had by now been deeply shaken.
Political bosses, railroad wreckers, stock manipulators, even
strike agitators were not being struck down for their sins;
industrious, humane businessmen were going bankrupt and
patient, humble, nonstriking workers were going hungry. The
religious preaching in the novels of the period becomes more
and more strident. Some of the novels, like Charles Sheldon's The Crucifixion of Phillip Strong (1894), Agibail Roe's
Free, Yet Forging Their Own Chains and R. F. Bishop's
Camerton Slope (1893) include long verbatim sermons, but
the reader cannot help wonder whether the novelists are not
really trying to persuade themselves.

The temperance theme also continues throughout the
period. Timothy Shay Arthur's The Strike at Tivoli Mills
(1879) is really a barely disguised temperance tract. No
drinking, no strikes. But even in novels with somewhat better developed plots and characters, the authors frequently
suggest that discontented workers have only themselves to
blame. Their wages would be adequate if they didn't squander them on drink. The strikers in Frances Hodgson Burnett's Haworth's (1879) are malcontents who meet at the

"Who'd ha' thowt it" pub.   John Hay's hero, Arthur Farnham,
in The Bread-Winners (1884), recognizes among the strikers
"the laziest and most incapable workmen in town--men whose
weekly wages were habitually docked for drunkenness, late
hours, and botchy work. "[2]   Thomas Bailey Aldrich's strikers
in The Stillwater Tragedy "squander a quarter of their week's
wages at the tavern. "   The tavern, the saloon and the pub
haunt the novelists not only as the places where the poor become poorer but as the meeting-rooms where sedition is
being plotted.

One of the most influential novels of this period was
Edward Bellamy's Looking Backward, published in 1887.   It
is an important landmark for two reasons: it introduces the
theme of socialism sympathetically and it sets the pattern
for a flood of Utopian novels to come which contrast a better
world of the future with the chaotic society of the present.
Henry Everett's The People's Program (1892), Thomas and
Anna Fitch's Better Days and Archibald McCowan's Philip
Meyer's Scheme (1892) all owe a debt to Bellamy, although
one wishes they had taken as much trouble in emulating his
style as they did in imitating his theme.

Bellamy's socialism in Looking Backward is not the
Marxian variety; Das Kapital had not yet been translated into
English.   His narrator, Julian West, awakes in the year 2000
to find Boston a transformed city.   Julian's last memory before his nap begins in 1887 is of his irritation at a series of
building trades strikes which have delayed the completion of
his new house.   When he comes out of his long sleep, he
tries lamely to explain strikes to his new friends, Dr. Leete
and his daughter Edith.   Julian's explanations do not make
much sense because, like most members of the middle class,
he has only the vaguest idea of what strikes are all about.

But in any case the explanation would fail because strikes
have become inexplicable to Bostonians of the 21st century.
With the elimination of classes and class antagonisms strikes
have become obsolete.   Bellamy, like his successors and im-
itators, uses the strike as an instance of a persistent evil
which will be obliterated by socialism.

Henry Everett's book, The People's Program, also
projects us into the future, 1893, the year after the book
was published.   The hero, George Streeter, leads a walkout
of 180,000 American building trade workers.   Strikes break
out in Vienna and throughout England.   In short order, an
international general strike is in progress.   Evidently, Streeter is meant to gain international renown through his strike
leadership, but the author apparently lost the thread of his
plot because the strike suddenly drops out of sight.   Streeter
plots for the Spanish throne, leads a cavalcade of college
students, is appointed Secretary of State, and finally organizes an International Peace Congress in Rome.

In Better Days by Thomas and Anna Fitch there is
another general strike.   Lorin French, an unenlightened capitalist, is instrumental in calling out the National Guard
against the assembled strikers.   He is caught in their cross-
fire and just before he dies, recognizes his mistakes.   The
hero, David Morning, is French's heir.   French's fortune,
plus a tremendously lucky gold strike, make Morning the
richest man in the world.   He uses his fortune to establish
profit-sharing and cooperative factories.   At one point he
buys up and razes all of lower Manhattan--an intriguing idea.

Archibald McCowan's novel, Philip Meyer's Scheme,
is as childish as his pseudonym: Luke A. Hedd.   His Utopia
comes into existence in 1906.   The book describes two
strikes, one of printers and another of construction workers.

The workers win all of their demands in both strikes because
they are so well organized that no strikebreakers are available.   The new and ideal society becomes a reality when all
the wage-earners in the country join a single universal union
and elect friendly legislators.   All three of these Utopian
novels are puerile and abominably written.   In all three,
strikes characterize the existing society and disappear under
the new order.   The new Utopias are not really very different from the America of the early Nineties, except for the
absence of strikes.   Edward Bellamy's ingenious descriptions
of twenty-first century amenities are completely beyond the
imagination of these pedestrian novelists.

A few of the post-Civil War novelists, Amanda M.
Douglas in Hope Mills, George Thomas Dowling in The
Wreckers, the Fitches in Better Days and Martin A. Foran
in The Other Side (1886), see the solution for labor unrest
in profit-sharing or cooperatively owned factories.   Still
fewer, Albion W. Tourgée in Murvale Eastman (1889) and
Amanda Douglas again in Hope Mills, advocate Christian
Socialism.   More see socialism as a threat against American society.   Socialism becomes a generic term, and the
novelists make no distinctions among socialism, anarchism,
communism or syndicalism, until after the Haymarket bomb
explosion on May 4, 1886, in which more than two hundred
people were injured and seven killed.   Fear of socialists
continues but fear of anarchists then becomes almost hys-
terical in the novels.   Anarchists lurk behind every bush
ready to blow up everything in sight with homemade bombs.
The fine ideological differences among socialists and anarchists make very little difference to the novelists.   They show
little evidence that they are even aware that socialists were
divided between those who wanted a secular cooperative so-

ciety and those who conceived of a socialist society based on
Christian principles.   They do not concern themselves, either,
with differences between anarchists who followed Johann
Most's call for direct violent action by an anarchist elite
and those who supported Albert Parsons, who advocated rebellion against capitalism only after extensive organization
of the working class.   The novelists know little and care
less about revolutionary theories.   They abhor and fear them
all.   They apparently do not realize, either, that most trade
unionists of the time were neither socialists nor anarchists,
only desperately scrabbling together organizations to protect
the economic interests of workingmen.

The single figure upon whom the novelists vent their
most bitter denunciations is the universally despised "walking
delegate."[3]   To Thomas Bailey Aldrich in The Stillwater
Tragedy the walking delegate is a "glib person disguised as
the Workingman's Friend," a "ghoul who lives off the workers," a troublemaker who "sets the place by the ears." To
Edward Fuller in Complaining Millions of Men (1886) he is
a scoundrel who "plays on the workers' necessities for his
own advantage," and is bent on "stirring up trouble." To
John Hay in The Bread-Winners he is a "human beast of
prey." And to Harold Frederic in The Lawton Girl he is a
disturbing influence who "spends altogether too much time at
the various bars" of the town.

William Dean Howells was one of the few who regarded the trade union, the strike, the walking delegate and even
the abuses by labor organizations as "a symptom;..not the
disease....   The real discontent is with the whole system,"
as he says in A Traveller in Altruria.   The execution of four
moderate Haymarket anarchists, applauded by most of the
novelists, led Howells to a shattering disillusionment with

capitalist justice.   He described the hanging of Parsons,
Spies, Fischer and Engel as "civic murder. "   As early as
1883 he was already referring sympathetically to a telegraph-
ers' strike in The Minister's Charge.   He was familiar with
both Bellamy's Looking Backward and Lawrence Gronlund's
The Cooperative Commonwealth in its Outlines (1884), a sort
of digest and forerunner in English of Karl Marx's Das Kapital.   Howells' interest in the fledgling labor movement led
him to produce what is probably the best novel in this period
in which a strike is used, A Hazard of New Fortunes (1890).

 Howells perceived that the strike could be used artisti-
cally in a new way.   He says in the author's preface to A
Hazard of New Fortunes: "Opportunely for me there was a
great street-car strike in New York, and the story began to
find its way to issues nobler and larger than those of the
love-affairs common to fiction. "[4]   His sympathy for the
strikers is all the more surprising when we recall his close
friendships with John Hay and Thomas Bailey Aldrich, both
of whom published novels which attacked strikers and trade
unions.   The strike in A Hazard of New Fortunes is crucial
to the development of the plot, but, more than that, Howells
uses it to reveal psychological changes in each of his main
characters.   Basil March, although he is humane and intelligent, remains a helpless and indecisive bystander during the
strike.   When enraged strikers attack a strikebreaker and
the police protecting him, March can only watch from the
sidelines.   His role as an onlooker is of a piece with his
personality.   He has already revealed his helplessness when
he capitulates to the arbitrary and unjust demands of Jacob
Dryfoos, whose money has launched the journal March edits.
The strike brings to the surface March's embitterment and
slow corruption in the contemporary competitive world:

> ...and so we go on, pushing and pulling, climbing
> and crawling, thrusting aside and trampling under-
> foot; lying, cheating, stealing; and when we get to
> the end, covered with blood and dirt and sin and
> shame, and look back over the way we've come to
> a palace of our own, or the poor-house, which is
> about the only possession we can claim in common
> with our brother-man, I don't think the retrospect
> can be pleasing. [5]

March's Socialist friend, Lindau, on the other hand,
while limited in judgment, is a man of conviction and integrity.   He knows he cannot affect the outcome of the strike but
nevertheless goes quixotically to the defense of the strikers.
His participation in the brawl ultimately costs him his life
but he defends his ideals with strength and nobility.   Conrad
Dryfoos, already burdened with a strong sense of guilt because of his father's reactionary and stubborn opposition to
change, is killed during the violence.   He is an innocent victim but his life is a necessary sacrifice for man's or, at
least, his father's redemption.   Jacob Dryfoos is a broken
man after his son's death.   His ideas have begun to waver
but his education has cost him a bitter price, the death of
his only son.   Howells is warning us that traditional Christian
virtues are no longer adequate.   They may even be our rationalization for an unwillingness to act decisively on the side
of justice.   His description of the strike violence is very
brief--a couple of pages--but they are among the best written pages of the novel, crisp and taut and completely free
of moralizing.   Howells' achievement in this novel should not
be underrated.   It took courage to adopt his lonely stand in
defense of strikes, and it took skill to make a strike an in-
tegral, not an incidental, part of the novel.

A few other novelists between 1870 and 1895 also expressed sympathy for the working class, but none of these

succeeded in using the strike creatively in their novels.
Their sympathy spills over into sentimentality, and their
strikes are hardly credible, let alone successful in deepen-
ing our insight into the characters.   Harold Frederic comes
closest to a realistic portrait of working class characters in
The Lawton Girl.   He tries hard to give a fair and honest
picture of a factory town.   Even the worthless drunks and
dreary slatterns in the town of Thessaly are not comic caricatures.   Jessica Lawton, his central character, has dignity
and strength in spite of her miserable surroundings.   She is
one of the few working class women in the novels of this
period who is not anxious to become a "lady" but who fights
for a life of dignity and independence as a working woman.
She has a kind of class consciousness which is very rare in
nineteenth century American fiction, a pride in her own worth
without either humility or envy toward her "betters."   Jessica
is in love with Reuben Tracy, a lawyer in Thessaly, and she
has a fit of very human jealousy when Reuben courts the
heiress, Kate Minster.   But Frederic has not been able to
resist some of the literary conventions of his time, and his
novel suffers.   When the Minster mill is struck, Jessica
learns by the sheerest coincidence that the strikers plan to
burn down the mill and the Minster house.   She struggles out
of a sickbed to warn Tracy.   Then, with the last remnants
of her strength, she drags herself through a blizzard in a
desperate effort to save her seducer, Horace Boyce, from
prison.   She finally dies in the comforting arms of Reuben
Tracy and Kate Minster.   Jessica has to die at the end of
the novel, as did all seduced girls of the period, but Frederic had the grace to regret his lapse.   In the preface to the
1897 edition of his works he wrote: "At the end I did...kill
Jessica, she who had not deserved or intended at all to die--

but I see now more clearly than anyone else that it was a
false and cowardly thing to do. "[6] Although Frederic's picture of Thessaly is more nearly realistic than the descriptions of most of his contemporaries, the strike itself is not
handled much better.   It becomes a convenient and melodramatic excuse to kill off Jessica.

In comparison with Frederic's novel, unsatisfactory
as that is, the others with some sort of sympathy for factory
workers come off much worse.   Elizabeth Ward's The Silent
Partner (1871), quite an early example of the use of a strike
in the novel, gives us some harrowing descriptions of working class life in a New England mill town.   But the novel
smells of printer's ink.   Mrs. Ward tells us in her preface
that she obtained her information from the reports of the
Massachusetts Bureau of Statistics of Labor, and it is easy
to believe her.   A carefully guided tour through a textile
mill and a slum street, a rummage through labor reports
and a few current magazine articles, and the novelist, properly horrified, is ready to shock her readers.   Mrs. Ward's
novel, synthetic and second-hand though her factory town is,
is actually a cut above most of her contemporaries.   If her
backgrounds are synthetic, her horror at the miseries she
describes obviously isn't, and she is sincerely trying to
arouse action on behalf of the factory workers.   Her heroine,
Perly Kelso, becomes not just a silent partner in the mill
she has inherited but an enlightened mill manager, after a
disastrous strike against a wage cut.   Perley's solution is
very simple.   All she needs to do is to explain honestly to
the strikers that the wage cut has been necessary because
several cotton companies have failed and the mill is losing
money and, of course, the striking workers return to work.
Mrs. Ward cannot resist winding up her novel with an excit-

ing set-piece: a burst dam and a flood, an obvious portent
of the violence unenlightened industrialists may yet unleash.

The second-hand knowledge of factory conditions is
characteristic of most of the novels in this period. We rarely see the workers actually inside the mills, and the central
characters are not workers. It is hardly surprising that the
novelists fail to show us authentic working class life. The
novelists themselves are from the middle class and have had
no first-hand personal experience with life in the factories.
Not only is their knowledge of factory work extremely limited, but in this period there is no reason for them to expand
their knowledge. Most of their readers are also middle
class and not at all interested in authenticity. Novelists,
publishers and readers are comfortably convinced that manual
labor is degrading and that the lives of factory hands are too
undignified to be interesting. Heroes and heroines have to be
above dirt and grime. They also need to display some kind
of intellect, and it is taken for granted that anyone grinding
away at a factory job is going to be both grimy and incapable
of thinking lucidly.

Apart from Jessica Lawton in Frederic's The Lawton
Girl, there is only one novel in this period with the distinction of honest-to-goodness working class protagonists. Edward King's Joseph Zalmonah betrays a deplorable lack of
writing talent and the author has obviously never been a
worker himself, but his hero is a garment worker on New
York's East Side, and the novel attempts to describe the
colorful, vigorous and pathetic efforts of the sweatshop workers to organize their union. They use plays and pageants,
community parades, songs, poems and the lively Yiddish
theater to dramatize the cause of the garment workers
throughout the noisy, smelly and lively East Side slum.

When they strike, it is in desperation, and they finance their
strikes with pennies contributed by workers already close to
starvation.   The novel is full of melodramatic devices--fires,
terrorist villains, insanity, epileptic fits, outrageous coinci-
dences.   Joseph gets involved in an affair with a married
woman who is conveniently disposed of in a typhus epidemic.
But in 1893 not many novelists were using union organizers
as their heroes, so in his clumsy way, Edward King is an
innovator.

In most of the novels in this group it is not only the
strike which is abhorrent but, in fact, any form of working
class organization.   For all their contempt of factory hands
the novelists are not callous monsters who want to see the
industrialists screw every last ounce of energy out of their
employees.   On the contrary, most of the novelists make
some kind of plea for humane factory management.   But
many of them are thoroughgoing proponents of individualism,
and it is this philosophy which deplores collective organized
action.   Each man, they say, must be free to develop his
own talents and to work out his own destiny.   The heroes of
many of these novels become mill owners or managers because they have both the capacity and the will to succeed.
They do not need to--or want to--combine with others to
reach the top.   They are, therefore, contemptuous of the
weaklings who need the support of an organization--be it a
trade union on the one hand or a trust on the other.   When
mill-owners in these novels refuse to deal with a union delegation, as they often do, they do so in defense of the virtue
of individual effort.   Alvan Relvason, a Chicago pork packer,
in Martin A. Foran's The Other Side says:

> 'We do not think it wise to treat with our men
> through an organization.   We are willing to treat

> with them as employés; to do otherwise would be
> to recognize a vicious principle--the right of the
> union to participate in the management of our pri-
> vate affairs.'7

Millowners in Clinton Ross' The Silent Workman (1886) and
in Timothy Shay Arthur's The Strike at Tivoli Mills take the
same position.   Each has become the head of an industrial
enterprise through his own efforts and ability.   He regards
his mill as his private domain, which he will continue to
run as he sees fit.   He will deal only with individual workers who each have the same right and responsibility as he
did to become a factory owner.   The union coerces not only
his free will but that of his workers as well.   John Hay in
The Bread-Winners also draws the same moral.   His vigorous hero, Arthur Farnham, is a man of substance because
he has made himself one.   Those who find themselves in an
inferior station have their own incompetence or ignorance or
laziness or incontinence, or a combination of all of these
vices, to blame.   A union only encourages the weak or the
vicious and eventually destroys all incentives for hard work
and superior ability.

        The novels are full of self-made men: Alan Prescott
in Frank L. Benedict's Miss Van Kortland, Stephen Garrick
in Elizabeth Stuart Phelps Ward's The Silent Partner, Maurice Graham in Abigail Roe's Free, Yet Forging Their Own
Chains, Jack Darcy in Amanda M. Douglas' Hope Mills,
Richard Shackford in Thomas Bailey Aldrich's The Stillwater
Tragedy, Richard Arbyght in Martin A. Foran's The Other
Side, and on and on and on.   They have all grown up in
relatively poor but respectable homes--not working class
homes.   A small inheritance or a loan from a friendly millowner or a job in the office of an industrial firm (not in the
factory or mill itself) starts them on the way up.   They are

all hard workers and they all become factory managers, often
opposing the rigid labor policies of their employers.   They
all end up as either superintendents in full charge of the factory or owners of their own factories which are undoubtedly
on the way to becoming successful enterprises.

     In only one of these novels is it even suggested that
the hard-working self-made man can, in spite of intelligence,
grit and perseverance, fail in his business venture.   Frances
Hodgson Burnett's novel, Haworth's, has a Lancashire foundry as its locale.   Jem Haworth, who begins life in a poorhouse, rises from foundry worker to the head of the Haworth
Iron Foundry.   The strike in his works is fomented by out-
siders from Manchester who stir up the incompetent, drunken
workers in Haworth's mill.   He faces the strikers, fearlessly
threatening them with his pistol and reminding them that he
has built good cottages for them and that he never insulted
them with hypocritical "benevolence" or "charity. "   Haworth's
courage is useless.   The strikers storm the house of Gerard
Ffrench, Haworth's silent partner, and attack his daughter,
Rachel, when she faces the enraged crowd alone.   Haworth's
fatal flaw is his singleminded infatuation for Rachel Ffrench,
who despises him.   Haworth's success is no recommendation
to Rachel, who cannot forgive him his lowly origins.   The
novel suggests that Haworth has overreached himself.   The
poorhouse boy has no right to seek an alliance with a true
lady.   When the strikers attack Rachel, Haworth loses his
head and beats up the man whose stone has wounded Rachel.
His devotion to Rachel has misled Haworth into trusting her
father, and after the strike he discovers that Ffrench has
absconded with the firm's money.   Haworth leaves the town
at the end of the novel as penniless as when he arrived.   His
financial empire lost, he is a ruined and disillusioned man.

Mrs. Burnett knows Lancashire and uses the colorful local
dialect well.   Like her contemporaries she is ignorant of the
life and work inside the foundry and avoids describing it.
The self-educated Haworth is one of the more interesting
examples of the individualist in action, made more credible
by his flawed personality and victimized by a rigid caste
system.

If the whole concept of the trade union is dangerous,
the one union which is feared and reviled above all in the
novels is the Mollie Maguires.   Strangely enough, the existence of an organized Mollie Maguire group in America was
never really proved.   In Ireland a secret group, called the
Mollie Maguires, had been active in organizing Irish farmers
to resist payment of outrageous rents to absentee English
landlords.   It was rumored that Irish immigrants to the
Pennsylvania coal regions had brought the organization with
them and were using it to plot the murders of mine owners
and superintendents.   The Mollies were also supposed to be
murdering "Modocs," miners who opposed the secret organization.   In 1877 the alleged existence of the Mollie Maguires
broke into the open during a Schuylkill County trial but there
is only one source of information about it--the testimony of
the undercover Pinkerton agent, James McParlan.   The miners on trial claimed that their only crime was militant trade
unionism, that they had never been involved in conspiracy or
murder and that there was no such organization as the Mollie
Maguires.   McParlan testified that he had infiltrated the Mollies under the name of McKenna and that he had personally
heard several murders plotted.   (McParlan turned up again
at the conspiracy trial of Bill Haywood and other mine union
officials in Colorado in 1902).   The state prosecutor, Frank-
lin B. Gowen, can hardly be regarded as an impartial seeker

after justice since he was simultaneously President of both
the Philadelphia and Reading Railroad and the Philadelphia
and Reading Coal and Iron Company, the employer of the
men on trial.   McParlan's testimony had a telling effect.
Nineteen miners were executed, and presumably the Mollie
Maguires had been wiped off the face of the earth.   Not for
the novelists, though.   The Mollies appear in at least five
of the novels of the time: Abigail Roe's Free, Yet Forging
Their Own Chains, Charles Benjamin's The Strike in the B--
Mills (1887), Patrick Justin McMahon's Philip; or, The Mollie's Secret (1891), R. F. Bishop's Camerton Slope and Mary
Hallock Foote's Coeur d'Alène.

      The novelists' sources of information about the Mollie
Maguires were undoubtedly current newspaper accounts of the
trial but, in addition, they depended heavily on Allan Pinkerton's book, The Molly Maguires and the Detectives (1877), in
which McParlan's story was immortalized.   R. F. Bishop
gives credit to the Pinkerton book as one of his sources but
it seems more than likely that the other novelists had also
read it.   It sold widely and seems to have had its effect
even in England.   The Scowrers, in Arthur Conan Doyle's
story, "The Valley of Fear, " are transparently Mollies, and
Doyle's Pinkerton spy, McMurdo, is a fictionalized McParlan.
The reliability of Pinkerton's book is certainly open to question.   Librarians have considerable trouble deciding whether
to catalog it as fiction or nonfiction.   Pinkerton was obviously capitalizing on the notoriety given the Mollies by the
Schuylkill County trial.   His book is full of furious action
but without documentation.   Pinkerton accuses the Knights of
Labor of being an "amalgamation of the Mollie Maguires and
the Paris Commune" in the book, a patent piece of nonsense.
McParlan was one of Pinkerton's own agents, and the book

is a defense of his trial testimony.   Pinkerton also claims
that two-thirds of all the workingmen in Scranton and Wilkes-
Barre belonged to the union, a statistic which would have
been a surprise to the struggling organization.

     The novelists who write about the Mollie Maguires
were not much interested in authenticity, however.   The
melodramatic aspects of the story--conspiracy, murder, secret passwords, midnight meetings--appealed to them and
they made lavish, if not very convincing, use of the Mollies.
In Free, Yet Forging Their Own Chains the Mollies shoot
Ned Malcome, a young miner who refuses to join the union.
The plot is complicated by Ned's worthless brother, who is
a member of the union, and by Bill McQuaid, leader of the
union, who lusts after Ned's fiancée, Bessie Walker.   In
Philip the Mollies plot to kill the mine superintendent but
are foiled when their plans are overheard by Philip Donahue,
who is discovered to be the superintendent's long-lost son.
The hero of the story is James McKenna, who joins the Mollies, then testifies against them at their trial.   In Camerton
Slope the Mollies meet in Barney Dillon's saloon, precipitate
a strike which none of the miners want, and are egged on by
Pat McCoy, the "Bodymaster," or union leader, to murder
the mine officials.   The conspirators are subjected to an
impromptu drumhead trial and expelled from Pennsylvania.
The author comments: "This 'extra-judicial' method of dealing with criminal conspiracy may not commend itself to some
people; but there is this to be said for it--the cure was ef-
fectual. "[8]   Of course, not every trial could expect to have
the miners' employer as prosecutor.

     The nineteenth century novelist who used the strike
was attempting to deal with basic philosophical questions.
Even when his novel was subliterary--as most of these are--

he was trying to dramatize important and vexing problems in a literary form.   Very often, however, the attitudes which become apparent in the novels reflect unconscious fears or prejudices.   There is a wide divergence between fact and fiction in these novels.   The strikes in the novels all become uncontrolled riots accompanied by death and violence.   Most real strikes of the time were dreary, undramatic rounds of meetings, picket lines and compromise agreements.   The strikes in the novels are, almost without exception, lost. Most strikes of the time succeeded.   The Commissioner of Labor reported in 1888 that in sixty percent of all strikes between 1880 and 1887 all the demands of the strikers were met. [9] The strikes in the novels are almost all spontaneous and break out in response to a sudden ruling by management or, at the worst, without any visible cause at all.   Most real strikes of the time came after long negotiations and a long period of union organization.   The novelists could not portray strikes realistically.   For one thing, they knew very little about strikes.   They depended for their information, most often, on the newspaper headlines of the day which, besides being biased against all strikes, dealt almost ex- clusively with those few strikes which did degenerate into violent clashes.   Most of the strikes of the time were never reported in the newspapers at all.   But more than the novel- ists' ignorance comes to the surface here.   The middle-class novelist, heir to a long Puritan heritage, cannot imagine a successful, carefully planned strike.   A factory hand was, to begin with, a failure, a brutish clod without spirit or in- telligence enough to become a successful entrepreneur.   A striker was a double failure, unable even to come to terms with his inferior station in life.   It was impossible to imag- ine him intelligent enough to plan a strike, disciplined enough to persist until a strike was won, and determined enough to withstand hunger in order to win the abstract right to bargain collectively.

What the novelist accepted as a reality made the strike a profoundly disturbing phenomenon. He saw the factory as a kind of family organization with the owner as the father and the workers as his children. Occasionally a father exercised his authority too rigorously and occasionally sons revolted against their fathers, even in pre-Freudian times. But the right, even the duty, of the father to assert his authority and the necessity to punish erring sons for their own good was beyond question. The nascent labor movement was beginning to insist that the factory system was an economic arrangement, unrelated to family organization, and that workers needed legal protections, not merely the paternal benevolence of the employers. Another reality for the novelist was an assured belief in the inherent superiority of American institutions. This was a period of growing national pride. Labor unrest in general and strikes in particular seemed to imply that all was not quite well in the nation and that beneath the visible stability lay chaotic forces threatening to destroy the order of American society as well as the laws which protected it.

Along with growing nationalism there was developing during this period a virulent fear of the foreigner. There were lots of foreigners around to become suspicious about. Throughout the nineteenth century millions of Europeans and Asians poured into the United States--the Irish after the potato crop failure, Hungarians after the defeat of Kossuth's nationalist movement in 1848, Germans escaping Bismarck's militaristic regime, Jews running from Polish and Russian pogroms, Cornish miners hunting jobs, Chinese recruited to

build the railroads, and men and women of all nations fleeing
from hunger and oppression.   They came in droves.   As long
as jobs were plentiful and cheap unskilled labor in demand,
these foreign settlers were tolerated.   Herded into their
dirty and crowded ghettoes, laughed at for their "quaint"
customs, but accepted.   Whenever depressions struck, however, the foreign laborer became a bitter competitor for dis-
appearing jobs and therefore a potential troublemaker.   The
one thing a middle-class already shaken by change least
wanted and most detested was a group who might make further trouble in American society.   To add to the distaste
immigrants aroused by being "different, " there was the fact
that many of them brought with them from the old country
revolutionary traditions.   The Irish had fought bitter battles
against English landlords; the Germans had organized trade
unions and socialist political parties; the Poles had rebelled
more than once against Russian authority; and the Jews had
learned organization as a survival technique everywhere in
Europe for centuries.   In their desperate desire to believe
that America was a stable and superior society the novelists
found it hard to accept that the native American worker could
be organizing trade unions and strikes.   It is no wonder that
so many of the novelists blame strikes on subversion by radicals from abroad.   Aldrich's agitator, Torrini, in The Stillwater Tragedy, is Italian; Pat McCoy in Bishop's Camerton
Slope and Dolan in Fuller's Complaining Millions of Men are
both Irish; Charles Benjamin's anarchist, Kohler, in The
Strike at the B-- Mills is German.   Robert Grant creates
a schizophrenic villain in Face to Face.   Andrew De Vito, who
combines intelligence with irrationality, is the illegitimate
offspring of an American father and an Italian mother, and
it is not hard to guess which characteristic each parent con-

tributed. Why so many American workers follow foreign
agitators into unplanned, disastrous strikes is never quite
explained except that workers--even American workers--are
by nature, childish and impulsive.

As distrust and fear grow the novelists begin to refer
to immigrants in more and more intemperate terms. They
become "hordes," "Huns," "strange, greasy, dirty-looking
men," "wild beasts," "foreign herds." By 1895 Henry Edward Rood's hero, Malcolm Curtis, in The Company Doctor
is fulminating:

> 'The ignorance, filth, and viciousness of these
> Poles, Italians, Sicilians, Tyroleans, Bohemians
> and Slovaks are absolutely appalling... the vast
> majority are cattle. ...   Is Congress mad in al-
> lowing these hosts to swarm over the land like
> the Huns of old?... they fight as do wild beasts,
> for the love of it.   They seem hardly human. '[10]

Distrust of the foreigner is not confined to working
class immigrants.   The European intellectual and the European aristocrat are also doing their share in subverting
American society.   European intellectuals import dangerous
foreign ideologies and the impoverished foreign noblemen
who marry American heiresses are no better.   Men like
Varemberg, the Belgian wastrel who marries Florence Lane
in William Bishop's The Golden Justice (1887), or the brutal
German Baron von Eulaw, who becomes Ellen Thornton's
husband in the Fitches' Better Days, lead their American
wives hellish lives.   Their greed for American fortunes,
their cruelty to their wives, and their arrogance and disdain
toward America is attributed to the degeneration of the European upper classes.

The attitude of the novelists toward the working class
is a fascinating study in contradictions.   On the one hand,
there is the sincerely held conviction that the "hand" be-

longs almost to a different species. He is a man with more
blunted feelings than the sensitive aristocrat or intellectual.
He is a violent, brutal, drunken, malicious, subhuman beast,
or, at best, an unreasoning child. Robert Grant's heroine,
Evelyn Pimlico, asks in Face to Face: "'Haven't you been a
clog to us by your ignorance and brutality and indolence?'"
and her employee, Andrew De Vito, answers: "'Yes, I could
have risen, perhaps, but the taint of my low origins would
have followed me.'"[11] "A parcel of children with no fore-
sight for themselves, " "These miners are as unreasonable
as children. "--the complaint is repeated a dozen times over
in the novels. Like pre-Civil War literature which argued
that the slave belonged to a subhuman species destined by
God to inferiority, these post-Civil War novelists also look
for comfort in the rationalization that the factory hand does
not really mind squalor or desire the luxuries his employer
enjoys. "'They did not mind the grime,'" muses the hero
of William Bishop's The Golden Justice. The workers who
wait on Arthur Farnum in The Bread-Winners cannot appreci-
ate the fine vintage wine he offers them and prefer beer or,
better yet, rotgut whiskey. The most cogent instance of the
workingman's malice and stupidity is the strike itself. If the
strike is troublesome and inconvenient to the employer, it
means outright starvation for the striker and his family, but
still he persists in striking.

    Side by side with the thesis of inborn inferiority, how-
ever, and sometimes in the same novel, exactly the opposite
view is also projected. All men are created equal, the more
admirable characters in the novels protest. There are no
class differences. Those who preach class warfare are deliberately sowing seeds of distrust among harmonious employers and their employees. Execrable novels like Charles Ben-

jamin's The Strike in the B--Mills, poor novels like Helen
Choate Prince's The Story of Christine Rochefort (1895), and
better novels like Harold Frederic's The Lawton Girl all
make the same point.   When the workers in each of these
novels are made to realize that there are no class differences, the strikes are settled in short order.   Darragh, a
moderate trade unionist in Benjamin's novel, recognizes that
"it is wrong as well as useless to array a part of the people
against the other, " denounces unionism and leads the workers
back into the mill.   In The Story of Christine Rochefort it is
the old Socialist shoemaker Sorel who sees the light under
the tutelage of Abbé Lemaire and pleads with the strikers to
recognize that we are all equally God's children.   In Frederic's novel the hero, Reuben Tracy, vehemently denounces
class divisions:

> 'Beware of men who preach the theory that be-
> cause you are puddlers or moulders or firemen,
> therefore you are different from the rest of your
> fellow-citizens.   I, for one, resent the idea that
> because I am a lawyer, and you, for example, are
> a blacksmith, therefore we belong to different clas-
> ses.   I wish with all my heart that everybody re-
> sented it, and that that abominable word "classes"
> could be wiped out of the English language as it is
> spoken in America.'[12]

What the novelists would like to see is a kind of gen-
tlemanly compact in which capital would recognize its role as
the fair but firm guardian of labor, while labor would trust
employers to look out for the worker's best interests.   The
industrialist must, of course, by virtue of his innate superiority, be the sole judge of what is fair and what is firm but
the interests of capital and labor are essentially identical.
The Commissioner of Labor, however, disagrees in his Annual Report of 1888:

> Much is said of the freedom of contract; that the

> workman has the same power to make contracts
> for his labor as the merchant has for the sale of
> his goods.   This idea is purely fallacious, for the
> merchant need not sell his goods today, while the
> workman must his labor, and he is, as a rule, at
> the mercy of the purchaser instead of being free
> to keep his labor if he cannot get his price....
> It is absurd to say that the interest of capital and
> labor are identical.   They are no more identical
> than the interests of the buyer and seller. [13]

If capital and labor could come to terms, then all decent

workmen would recognize that they owe a debt of gratitude

to their employers.   The problem of "gratitude" looms large

in many of the novels.   Strikers are accused of breaking

some undefined bargain in which employers have benevolently

provided them with jobs for which they should be grateful.

The nineteenth century novelists who picture strikes

are caught in a peculiar paradox.   Strike leaders are repul-

sive and monstrous creatures to many of them.   At the same

time they have a kind of compelling fascination which the

novelists spin out in a variety of rape fantasies.   Rape is, of

course, a forbidden word but attempted rape is frequent and

the novelists display considerable ingenuity in talking about it

without ever naming it.   At the least thoughtful level the

strike leader lusts after the chaste heroine.   She is always

several social cuts above him, so his lust is part of his mad

ambition.   He wants to take by force not only the money,

home and factory of his master but the most sacred property

of all--his woman.   Offitt, McQuaid, Baretta, the union lead-

ers in John Hay's The Bread-Winners, Abigail Roe's Free,

Yet Forging Their Own Chains and Edward Fuller's Complain-

ing Millions of Men all have lascivious designs on attractive

ladies in the novels.   But the rape element is not one-sided.

Upper class men in many of the novels seduce poor and inno-

cent working girls.   Frank Lyster seduces Marcia Nullus, a

poor seamstress in his shirt factory in The Other Side, and
Horace Boyce, a rich young wastrel, is the father of Jessica
Lawton's illegitimate son in The Lawton Girl.   John McDowell
Leavitt carries the seduction theme to absurd lengths in his
absurd novel, Kings of Capital and Knights of Labor for the
People (1885).   When the son of the company president betrays Belle Standfast, daughter of a worker in the Alma Locomotive Works, the workers go mad and call a violent
strike in which "mobs were incited, shops were occupied,
railroads were seized, trains were plundered, depots were
destroyed, cities were in a blaze. "[14]   Meanwhile, poor
Belle, the innocent cause of all this upheaval, has, of course,
died (as do all betrayed girls in these novels).

The upper class women desired by labor leaders are
not always averse to the attentions of their lowly lovers.
Charles Bellamy's Bertha Ellingsworth in The Breton Mills
(1879) elopes with the fascinating Curran.   Although she
leaves him and marries the hero, Philip Breton, bigamously,
Bertha continues to be attracted to Curran.   Bertha doesn't
have to die at the end of the novel because she has had the
practical sense to insist on Curran's marrying her, and her
dilemma is finally resolved when Curran is killed attempting
to save her from a runaway horse.   Evelyn Pimlico in Robert Grant's Face to Face is also fascinated by a labor leader, the ambivalent Andrew De Vito.   As a matter of fact,
Evelyn offers to kiss him before she knows who he is, when
they accidentally meet in a wood.   Andrew is tempted but
refuses her offer.   Later, when she inherits a mill, she is
still so taken with him that she appoints him her superintendent.   He repays her generosity by organizing a strike, and
Evelyn marries another, more suitable, man.

All of these sexual crossings of class lines reflect in

literary terms the novelists' ambivalence toward that alien
unknown breed, the workingman.   Precisely because he is
mysterious, he--or his woman--becomes desirable.   Because
sexual experience with despised peoples is forbidden, it becomes all the more tempting.

An obsession with sex, especially illicit sex, goes
hand in hand in many of these novels with a passionate interest in death.   The unmarried girl who indulges in sex invariably dies, although the man who seduces her suffers, at
most, a few pangs of conscience.   The girls are always pictured as innocent dupes or victims, not adventuresses.   It
is not exactly evident why gullibility or foolishness should be
a capital crime while seduction is not punishable at all.
These novelists are no better able to deal realistically with
sex than with the strike.   Obviously, not every girl who gave
birth to an illegitimate child or had an affair with a man,
immediately sank into a decline, although the law often did
deal harshly with her.   Some of the novelists who kill off
their erring women do so because of their conviction that
death is the proper punishment for the sexual sinner or because they hope that their novelistic examples will serve as
deterrents to girls contemplating sexual adventures.   More
of them let the girls die because they cannot imagine what
kind of life could be possible for a girl who is no longer a
virgin.   They would like to think that once she has fallen, a
woman would no longer want to live.   A man goes on with
his work, but a woman who has lost her one saleable com-
modity--her chastity--can have no conceivable future.   Death
for the woman is not entirely a punishment.   It also serves
as a release from a life that is no longer tolerable.   In her
afterlife the foolish girl will receive the justice she cannot
expect on earth, so most of the dying girls in the novels

are both repentant and serene in their last moments.

Death is also a fitting punishment for the many strike agitators in the invariably violent strikes in these novels. It is their irresponsible strike leadership which has stirred up the trouble in the first place, so they pay for their crimes by dying. Best of all is the dying agitator who repents just before he breathes his last (like Torrini in The Stillwater Tragedy and Curran in The Breton Mills), but often the strike leaders die too suddenly to permit a conversion. Many of the deaths are obvious literary wish fulfillments. The novelists have been caught helplessly in the violent currents disturbing industrial America. In their novels, at least, they can impose order, justice and retribution.

Death is not regarded only as a punishment, however. Innocent nonstrikers also die frequently in the course of these novels, and the novelists indulge themselves in long heartrending descriptions of the deaths of cripples, young children and girls approaching puberty. Thomas Denison devotes many pages to the lingering death of the hunchback, Johnny Hackett, and the tubercular May Bryce in An Iron Crown. In The Wreckers poor Jane, slaving away at her sewing machine, finally coughs away her young life. Young Freddy, born a cripple, wastes slowly away throughout most of Katherine Pearson Woods' Metzerott, Shoemaker (1889), and in the same novel Tina Kellar's death from overwork and exposure precipitates the climactic strike. These deaths are often seen as the happy release of an innocent from earthly suffering into a better world. They are also used to set an example of patient resignation. If these young people can endure the slow tortures of tuberculosis, why can't ablebodied workers bear with equal fortitude the deprivations of their lives without resorting to disturbing strikes?

Sometimes the sacrifice of an innocent victim, the novelist
hopes, will bring about the redemption of many sinners.
This pious hope is not often realized. Conrad Dryfoos'
death in A Hazard of New Fortunes does chasten his father,
but Phillip Strong's sudden collapse at the foot of the cross
in his church, in The Crucifixion of Phillip Strong, has, at
best, converted only the mill-workers who have come to hear
his sermon. His rich parishioners are still obdurate sinners.
Margaret Henderson's death in childbirth in A Little Journey
in the World, if it is meant to redeem her unscrupulous husband, is a failure. He remarries and goes merrily on his
stock-manipulating way.

Most of the novels handle serious themes with deadly
seriousness. Frank Benedict makes a lame and vain attempt
at humor in his Miss Van Kortland. He throws together a
garrulous Irish-woman with a wart on her nose, a servant
who is subject to fits, and an ugly taciturn handyman. Their
ridiculous antics miss comedy by a mile because the characters are nothing more than stereotyped caricatures. Frank
Stockton's novel, The Hundredth Man (1886), is a notable exception, the only one to use a strike humorously. The strike
has no real relevance to the plot, which deals with Horace
Stratford's search for that one in every hundred men who is
"preeminent" by virtue of his inborn qualities. One of the
characters in the novel, John People, manages Vatoldi's
Restaurant, and it is the waiters in the restaurant who stage
a strike. Their main grievance is an order forbidding them
to wear dress-suits because they cannot be distinguished
from the diners. In the course of the strike they think up
some amusing tactics. They begin by distributing circulars
to passers-by and proceed to threaten patrons of the restaurant and strike-breaking waiters. But when they get nowhere

with these methods, they and their sympathizers enter the
restaurant, order meals, then make noisy and fairly funny
demonstrations inside the place, complaining about the food
and the service.   Finally, as a last resort, they hire a man
to eat at Vatoldi's, who then doubles up outside the restaurant, loudly protesting that he has been poisoned.   When the
restaurant is forced to close, George Bencher, the strike
agitator, gets a sound beating from the striking waiters, who
have now done themselves completely out of jobs by their
antics.   No comic genius, Stockton still manages to extract
some fun out of the situation.

        With the exception of A Hazard of New Fortunes, none
of these novels is a memorable, nor even a particularly competent piece of literary craftsmanship.   Characters, plots,
even grammar are amateurish.   The characters remain stat-
ic.   The good generally stay good; the bad may become a
little worse.   Workers are never really shown except as
threatening masses in the background or as caricatures, but
we are rarely partners to their inner feelings, emotions or
conflicts.   A few strike leaders talk about or act out their
ideas, but it is never clear what power they possess (except
outright intimidation) that impels masses of workers to support them.   Industrialists in the novels rarely come off any
better.   We are given few insights into what drives them.
The only characters--and those are few enough--who come
through with any credibility at all are those whom the novelists best understand, the middle class preachers, doctors,
teachers or petty entrepreneurs they themselves derive from.

        The plots of most of the novels are frenzied collections
of all the melodramatic devices the author can cram into four
hundred pages or so.   It would be difficult to match the assortment of floods, snowstorms, fires, cave-ins, landslides

and other disasters packed into these novels.   The strike is
usually treated as just another natural disaster.   We are
never brought inside it, never made aware that it is a human enterprise.   The strikes are often climactic devices but
the plots could have been worked out just as well (or poorly)
by the substitution of any other "gimmick"--a tornado, a runaway horse, a railroad wreck.

Purple passages, stilted dialogue and almost indeci-
pherable dialects are the general rule.   The symbolism is
painfully obvious, especially in the choice of names.   Strongs,
Stirlings, Standfasts and Keans do battle against stubborn
Thornes, petty Smallwoods, prickly Briarleys or feckless
Norwells.   One of the reasons for the subliterary quality of
most of these novels probably lies precisely in the novelty
of the strike theme.   The authors who used it were novices.
Most professional novelists of the time were exploring human
dynamics within their own class, and most of the middle
class had rarely been touched directly by industrialization
or strikes.   Another reason for the novelists' ineptitude is
their motivation.   They are really more interested in writing
tracts than novels.   They want to preach a sermon to their
readers, and they incessantly do just that.   They use the
novel as their vehicle because nineteenth century Americans
were reading more novels than sermons.   The one important
contribution of this group of novelists is their experimentation with new literary material.   Their fumbling attempts to
introduce the strike into the novel pave the way for a more
sophisticated and effective use of such material in the future.

Notes

1.   U. S. Commissioner of Labor, First Annual Report
      (Washington, D. C. :   Government Printing Office,

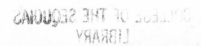

1886), p. 1061.

2. John Hay, The Bread-Winners; a Social Study (New York: Harper and Bros., 1884), p. 82.

3. The term, walking delegate, fallen into disuse since the advent of the Cadillac, vividly describes the life of a union officer in the nineteenth and early twentieth century. He was elected by the union membership to walk--literally--from one shop to another checking on adherence to the union contract, collecting union dues and processing grievances. The first reference to a walking delegate occurs in 1799 in documents relating to the Philadelphia Cordwainers' Association.

4. William Dean Howells, A Hazard of New Fortunes (New York: E. P. Dutton and Co., 1952), p. xxii.

5. Ibid., p. 486.

6. Quoted in Heinz Wüstenhagen, "Harold Frederics The Lawton Girl," Zeitschrift für Anglistik und Amerikanistik, XII:1 (1964), 41.

7. Martin A. Foran, The Other Side (Washington, D. C.: W. A. Ingham, 1886), p. 197.

8. R. F. Bishop, Camerton Slope, a Story of Mining Life (Cincinnati: Cranston and Curts; New York: Hunt and Eaton, 1893), p. 316.

9. U. S. Bureau of Labor Statistics, Bulletin, no. 651 (Washington, D. C.: Government Printing Office, 1932), p. 34.

10. Henry Edward Rood, The Company Doctor, an American Story (New York: Merriam Co., 1895), p. 223, 239, 241.

11. Robert Grant, Face to Face (New York: Charles Scribner's Sons, 1886), p. 340.

12. Harold Frederic, The Lawton Girl (New York: Charles Scribner's Sons, 1897), p. 444.

13. U. S. Commissioner of Labor, Third Annual Report, (Washington, D. C.: Government Printing Office,

1888), p. 1051.

14.   John McDowell Leavitt, <u>Kings of Capital and Knights of</u>
      <u>Labor for the People</u> (Cincinnati: Shelton and Bulkley
      Book Co. ,   1886), p.   518.

Chapter 3

UNEASY CHANGE: 1895-1910

By the mid-Nineties the first signs of subtle changes in the American mood appear. Materially, the United States had advanced with almost incredible rapidity. A full-fledged industrial power, bustling, vigorous, adventurous, experimental, America was moving into the Machine Age. Ingenious inventions and bold industrial innovations had spurred great masses of the population to move off the land into urban factories. Great fortunes excited admiration but made all the more evident the terrible contrasting poverty. The economic advances of the country were soon transferred to the international political scene. America's first full-scale venture into imperialism occurred in 1898 with the outbreak of the Spanish-American War. American victory came quickly and easily. Robert Herrick catches the busy optimism of the post-war period briefly in The Web of Life (1900):

> As he sauntered down La Salle Street, the air of the pavement breathed the optimism of the hour. Sommers was amazed at the number of brokers' offices, at the streams of men going and coming around these busy booths. The war was over, or practically over, and speculation was brisker than ever. To be sure, the bills for the war were not paid, but success was in the air, and everyone was striving to exploit that success in his own behalf. [1]

But underneath, an uneasy doubt was growing. Something appeared to be wrong. While most writers still regarded poverty with traditional attitudes, a few here and

55

there were beginning to question. Was it really true that
the poor were only reaping the harvest of their own incompetence, that the rich had been rewarded for their superior
ability and intelligence, that the status quo had been divinely
ordained? Some of the novelists were now doubtful that poverty automatically meant moral degradation. The converse
also appeared very tentatively in the novels. Simply being
rich did not necessarily imply moral superiority. As in
earlier novels, financial czars are still pictured as sinners.
Elliot Gardwell, the railroad tycoon in Charles K. Lush's
The Federal Judge (1897), for example, is discovered after
a heart attack to have been living a double life. But now,
for the first time, lawlessness or questionable practices are
no longer the monopoly of villains in the novels. Christopher
Kenyon, the hero of Florence Converse's The Burden of
Christopher (1900), misuses a trust fund, although out of
noble motives. Dr. Harold Sommers in Robert Herrick's
The Web of Life succumbs to the temptations of a lucrative
but socially useless medical practice for a while. If even
well-meaning middle-class heroes could be corrupted, then
moral debasement could no longer be equated with poverty.
The novelists were beginning to look for more complex
sources of both poverty and corruption.

        The novelists began to change their attitudes toward
manual labor, too. To the nineteenth century novelist menial
work was not only distasteful but degrading. The man who
had to work with his hands was not likely to have developed
finer sensibilities or much intellectual curiosity. At the turn
of the century it was just beginning to seem possible that a
laborer and a creative artist were not so very different from
each other. Any work, even factory work, might provide a
sense of pride in a job well done, joy in creating something

new, and an appreciation of the drama implicit in a man's
triumph over formless raw materials.   Amid the ugliness of
the factory the novelists also catch glimpses of something
else.   John R. McMahon's steel workers in Toilers and Idlers
(1907) take pride in an intricate molding job.   Gwendolen
Overton's workers in Captains of the World (1904) know they
have accomplished something creative when they cooperate in
tapping a Bessemer furnace with split-second timing.

    Most factory jobs offered no opportunities for pride
or joy, of course, either in real life or in the novels.   The
work was dirty, backbreaking and dangerous, or, at best,
repetitive enough to be soul-destroying.   The novelists began
to see a connection between the sullen, angry, rebellious
worker and his alienating, uncreative work.   Perhaps the
factory hand struck not because he was innately vicious or
childish enough to be misled by malicious agitators but because he wanted to assert his own dignity.   Thomas Nelson
Page claims in John Marvel, Assistant (1909):   "That cause
was not, as some thought, so much money a day, but was
the claim to justice and consideration and brotherly kindness."[2]
Or, "It isn't empty stomachs and bare backs that is the chief
grievance: it is simply degraded manhood and lost freedom,"[3]
Edwin Brenholtz suggests in The Recording Angel (1905).
Mary Wilkins Freeman sees labor as necessary not so much
for the production of goods or "its equivalent in silver and
gold" but "for the growth in the character of the laborer."[4]

    The novelists were changing and softening but were
not quite ready to accept that empty stomachs were creating
strikes.   Most real strikes were about money.   But to the
novelists there is something essentially mean in mere money-
grubbing, so they look for more high-minded motives: dignity
or justice or growth in character.   The very fact that they

are searching for the causes of labor unrest, and for noble
causes at that, signals an important change in attitude. Some
of the novelists, at least, are no longer content to regard
the worker as another, and lower, species.

In the course of re-examining labor the novelists of
the new century were also looking at other aspects of American life with new insight. Several of the novels scrutinize
in a new light the role of women in American society. The
society girl of the past, dedicated to snaring an eligible husband, was now beginning to seem selfish and parasitic. In
real life, as in the novels, she was beginning to devote part
of her time to work in the settlement houses which were
springing up everywhere in the urban slums. The early
volunteer social worker saw her role not only as helping to
alleviate some of the miseries of slum life but as developing her own independence at the same time. Her working
class sister was also expanding her sphere of action. Many
working women of the time, especially in the sweated garment industry, threw themselves into the organization of
women's trade unions and showed great skill and courage
as trade union leaders. The novels of the period were slow
to accept women in these new roles but the ideas seeped
through gradually.

Francis Hopkinson Smith portrays an unusual woman
in his novel, Tom Grogan (1896). "Tom" in this case is a
woman stevedore and contractor supporting her children and
an invalid husband. She valiantly defies a corrupt union
walking delegate and in the ensuing strike deliberately gives
up a lucrative contract to spare the families of her striking
employees hunger and want. Smith, a popular novelist of
the period, has written an old-fashioned melodramatic novel
but has shrewdly recognized that the time is ripe for popular

acceptance of an unconventional working woman like Tom
Grogan.

The woman trade unionist makes her first appearance
in novels like Theresa Serber Malkiel's Diary of a Shirtwaist
Striker (1910) and Marie Van Vorst's Amanda of the Mill
(1905). Diary of a Shirtwaist Striker is a naive story based
on some actual incidents in the organization of New York's
garment industry. Mary, the heroine, begins her diary as
she joins the other girls in her shop in a strike. From a
rather timid and thoughtless youngster she quickly matures
into an active fighter defying both her father and her fiancé
who think woman's place is at the sewing machine, not on
the picket line. Before the strike is over Mary has led a
picket line, been arrested and served a term in the work-
house. Finally, the owner of her shop signs a contract with
the union Mary has helped to organize. She marries her by-
now-converted Jim. Amanda of the Mill is one of the earliest
novels to deal with the uprooting of South Carolina hill people
by the voracious textile mills of the South. The complicated
plot centers on Amanda Henchley's love affair with the union
organizer, Henry Euston, but the novel describes the active
work of women millhands in the course of a series of ugly
strikes.

Middle and upper class women working in settlement
houses appear in several of these novels. The original purpose of the settlement house was the establishment of educational and cultural centers in the working class ghettos, but
many of the settlements soon became centers for union organization as well. Settlement houses in Chicago and in New
York actively cooperated in the planning and financing of industrial strikes. Under the dynamic leadership of Jane
Addams, Hull House in Chicago began by offering classes

in home economics, manual training, music and English to
slum dwellers, but went on to mediate labor disputes and
to lobby for the establishment of government arbitration
boards.   The settlement appears prominently in Isaac Kahn
Friedman's By Bread Alone (1901), Vida D. Scudder's A
Listener in Babel (1903), Alice French's The Man of the
Hour (1905) and Arthur Jerome Eddy's Ganton and Co. (1908).
It is also mentioned in Gwendolen Overton's Captains of the
World, Thomas Nelson Page's John Marvel, Assistant and
Charlotte Teller's The Cage (1907).

    The novelists are by no means unanimously favorable
to the settlement house and its work.   Some of them see it
as a nest of sexually frustrated, incompetent, interfering fe-
males who poke into areas they know nothing about.   Arthur
Jerome Eddy bitterly attacks the "Ruskin Settlement" in his
novel, Ganton and Co., for proposing arbitration during the
packing-house strike.   His hero, Allan Borlan, accuses the
officious ladies of Ruskin House of interfering in the strike
only as a way of solving their own personal frustrations.
For Vida Scudder's heroine in A Listener in Babel, on the
other hand, Langley House is both a refuge for Chicago
workers and a source of salvation for Hilda Loring herself.
Hilda's busy, useful life is contrasted with the rather pointless existence of her best friend, Dorothy Ferguson.   Dorothy has married the man Hilda loved, has two thriving children and lives in middle class comfort, but she is haunted
by a sense of loneliness and frustration because, unlike Hilda, she has never experienced the joys of dedicating herself
to others.

    The rise of the settlement movement and its reflection
in these novels brings several contemporary paradoxes to the
surface.   The most acceptable role for a woman is still a

quiet dedication to home and family but idleness is both sin-
ful and irresponsible, and the upper class woman surrounded
by a small army of household servants ought to be doing
something more useful than idly planning dinners and balls.
The settlement house, dispensing benevolent charity to the
poor, might be a useful solution for her if only she could
resist expanding its role into labor struggles.

      Charity itself has become paradoxical in this period.
The old belief that the benevolence of the rich would ultimately solve the vexing division between capital and labor has
been shaken. Some of the novelists have begun to think
charity is not the path to justice. Workers in some of the
novels, like Captains of the World and A Listener in Babel,
angrily reject the philanthropy of their employers. They do
not want a company hospital or an accident fund. They insist on an eight-hour day to cut down the number of accidents
and an employer's liability act to guarantee sick benefits.
'"The more "sweet charity" you pour out on the wives and
children of the workers, the more the men organize and
strike, and destroy our property,'"[5] complains Joel Holden
in James H. Brower's Mills of Mammon (1909). Workers
and a few novelists are insisting that an appeal to the employer's conscience is shaky insurance for the worker. They
are calling for legislation which will impose responsibility on
the manufacturer.

      The role of women was changing in the novels but not
entirely for the better. One woman became an obsessive
symbol of evil. Emma Goldman, born in Kovno, Russian
Lithuania, in 1869, one-time garment-worker active in the
Jewish trade union movement, became a leading figure in
American Anarchist circles in the 1880's, soon after the
Haymarket incident. A dynamic speaker and a forceful per-

sonality, she used her undeniable talents and intelligence to
propagandize for anarchism, free love, birth control, the
rights of women--all horrifying causes to most of her contemporaries.   In the novels she appears in many guises--as
Ida Fisher in Gertrude Potter Daniels' The Warners (1901),
as Sophia Goldstein in Isaac Kahn Friedman's By Bread Alone,
as Catherine the Scarlet Nun in Thomas Dixon, Jr.'s Comrades (1909), as Sonia Sofronsky in John R. McMahon's Toilers and Idlers.   In all of the novels she is an evil spirit.
She plots violence out of sheer malice.   She uses her sex
appeal to ensnare co-conspirators.   She finds the way infalli-
bly to the heart of any dissension and fans it into an uncontrollable explosion.   Friedman says of his Sophia: "she had
the scent of the vulture for carrion."   And in all the novels
she comes to a bad end.   Mrs. Daniels' Ida sees her young
son killed in a strike riot she has herself fomented, and she
dies crooning over his dead body.   Dixon's Catherine queens
it over a Polish Socialist community in Anaheim until her
lover deserts her for a younger girl and the community is
destroyed by an invasion of armed soldiers.   McMahon's
Sonia sees her lover killed during a strike and becomes a
fugitive from the police.   Friedman's Sophia also witnesses
the death of her Anarchist lover by suicide and ends up a
lonely, friendless outcast.

The tremendous appeal of Emma Goldman for the
novelists lies partly in her personality and partly in the outrageously unconventional ideas she espoused.   An impassioned
orator of immense vitality and energy, she gave an over-
whelming impression of courage and integrity.   Edward Cor-
so, Commissioner of Immigration, called her "the most interesting radical ever to pass through the gates of Ellis
Island."[6]   She boldly defied accepted contemporary mores,

boasting of her love affairs, publicly defending President Mc-
Kinley's Anarchist assassin, Leon Czolgolsz, and serving
several prison sentences, absolutely unrepentant for her
"crimes. " She lived until 1940, a wandering self-exile, pro-
claiming until the end of her life her conviction that she had
always been true to her principles and that she regretted nothing she had done.

The hatred of the novelists for Emma Goldman is not
without its irony.   Her bright vision of a better world curiously reflects a view which the novelists themselves were
beginning to articulate.   In her address to the 1907 Anarchist
Congress in Amsterdam she spoke eloquently of work in a
free society as "a creative force. " "What painting is to the
artist and the discovery to the scientist, " she said, "the
making of a table, the building of a house, or the tilling of
the soil" could be to a man free to choose his work. [7] Some
of the novelists who portrayed her so mercilessly had the
same vision of the free and creative worker.

The novelists were both electrified and enraged by
her.   The new woman, already appearing on the American
scene, was troubling enough to many intellectuals.   It was
all very well to encourage women to seek a measure of independence and even a tiny degree of sexual freedom, but
where would it all end?   With thousands of Emma Goldmans?
Not if the novelists could help it.   So they kill her off, send
her into wandering exile, cut her off from all decent people
or consign her to a lonely outcast's life, as a warning and
an object lesson.   Even many nominal Socialists of the time
were beginning to worry about the appeal of violent revolution
as a solution to capitalist injustice, and Emma's frank defense of terror as a working class weapon was extremely
disturbing.   Isaac Kahn Friedman and John R. McMahon,

both Socialist novelists, are no kinder to their Sophia and
Sonia than the novelists who abhor Socialism and anarchism
equally.

Some of the novelists in this period were taking a new
look at the theories of Socialism. As disenchantment with
industrial capitalism grew, Socialism began to attract some
intellectuals. Christian Socialism, deeply influenced by the
movement in England, continued into the new century. The
collective rearrangement of society under the guidance of an
active and enlightened Christianity could become the means
for making the morality of the New Testament a contemporary
reality. By now, Marxist theory had made some impact on
American political thought. To the Marxists the Christian
church as well as all organized religion was suspect. The
church was only another arm of the capitalist class, serving
to impress resignation instead of revolution on the working
class. Essentially, the Marxists saw themselves as the
heirs of Judeo-Christian moral values. Through the economic re-ordering of the state, they believed, justice would
triumph on earth. Socialists and anarchists were by this
time divided by a wide ideological split. Anarchists, who
also looked to the ultimate establishment of a just, cooperative society, countenanced, and sometimes engaged in, acts
of terror as the way to educate and unite the masses in
preparation for the coming revolution, while Socialists believed that the revolution could only come about through the
organization of the working class. Violence, if it came,
would be imposed by the capitalists, who would not willingly
surrender power.

The Socialist novel, usually a blatant political tract,
enters American fiction during this period. The novel propagandizing for Socialism substitutes for the earlier novels

which had propagandized for Christianity, and often uses the
very same techniques: pages of undigested sermons, sudden
dramatic conversions and intimations of a serene and peaceful society to come.   The characters of both Christian and
Socialist novels are often one-dimensional.   The older irreligious, lustful villain becomes the ruthless exploiting capitalist painted in several shades of black, and the saintly
Christian hero becomes the self-sacrificing Socialist portrayed in varying shades of white.   Most of the Socialist
novelists are firmly convinced of the imminence of the revolution.   It will come by the next presidential election, "which
the Socialists will certainly win, " predicts Edwin Brenholtz's
Socialist agitator in The Recording Angel.   Or, at least, in
the very near future, since capitalism is already in a rapid
decline, Tom Keating assures Ruth Arnold in Leroy Scott's
The Walking Delegate (1905).   Like early Christians, the novelists indicate that martyrdom for the cause can be the way
to salvation--for society, if not for the individual.   Many of
their characters seek martyrdom willingly and sometimes
joyfully, again like early Christians.   A dedicated Socialist
like Leo Wolffert in Thomas Nelson Page's John Marvel,
Assistant deliberately turns his back on a potentially brilliant
career to organize workers in the slums and eventually to
die during a strike.   Christopher Kenyon, in Florence Converse's The Burden of Christopher, runs his factory as a
cooperative even when it means bankruptcy and suicide.
Isaac Kahn Friedman's Blair Carrhart, in By Bread Alone,
sacrifices his career as a minister, his engagement to the
girl he loves, and even his health to his conviction that he
must devote himself to the Socialist cause.   Ernest Everhard,
the Socialist hero of Jack London's The Iron Heel (1907), willingly goes to his death in the struggle against the tyranny of

the Iron Heel regime. The Christian parallels in the Socialist
novels are not surprising. Many middle class Socialists began with strong Christian church affiliations, and all of them
had been deeply influenced by Christian morality. The Socialist Eden they envision is an earthly realization of the Christian heaven. Socialism promises the universal brotherhood
of man, a just reward for the virtuous, a release from dull
and uncreative work.

Socialist novels are invariably pro-union, of course,
and sympathetic to strikes. They see the strike as a necessary step toward the radical reorganization of society, but
only a first step. Without ultimate state ownership of mines,
mills and factories, the trade union is only a temporary stop-
gap. Strikes help the worker to a more equitable share of
the profits his labor has created, but the real solution can
never come until capitalism is replaced by socialism, and
competition by cooperation.

The best Socialist novel of the period, far and away,
is Upton Sinclair's The Jungle (1906). Sinclair describes, in
great detail, the nauseating processes of the Chicago stockyards and the intolerable conditions of the workers in the
meat-packing plants. He also pictures vividly the home life
of the workers, contrasting the filthy crowded slums with
the gusto of an immigrant wedding party and the tender concern of family members for each other. Jurgis Rudkis, the
powerful young immigrant hero, is not a failure because of
his innate inferiority. He is energetic, intelligent and responsible; he has, in fact, all the prerequisites for success.
He struggles to keep his family alive but fails nonetheless.
The meat-packers' trusts kill animals and men with equal
indifference. The strike is not a central incident in the
novel, but Sinclair uses it to make a telling point. The

meat packers have brought strikebreakers into the plant to
keep it going during the strike, and suddenly are faced with
the problem of feeding, housing and controlling several hundred rough and uncouth men. They advance Jurgis, one of
the strikebreakers, to a position of authority, and he succeeds admirably in organizing the scabs. But in the process
he realizes bitterly that his employers can only make use of
his intelligence and ability when they pit him against the men
of his own class. In all his years as a worker he has never
been given the chance to use or develop his talents. The
realization utterly demoralizes Jurgis. He begins to drink
heavily and drives the strikebreakers unmercifully. When
the strike is over, Jurgis leaves, once more unnecessary to
the factory owners and once more out of a job. His family
scattered, full of self-disgust because he has allowed himself
to be used, Jurgis wanders aimlessly from job to job, seeking release in heavy drinking bouts. He is saved from complete despair when he discovers Socialism and dedicates himself to the Socialist cause.

      Thereafter, the novel degenerates into a talky Socialist
tract, but Jurgis has learned an important lesson from his
strike experience. The most powerful, intelligent and ambitious individual can still be helpless against capitalist exploitation. A few such individuals may be able to escape and
themselves become capitalists but, for most, the only real
escape lies in learning to work collectively with others for
a new political and economic order. The Jungle is a superb
piece of muckraking reportage and rightfully became a sensation soon after it was published. It contributed to the passage of the first Federal pure food and drug laws, a step
which gave public acknowledgment to the government's right
and responsibility to regulate industry for the public welfare.

The novel uses a strike for a new unusual purpose. It is
Jurgis Rudkis' university, through which he discovers his
crucial relationship as an individual to his class.

Nineteenth century ideas persisted in the novels during
this transitional period, although we can trace a few embry-
onic changes. The industrialist is still the empire-builder,
wealthy because he is superior--in skill, intelligence and in-
dustriousness. His right to rule his hard-won enterprise
without interference is not often questioned by the novelists.
Peter Rathbawne, the millowner of Guy Wetmore Carryl's
The Lieutenant Governor (1903), Captain Amos Williams,
president of the Latin-American Steamship Line in Eugene
Walter's Paid in Full (1908), Allan Borlan, the meatpacker
in Arthur Jerome Eddy's Ganton and Co. all insist they will
not be dictated to by the unions. Their intransigence in
these novels is part of their strength. They dig in their
heels, refuse to knuckle under and, by their example, rally
other weakening industrialists against the threatening growth
of trade union power.

But they are fighting a losing battle. In a number of
the novels of this period the entrepreneurs and the novelists
are beginning to soften. Great wealth imposes great responsibility, they are now willing to admit. The man who wields
power over the livelihood of the men in his employ has to
submit to some controls. John Ganton, the ruthless old
meatpacking tycoon in Ganton and Co., wants no truck with
the union because his employees should know that he can be
trusted to care for their interests with fatherly concern
while he is tending to his own. Even in Roy L. McCardell's
ridiculous novel, The Wage Slaves of New York (1899),
Arthur Barriston, the silk mill owner, tries to cope with
the problem of his responsibility toward his "hands. " He

regards his position as "a sacred trust." In Charles King's
A Tame Surrender (1896), George Pullman's refusal to arbitrate the bloody strike at his plant is considered a bit em-
barrassing.   One of the characters comments on the Pullman
strike:

> '...the company refuses to hear of arbitration.
> From a purely business point of view I cannot
> deny their right to do so, but the very attitude
> assumed by the corporation makes many of the
> labor-leaders' accusations true.'[8]

Even though the entrepreneur has the right to order his own
affairs without hindrance, his insistence on absolute control
is unseemly and irresponsible.   A few of the novelists hesitantly take the next step.   If the inner compulsions of the
industrialist are weak or absent, then perhaps society has
the right to make up for his deficiency and to compel him
to treat his employees fairly.

Writers like Guy Wetmore Carryl, Arthur Jerome
Eddy and Charles King have by slow degrees come a long
way from John Hay, Thomas Bailey Aldrich and Charles Benjamin in their attitude toward the industrialist.   Although
they are all superficially alike in their admiration for the
successful captain of industry, the novelist of the early years
of the twentieth century has a somewhat different kind of man
in mind.   The nineteenth century novelist often contrasted
his millowner hero to other factory owners who were dishonest or conniving.   Now, in the early twentieth century,
the millowner is a hero because he is not only honest but
responsible.   His responsibility takes the form of working
hard himself, and of paying his workers decent wages and
giving them tolerable working conditions.   Peter Rathbawne
in The Lieutenant Governor, the same man who will not accept union interference, claims:

> 'No one can say that I ever clipped wages, even when
> I had to run the mills at a loss, as I've had to do
> more than once.   I gave my people an eight-hour
> day long before the law of Alleghenia jammed it
> down the throats of other mill-owners. '[9]

If Rathbawne did voluntarily establish an eight-hour day in
his mill he was a unique specimen.   Most of the millowners
had to have it "jammed down their throats, " as he himself
admits.   The new-found responsibility of the employer, which
the novelists now calmly assume to stem from the industrialists' enlightened self-interest, is the result of some of the
bloody strikes of the past and the growth in the organization
and power of the trade unions.

   Another example of the newly responsible employer is
Clarence Haydon, superintendent of the mine in James North
Wright's Where Copper Was King (1905).   Haydon puts the
safety of his miners ahead of his property when he orders
fans turned on to create a back-draft in the copper mine
where four miners have been trapped by a fire.   The fans
do irreparable damage to the mine but three of the men are
saved.   Here again, Wright assumes that it is the industrialist's concern and not the power of the union which enforces
safety measures.   The novelist of the new century no longer
accepts success as an unqualified virtue.   The successful industrialist must also accept responsibility.   The unspoken
threat behind this new concern for the workers is that if the
capitalist does not voluntarily accept the responsibility, the
unions or the government, or both, have the right to impose
controls upon him.

   Most of the novelists would still like to think that
there is a traditional father-son relationship between masters
and men, and that if only unions and union organizers would
stay out of the picture, reasonable solutions could be worked

out without resorting to strikes or lockouts. But it is getting
harder to maintain such a belief. Allan Borlan in Ganton
and Co. accuses the unions of destroying confidence, good-
will and esteem between employers and employees, and
Marie Van Vorst's millowner in Amanda of the Mill thinks
mutual understanding will avoid the necessity for unions or
arbitration. Frank Nason, the author of The Blue Goose
(1903), believes unions "knock together the heads of the laborer and his employer and impartially pick the pockets of
each in the general mêlée which is bound to follow."[10] But
the novelists reflect the first signs of doubt. Where was
contemporary society heading and how was it achieving material success? Perhaps strikes were symptoms of hidden
dislocations, perhaps they were forced on desperate workmen.
Amanda of the Mill, By Bread Alone, Captains of the World,
Herbert Elliot Hamblen's The General Manager's Story (1898),
The Walking Delegate all suggest that the workers have legitimate grievances and that they strike only when other measures
fail. As a matter of fact, suggests Neil Manning, Gwendolen
Overton's union officer in Captains of the World, it is the
union that restrains, rather than inflames violence. The
union discourages violence because it is the strikers who
suffer most from it. Manning also suggests that the strike
is an educational process. The men learn from their experience what no amount of philanthropy from their employers
could ever teach them.

The demands of the strikers now begin to make some
sense, too. Some are still outrageous or silly or irrational.
(One striker in Alice French's The Man of the Hour wants
"a nice house with a piazza and a bath-room with a white
china bath-tub, and a horse and buggy and...a hired girl,"[11]
and the author leaves us in no doubt that she thinks he is

slightly mad).   But a few of the novels suggest that the striker wants conditions which will let him be a man.   The most
poignant expression of the strikers' reasonable demands is
Henry Euston's speech to the textile strikers in Amanda of
the Mill.

> 'Our point is only--Recognition.   Only--that when
> a picked few of us present ourselves at the mill-
> owner's door we shall be received, conferred with,
> man to man--Recognition! Then we will ask for
> shorter hours--a working day that will permit you
> to breathe, to rest, to keep clean--to read, per-
> haps; to think, to remain human beings in spite of
> benumbing machinery. '[12]

Along with a dawning sympathy for the workingman's
demands an uneasy fear of the machine also begins to in-
trude.   The machine-tender has been turned into a dull
drudge by his simple repetitive taks.   Mary Wilkins Freeman's description of the women leather-workers in her novel,
The Portion of Labor (1901), is harsh and ugly, but her re-
pulsion is tempered by a kind of pity which has not been evident in the novel since Rebecca Harding Davis's Margret
Howth or Elizabeth Phelps Ward's The Silent Partner, written
thirty and forty years earlier.

> ... girls and women in dingy skirts and bagging
> blouses, with coarse hair strained into hard knots
> of exigency from patient, or sullen faces, accord-
> ing to their methods of bearing their lots; all of
> them rank with the smell of leather, their coarse
> hands stained with it, swinging their poor little
> worn bags which had held their dinners. [13]

In Mrs. Freeman's novel, as well as in John McMahon's
Toilers and Idlers, we get the first whiff of disillusionment
with technological and industrial progress.   Has it perhaps
been too dearly bought at the expense of individual creativity?
Years later, Sherwood Anderson would once more take up
this theme in far better novels.

The professional union organizer or walking delegate still comes off very badly. Most of the union leaders in these novels are driven by low and selfish motives. They hunger for power; they envy the success of hardworking industrialists; they lust after upper class women; they use their positions of trust to extort money; they enjoy mischief for its own sake; a few end up clearly insane. Bribery of the walking delegates and business agents is frequent in the novels. Grady, in Calumet "K" (1901) by Samuel Merwin and Henry Kitchell Webster, demands five thousand dollars from Charlie Bannon, foreman of the Calumet "K" construction job, in return for preventing a strike, while Buck Foley in Leroy Scott's The Walking Delegate gets a thousand dollars for ending one. Allan Borlan, in Arthur Jerome Eddy's Ganton and Co., refuses to hand out bribes despite union threats against his meat-packing firm. Some of the union officers in the novels are not only corrupt but irrational. Kirby, in Gertrude Potter Daniels' The Warners, becomes a raving maniac when his wife and son are killed in a strike he himself has whipped up. McGrath, in Guy Wetmore Carryl's The Lieutenant Governor, forces a strike out of sheer "wounded vanity." The men have no real quarrel with their employer but McGrath has been discharged as a bad influence on them. The union organizers in Charles King's A Tame Surrender are accused of stirring up "tramps and loafers" with "no end but mischief in view."

But a new note is slipping in. A few of the walking delegates are sincere and honest. Leroy Scott's hero, Tom Keating, in The Walking Delegate, is by no means faultless but his dedication to the union is plainly motivated by his own personal experience as a construction worker and he learns his job as a walking delegate slowly and painfully,

making many mistakes. His pathetic dead-ended love affair
with a sympathetic secretary and his eventual return to his
rather silly wife help make Keating a credible human being.
Marie Van Vorst's organizer, Henry Euston, in Amanda of
the Mill, is also sympathetically sketched. A reformed al-
coholic, yoked to a slatternly wife, Euston is driven by the
vision of a better life for the millworkers. The novelists
are beginning to make two important literary changes: they
can visualize sympathetic strike leaders and they can see the
strike from the workers' point of view.

    If at least some of the novelists can think of the work-
er as a human being, fewer of them are willing to accept the
foreign-born worker as equally human. Distrust of the immigrant not only carries over into the new century but becomes,
if anything, more virulent. Novelists like Arthur Jerome
Eddy and Charles King see the foreigner as little more than
a wild beast ready to "knife a man" or "eagerly awaiting the
next opportunity to preach sedition and rebellion. " Isaac
Kahn Friedman assumes that his hero's Anglo-Saxon heritage
makes him morally superior to his Polish antagonist in By
Bread Alone. Blair Carrhart will fight Vorlinski with his
fists like a man but "atavism, the inculcated lesson of fair
play, heredity or a superior race"[14] prevent Carrhart from
using a knife as Vorlinski does. Naturally, Carrhart, being
a superior American, wins the fight anyway. Alice French,
writing under the pseudonym of Octave Thanet, invents a
schizophrenic hero for her novel, The Man of the Hour. John /
Ivan Winslow is the offspring of a mésalliance between a bluff
New England manufacturer and a Russian princess with Nihilist sympathies. In his early life his foreign mother's evil
influence propels him into a career as a socialist agitator,
Pullman strike organizer and roisterous walking delegate in

a steel workers' union.   But the solid heritage from his father constantly pulls him in the opposite direction.   Even
during his most active socialist period he decides he can
try "to make the unions stand for something better than
striking."[15]   Before the story ends, his American heritage
wins out, and he switches sides abruptly.   He becomes an
active strikebreaker, threatening and intimidating the disloyal
strikers.   He personally organizes a band of Negro strikebreakers and heroically leads them inside the struck plant.
("'The darkies amuse me.... (they) play cards and craps.   I
tell them stories,'"[15] Winslow comments).   When he has
fully atoned for his earlier aberration by preventing the steel
strike from coming before an arbitration board, he is at
last sure he has eradicated the alien strain from his personality.   "The Anglo-Saxon in me has conquered," he exults.

      The outright villains in this group of novels are still
foreign-born--the Pole Vorlinski and the French anarchist La
Vette in Friedman's By Bread Alone, the German socialist
Elmendorf in King's A Tame Surrender, the Cornishman,
Dick Jeffrey, in Wright's Where Copper Was King.   Some
of the villains are American-born, but their names--McGrath,
Wolf, Grady, Luna, Rubinovich--seem to suggest that they
are only first generation Americans and not of good Anglo-
Saxon stock.   The novelists assume that foreigners are
ashamed of their background.   Young Paul Brodski in By
Bread Alone reluctantly admits he is Polish "as if not overly
proud of the fact."   Leo Wolffert in Thomas Nelson Page's
John Marvel, Assistant quietly eats his heart out for Eleanor
Leigh but will not tell her he loves her because, as a German Jew, he knows he is unworthy of her.   But one small
suggestion of a change in attitude begins to be evident.

      A few of the novelists wonder whether the sullen un-

grateful foreigners might not be reacting to what they have
found in America. Coming here with high hopes, they have
found only corrosive disappointment. Upton Sinclair's uprooted Lithuanian immigrants in The Jungle are overworked,
cheated and destroyed in the Chicago slums. Mary Wilkins
Freeman describes a high school graduation in The Portion
of Labor. As Ellen Brewster delivers a valedictory address
full of praise for the rich promise of American democracy,
the author wonders what the foreign-born graduates and their
parents in the audience are thinking. Are they contrasting
American ideals with their own unfulfilled lives? Isaac Kahn
Friedman, the same Friedman who was touting his hero's
Anglo-Saxon virtues in By Bread Alone in 1901, has a few
second thoughts in his novel, The Radical, published six
years later. In 1907 he notes that the foreigners "had toiled
and spun during their youth, and in their old age were neither fed by the fruits of their labor nor warmed by the fibres
of their spinning. "[16]

The church and organized religion continue to play a
role in the novels at the turn of the century but a much di-
minished one. Actual word-for-word sermons almost disappear. There are still occasional passages blaming strikes
on godlessness. Ellen Brewster, for example, in Mary Wilkins Freeman's The Portion of Labor, wonders whether any
one who questions inequality is not "'usurping the part of the
Creator, and bringing down wrath and confusion not only upon
his own head, but upon the heads of others?'"[17] There are
still a few outright religious tracts, but very few. In Henry
Cherouny's The Burial of the Apprentice (1900), for example,
young Charley, the son of an anarchist, attends the Sunday
School of his local Episcopal Church but under his father's
influence he leaves the church, participates in a useless ap-

prentice's strike and eventually dies of tuberculosis. His
father, consumed with guilt for turning his son away from
religion, goes mad.   There are also a few Christian Socialist tracts.   Cortland Myers' Would Christ Belong to a Labor
Union? (1900) takes place during a violent street car strike.
To a congregation which includes several officials and stockholders of the streetcar company, the Rev. David Dowling
preaches a sermon advocating public ownership of public utilities and the establishment of permanent arbitration boards.
Dowling maintains that Christ would join a union, might even
reluctantly go out on strike, but would definitely not engage
in violence.   The industrialists are impressed enough by the
sermon to agree to negotiate with the strikers, and the union
leader, Henry Fielding, joins Dowling's church.

        For the first time novelists criticize the church and
churchmen.   Isaac Kahn Friedman portrays a malicious
priest, Father Kozma, in By Bread Alone, who threatens
his parishioners with excommunication if they associate with
Blair Carrhart, who is organizing a union.   Friedman also
intimates that the company has been contributing money to
the church in return for the priest's help in preventing
strikes.   By itself, this would not be a significant example,
since Father Kozma's church is a Catholic church.   Anti-
Catholic feeling is not new to the American novel and Catholic clerics in the novels had often been pictured as malign
influences.   What is new, however, is the growing number of
Protestant ministers in the novels who are being arraigned
for neglecting the poor and pandering to their rich congrega-
tions.   Thomas Nelson Page's Dr. Capon, in John Marvel,
Assistant, the rector of a fashionable church, is described
as one "who dealt more with the rich and less with the poor."
Capon consorts with industrialists and warns his assistant,

John Marvel, that he is spending too much time ministering
to the women and children in a strike-ridden slum.   Jack
London paints an acid picture of Bishop Morehouse in The
Iron Heel.   The Bishop is utterly ignorant of the lives of
workers until Ernest Everhard takes him on a guided tour
of the slums.   The Bishop has never bothered to translate
Christianity into a concern for the poor.

    The novels of this period reveal how slowly change
comes about.   The ideas, attitudes and themes of the nineteenth century still persist.   Whatever changes do become
evident are hesitantly introduced and only tentatively developed.   Among the themes which continue with almost no dis-
cernible change is, somewhat surprisingly, the 1886 Haymarket affair.   More than twenty years after the McCormick
Strike and its violent aftermath, the trauma has not yet been
fully healed.   Several of Robert Herrick's characters if The
Memoirs of an American Citizen (1905) are intimately con-
nected with the Haymarket riot.   Van Harrington, the narrator, gets involved in discussions of the affair with his fellow
boarder, Jaffrey Slocum.   Another boarder, Hillary Cox, is
scarred for life in the mêlée. Harrington eventually serves
on the jury trying the Haymarket anarchists, and lays the
foundation for his future fortune when his vote for the death
sentence earns him the esteem of his employer, Henry Dround.
Alice French also reverts, with horror, to the Haymarket affair in The Man of the Hour.   Walter Tyler, a leader in the
Molders' Union and the hero's vicious antagonist in the novel,
is suspected of having had a hand in the riot.   '"He's hand
in glove with the old Spies-Engel-Parsons gang; and he is a
pretty thoroughgoing rascal, to my mind,'"18 a fellow-worker
says of Tyler.   Charlotte Teller uses the Haymarket trial as
a pivotal incident in the plot of her novel, The Cage.   Alex-

ander Sloane, the millionaire lumber dealer, and his son
Alec have been estranged for a long time. Alec accuses his
father of callous disregard for his striking workers' welfare
and Sloane thinks his son is foolishly committed to the cause
of the strikers. On the day the four Anarchists are hanged,
both come to their senses and admit they have been wrong.
The execution has reunited father and son.

Another nineteenth century theme which continues to
be important in this group of novels is the persistent idea
that any worker who really wants to, can become successful.
Unions may be necessary to protect the weak or the stupid
but the worker who develops a skill, who works hard, who
produces more will be rewarded materially. The trouble
with unions, says Johnny Winslow in The Man of the Hour,
is that they force a worker "to stop work to help somebody
else. " He deplores the trend in which '" the old notion that
any saving, self-denying industrious workingman might rise
to something better and employ men, on his own account, is
almost gone. '"19 Matthew Kelly, the gold miner in Hamlin
Garland's Hesper (1903), has nothing but contempt for men
who go to work for mining companies and then resort to
unions to win better wages and conditions. He pans for gold
on his own claim and is quite willing to endure loneliness,
hard work and a period of deprivation. He is finally rewarded with a rich gold-strike. Robert Herrick's narrator, Van
Harrington, in The Memoirs of an American Citizen, is a
fine example of the man who has his own efforts to thank for
material success. Harrington has little patience with the
strikers at the McCormick plant and even less with the
strikers, later on, in one of his own meat packing plants.
When they attack him, he uses his fists to good advantage,
then treats them to a lecture on his own "dog-eat-dog" phi-

losophy. "'That experience was the greatest bracer I ever
had in my life,'" is his comment. The real man relishes
a hand-to-hand combat in a physical encounter, in a factory
or in the scramble of the wheat pit or stockmarket, and if
he has spirit and backbone he will win out in the end. The
epitome of the man who makes it on his own, without snivell-
ing and without expecting help from unions, is the fast disap-
pearing cowboy, last of the Western frontiersmen. Owen
Wister wrote:

> I have liked several of Duke's cowboys. They are
> of the manly, simple, humorous, American type
> which I hold to be the best and bravest we possess
> and our hope for the future. They work hard, they
> play hard, and they don't go on strike. [20]

Another example of the man who works hard, plays
hard and doesn't go on strike or join unions is the Army officer, and it is not surprising to find a number of active or
reserve officers sympathetically portrayed in the novels.
Lieutenant Randy Merriam in Charles King's An Army Wife
(1896) is assigned to make sure the mails go through during
a railroad strike. King's A Tame Surrender describes Captain Floyd Forrest's participation in the Pullman strike. John
Barclay, in Guy Wetmore Carryl's The Lieutenant Governor,
declares martial law and orders out the troops under the command of his close friend, Colonel Broadcastle. Rob Raymond,
the hero of Hamlin Garland's Hesper, has attended West Point,
and John Winslow in Alice French's The Man of the Hour is
a graduate of a military school. Allison, the railroad magnate, in A Tame Surrender, suggests a solution that would
make strikes an impossibility:

> 'What I wish could be done with our hands would
> be to have them regularly enlisted for the work, --
> so many years unless sooner discharged, --just like
> the soldiers, by Jove! Then when a man quit work

it would be desertion, and when he combined with
others to strike it would be mutiny.   Ah, we'd have
a railway service in this country then that would
beat the world. '21

The virtues inherent in military organization were very
attractive to the novelists.   Unquestioning obedience, training
in quick response to crisis, dedication to the upholding of law
and order were appealing in a time of disorder.   Predictable,
controlled ranks of massed soldiers were infinitely preferable
to disorderly mobs of strikers.   Jack Monro, a cashiered
West Pointer in Hesper, says, '"I want to show them a hundred men trained in unhesitating obedience to a leader are
better than ten thousand men whooping and yelling in a
mob. '"22   It was only in the Socialist novels that the military
was not considered praiseworthy.   Socialists opposed the
army for two reasons.   They regarded it as a tool of the
bourgeois state, imposing the will of the capitalist class upon
the oppressed working class.   In addition, most Socialists of
the period were strongly pacifist.   They opposed not only the
use of military force but the use of counterforce by strikers
as well.

The one entirely new element introduced into many of
the novels of this period is the authenticity of the factory set-
tings.   Not only do the novelists actually take their readers
inside the mines and the mills but some of them know what
really goes on there.   Upton Sinclair's stockyards, Isaac
Kahn Friedman's steel mills, Marie Van Vorst's cotton mills
are real places.   Herbert Elliott Hamblen's railroad slang in
The General Manager's Story or Marie Van Vorst's Southern
hill dialect in Amanda of the Mill have an authentic ring.
Theodore Dreiser's description of the machines stamping out
shoe parts in Sister Carrie (1900) is detailed and recognizable.   The jobs, the clothes, the slang, the union meetings

in some of these novels are obviously based on experience
and not on second-hand reports.

The new authenticity in descriptions of working class
life reflects a change in the class origins of both the novelist and his readers. Industrialization and technological advances require a corresponding increase in the literacy of
the workers. The machinist has to read a blueprint, and
from blueprint to novel is not such a giant step. The literate worker begins, early in the twentieth century, to become
part of the novelists' public. The novelist himself may in a
few rare instances have come out of the working class (Jack
London is the most notable example). More often, he continues to come from a middle class background but he is less
and less likely to be an amateur, scribbling novels to add to
the family income. The novelist, especially one who is writing about factories, is usually a professional writer who began his career as a journalist. He knows his steel or cotton
mill because he has seen the inside of it as a reporter. Sinclair, Friedman, Scott were all at some time working journalists. Marie Van Vorst actually went to work in a South
Carolina cotton mill to collect her data, as she reports in
her book, The Woman Who Toils (1903).

The novel had by now been fully accepted as a creative art form in America, and factory life and the strike as
legitimate themes for the novelist to explore. For a few
novelists the strike had already become a sophisticated literary technique--but for only a very few. Robert Herrick uses
the Pullman strike of 1894 in The Web of Life to reveal both
the inner life of his main character, Dr. Howard Sommers,
and the corroding social milieu in which Sommers tries to
function. Sommers has managed to build a fashionable medical practice and has been accepted into upper class society,

but he is uneasy. The young doctor listens in growing disgust to the pompous, self-satisfied dinner conversations of
the society leaders among whom he carries on his lucrative
practice. As the strike develops, the financiers become
more and more incensed, and begin to call for Federal
troops to be used against the strikers. Their callous sel-
fishness troubles Sommers, but so do the corruptness of the
labor leaders and the brutality and ignorance of the strikers.
He predicts that '"the rich will buy out the leaders. . . . and
we shall all settle down to the same old game of grab on
the same old basis.'"[23] Sommers' personal life becomes
a kind of counterpoint to the power struggle developing in
the strike. He is caught up in an obsessive liaison with
Alves Preston, a widowed schoolteacher, whose neurotic
needs he cannot satisfy. Unable to make a clear choice between industrialists and strikers, Sommers becomes the victim of both. Distrusted and isolated, he removes himself
more and more from all relationships except his love affair
with Alves. His medical practice among the rich has been
wrecked, while his medical skill is refused by suspicious
strikers. When Alves commits suicide, Sommers leaves
Chicago to tend Cuban war veterans in a Florida fever-hos-
pital, and there finally regains some kind of equilibrium.
Through his involvement with the strike Sommers has learned
that the individual is helpless in the face of tremendous and
uncontrollable social forces. The strike disaster is Sommers' disaster, too. All he has left are the remnants of
his integrity. His brief and tragic revolt is over.

　　　　The most successful use of a strike in this period is
Theodore Dreiser's in Sister Carrie. A Brooklyn streetcar
strike becomes in Dreiser's hands a powerful artistic device
through which a man's gradual breakdown is detailed. When

Hurstwood meets Carrie Meeber, he is a strong and successful man.   His illicit passion for Carrie overwhelms him and
he begins to deteriorate morally as well as physically.   When
he decides to steal some of his employer's money, he begins
to lose some of his great vitality.   His decision to return
what money is left is not a sign of redemption.   On the contrary, he has sunk a little lower because he is not prompted
by any ethical principles.   He is simply afraid.   His sturdy
independence diminishes steadily until he is reduced to un-
ashamed cadging on Carrie's earnings.   Against the backdrop
of the strike Hurstwood plays out his last desperate effort to
regain his manhood.

Dreiser stresses Hurstwood's sympathy with the strikers.   Even the police secretly sympathize with the strikers
and despise the strikebreakers they are detailed to protect.
But Hurstwood has by now sunk so low that in spite of his
sympathies he agrees to become a strikebreaker.   When violence begins, he deteriorates a little more.   While the streetcar conductor is being beaten unconscious, Hurstwood cowers
helplessly, very different from the man of action he used to
be.   As the ambulance clangs off, Hurstwood slinks home in
a driving snowstorm.   (Dreiser could not quite manage to
resist this anachronistic touch of melodrama.)   The strike
has marked the end of Hurstwood's existence as a strong and
decent human being.   It is after this escapade that Carrie's
contempt for him becomes unbearable and she leaves him for
good.   The pathetic twenty dollars she leaves behind for the
wreck of a man he has become is the final coup-de-grâce.

Dreiser's own sympathies with the working class are
evident in the novel.   He believes that the strikers' demands
are justified.   (He includes a long passage describing the
grievances of the "trippers. ")   He thinks even their violence

is understandable, coming as it does out of hunger and exas-
peration.   But he has not set out to convert us to any sort
of sociological or economic theory.   He uses the strike entirely for artistic purposes, and he does so responsibly and
superbly well.   The drama of the novel lies in each individual's moving struggle to survive.   Hurstwood's fails, and we
see the dramatic end of his struggle through his involvement
in the strike.   Dreiser's uses of the strike in this novel sur-
passes all the earlier examples, including William Dean Howells' in A Hazard of New Fortunes.   The Dryfooses, Basil
March and Lindau in the earlier novel, although affected by the
strike, are not really intimately concerned with it.   Hurstwood is.   His participation is not an accidental one.   The
consequences of the strike in Howells' novel are too melodramatic: the deaths of two people who are not themselves
strikers or strikebreakers.   Dreiser, for all his addiction
to melodrama, does not overdramatize the strike.   The violence is realistic, the consequences are credible.   Howells
has tried to draw too many diffuse conclusions from his
strike.   Dreiser uses his for one purpose only: Hurstwood's
moral disintegration.

By 1910 American society had undergone some fundamental changes.   A predominantly rural society had become
industrialized.   The frontier had disappeared.   The factory
worker was beginning to organize and his demands were beginning to be heard.   In the novels which used strikes change
came slowly, but by 1910 many were visible.   The novelist
had begun to look at the worker as a human being and at the
strike as a social phenomenon which could be analyzed and
explained.   The strike was becoming an artistic device which
would be used to deepen insight and understanding.

Notes

1. Robert Herrick, The Web of Life (New York: Macmillan
    Co. , 1914), p. 342.

2. Thomas Nelson Page, John Marvel, Assistant (New York:
    Charles Scribner's Sons, 1909), p. 462

3. Edwin Arnold Brenholtz, The Recording Angel (Chicago:
    Charles H. Kerr and Co. , 1905), p. 173.

4. Mary E. Wilkins Freeman, The Portion of Labor (New
    York: Harper and Bros. , 1901), p. 563.

5. James H. Brower, The Mills of Mammon (Joliet, Ill. :
    P. H. Murray and Co. , 1909), p. 13.

6. Cecyle S. Neidle, The New Americans (New York:
    Twayne Publishers, 1967), p. 179.

7. Richard Drinnon, Rebel in Paradise (Chicago: Univer-
    sity of Chicago Press, 1961). p. 104.

8. Charles King, A Tame Surrender (Philadelphia: J. B.
    Lippincott Co. , 1896), p. 156.

9. Guy Wetmore Carryl, The Lieutenant Governor (Boston:
    Houghton Mifflin Co. , 1903), p. 72.

10. Frank Lewis Nason, The Blue Goose (New York: Mc-
    Clure, Phillips and Co. , 1903), p. 36.

11. Alice French (Octave Thanet), The Man of the Hour (New
    York: Grosset and Dunlap, 1905), p. 177.

12. Marie Van Vorst, Amanda of the Mill (New York: Dodd,
    Mead and Co. , 1905), p. 206.

13. Freeman, op. cit. , p. 226-227.

14. Isaac Kahn Friedman, By Bread Alone (New York: Mc-
    Clure Phillips and Co. , 1901), p. 85.

15. French, op. cit. , p. 342, 434, 438.

16. Isaac Kahn Friedman, The Radical (New York: D. Apple-
    ton and Co. , 1907), p. 14.

17. Freeman, op. cit., p. 519.

18. French, op. cit., p. 201.

19. Ibid., p. 346.

20. Fanny Kemble Wister, ed., Owen Wister Out West
     (Chicago: University of Chicago Press, 1958), p.
     246.

21. King, op. cit., p. 157.

22. Hamlin Garland, Hesper (New York: Harper and Bros.,
     (1903), p. 245.

23. Herrick, op. cit., p. 140.

Chapter 4

NEW ATTITUDES, NEW TRACTS: 1910-1929

By 1910 the nation was enjoying a period of renewed exuberance and optimism.   The Spanish-American War in 1898 had marked a significant victory for the United States; it was her debut as an important international power.   After the panic of 1907 the economy had recovered quickly.   There were new technological advances at home and new markets abroad waiting for full exploitation.   When World War I began, America stayed prudently aloof for a while from the European quarrels--and made money.   In 1917, when the United States entered the war, nationalism and euphoria reached an unprecedented peak.   It took less than two years of war to change the cheerful optimism of 1910 into a new mood of gloomy disillusionment.   Throughout the Twenties a brooding alienation simmered under the surface prosperity.

Economic and political successes and the new international status of the United States before World War I led quite directly to a belief in the natural superiority of Americans and, by easy stages, to an identification with the concept of the Superman.   The nation could point to some very real supermen--men like Gould or Rockefeller or Morgan or Doheny or Hearst, who literally ruled financial empires, or, on the opposite side of the economic battlefield, a man like Big Bill Haywood, leader of the Western Miners' Federation and, a little later, organizer of the Industrial Workers of the World.   Haywood appeared as a character in no fewer

than five novels of the period, either under his own name or
barely disguised: Carl Van Vechten's Peter Whiffle (1929),
Max Eastman's Venture (1927), Ernest Poole's The Harbor
(1916), Idwal Jones' Steel Chips (1929) and Clement Wood's
Mountain (1920). The unbeatable industrialist, the two-fisted
outdoorsman or the tough labor organizer became a cliché of
contemporary American fiction in novels by Jack London,
Zane Grey, Robert Chambers, Upton Sinclair and many others. The novelists were charmed by the romance of the ruthless leader of men, whatever his political or economic affilia-
tion, whose physical strength and indomitable will could sway
masses of lesser men.

    Post-war disillusionment, however, posed some new
problems. Not everyone was convinced that conditions were
really as satisfactory as the surface seemed to indicate.
Veterans wondering whether the war had really been worth
its cost, workers barely scraping a living despite a financial
boom, intellectuals alienated from a crass business ethic
were, more or less articulately, disenchanted with America
in the Twenties. Cynical, indecisive, uprooted protagonists
began to make their appearance in the novels. Pelham Judson in Clement Wood's Mountain and Harris Burnham in
Charles Rumford Walker's Bread and Fire (1927), who both
end up jobless and hopeless, Marie Rogers in Agnes Smedley's Daughter of Earth (1929), whose marriage fails misera-
bly, Sinclair Lewis' Babbitt in his novel, Babbitt (1922),
whose name has become the byword for the shallow, self-
deceiving small town businessman, and Paulus Kempf in
Leonard Cline's fantastic God Head (1925), whose complete
loss of faith in humanity turns him into a Lemminkainen, a
malicious spirit who wrecks human lives, are new kinds of
"heroes" in American fiction.

Some of the novelists of the post-war period began to
look with interest toward Socialism and, in particular, to the
Soviet experiment in the U. S. S. R. Interest in Socialism already had a relatively long history among American intellectuals, beginning in the Eighteeen Forties with early Socialist
experiments like New Harmony and Brook Farm. In the
period just before World War I Socialist ideas had had a
fresh spurt of growth and influence. Eugene Debs, campaign-
ing for president in 1916, polled more than a million votes,
an impressive total, especially since the candidate was then
serving a sentence in a Federal prison. In 1911, the Socialist periodical, The Masses, was founded. Until its demise
in 1917 it attracted a magnificent roster of writers, journalists and artists. The work of Sherwood Anderson, Wilbur
Daniel Steele, Floyd Dell, Max Eastman, John Sloan, Art
Young, Arthur B. Davies, John Reed, Louis Untermeyer,
Charles Erskine Scott Wood, George Bellows all appeared in
The Masses during its brief existence. It was not accidental
that Socialism attracted so many artists, nor that Socialists
concerned themselves almost equally with politics and art.
The artist who felt and could articulate his discontent with
capitalist values looked to Socialism as a possible way out.

Writers of many different political persuasions were
exploring the subsurface injustices of capitalist society with
increasing disillusionment--frankly Socialist writers like Upton Sinclair, David Graham Phillips, James Oppenheim, Jack
London, increasingly vehement "muckrakers" like Lincoln
Steffens and Ida Tarbell, and politically uncommitted but
thoughtful and observant writers like Sherwood Anderson and
William Allen White. Socialism seemed to offer the possibility to create a new and equalitarian society.

World War I shattered such organization as the Social-

ist movement had managed to develop.   The Socialist Party
fell apart over the issue of American participation in the
war.   Those who opposed the war had a rough time of it--
several I. W. W. leaders were lynched; the editors of The
Masses were tried twice in Federal courts for their editori-
als against the war; conscientious objectors remained in Federal prisons years after the end of the war.   In the Twenties,
under Attorney General Mitchell Palmer's direction, a series
of blatantly illegal arrests and deportations was carried out
against foreign-born Socialists.   The single greatest concentration of political activity by American intellectuals during
the Twenties centered around the Sacco-Vanzetti cause célèbre.
Niccolo Sacco and Bartolomeo Vanzetti, two Italian anarchists,
were arrested, tried and, in 1927, executed for their alleged
participation in an armed payroll robbery in Massachusetts.
Many artists, jurists, writers and philosophers became involved in the case.   Many of those who spoke, demonstrated
and wrote during the legal proceedings were not primarily
concerned with Anarchist or Socialist ideology.   They had
concluded in the course of the trial that the official handling
of the case was flagrantly ignoring American ideals of justice and equality.   Upton Sinclair makes the most direct use
of the case in Boston (1927).   Bartolomeo Vanzetti appears
as one of the important characters in the novel, the leader
of a strike in a cordage factory.   The heroine, Cornelia
Thornwell, member of a prominent Boston family, throws
herself passionately into the organization of the Sacco-Vanzetti defense apparatus when the two Anarchists are arrested.

        The interest in Socialism among novelists of the period
expressed itself frequently in the Socialist tract-novel which
by now had almost completely superseded the earlier religious
tracts.   In the Socialist novels the strike became a convenient,

and inevitable, device to show a confrontation between working class and capitalist class, a microcosmic portent of the
imminent Socialist revolution.   These novels are primarily
important as the historical forerunners of those in the Thirties which also used the strike as an example of revolution
in miniature, although the novelists of the Thirties changed
and expanded both their viewpoint and their techniques considerably.   Curiously, the Socialist novelists tended to view
the confrontation through the eyes of very rich strike sympathizers.   Lucian Emery, in Florence Converse's The Children of Light (1912), is a millionaire Socialist who leads a
garment worker's strike and goes to jail at the end of the
novel.   Jim Ross, in Upton Sinclair's Oil! (1926), is a millionaire oilman who supports several strikes with substantial
financial contributions as a result of his lifelong friendship
with Socialist Paul Watkins.   Another of Sinclair's heroes
is millionaire Hal Warner in King Coal (1917), the son of a
coal magnate, who uses his connections to help the strikers.

    For the Socialist novelists of this period, as for their
Socialist predecessors, the strike is not a real solution to
the problems inherent in capitalism.   Rather, it is a training school in which the working class learns two important
lessons.   One is the consciousness of class.   During a
strike workers learn that they are economically and politically bound to each other and that only their own collective
efforts will free them from their exploitation by the capitalist class.   Secondly, the workers learn from the strike the
elements of military strategy in preparation for the coming
battle.   With this lesson, however, the novelists are caught
in something of a dilemma.   The "final conflict" of the revolutionary anthem, the Internationale, is inevitable since the
capitalists will never voluntarily relinquish power, but the

conflict will be precipitated by the capitalists, so strikers must always be shown as the victims of violence, never the aggressors. In novel after novel the strikers are always instructed to avoid violence; time and again the strikes erupt into violence. Brooklyn sugar refinery workers fight "little pitched battles" in James Oppenheim's The Nine-Tenths (1911), the strike degenerates into a riot in David Graham Phillips' The Conflict (1911), Cyrus Emery is killed during the strike in Florence Converse's The Children of Light. Each time, the violence is forced upon the strikers. The dilemma of the novelists lies in an unresolved philosophical conflict in the Socialist thought of the period, unresolved at least for the many middle class Socialists with strong Christian backgrounds. Force of any kind was abhorrent to them and somehow they hoped for nonviolent change even though they recognized that this was not a likelihood. Socialist ideology, influenced by two equally powerful currents--the revolutionary and the humanist--caught the novelists between its contradictions.

The close relationship between Christianity and Socialism continued to interest the novelists during this period. There is a strong Socialist bias against all religions, especially the mystical and unscientific elements, but most of the attacks on the Christian church in these Socialist novels are directed against the institution and not against the religion. A number of the Socialist novelists were themselves exseminarians, Christian ministers or the sons of ministers. To those who took Christian teachings seriously--and somewhat literally--Socialism seemed to offer a purer life, a society organized to give everyday reality to the promises of the New Testament. There are constant analogies in the novels between Socialism and early Christianity. Many of

the novelists are saying that it is Socialism which is trying
to make Christian morality a contemporary actuality, while
the organized Christian church has betrayed the ideals of
the Redeemer.   Daniel Poling's hero in The Furnace (1925)
eloquently defends both the strike and the "United World
Movement. "   "'It is dollars and dolomite and slag and scrap
against the immortal soul, '"[1] he says.   The Christian ethic,
elevating the human soul above commodities and profits, has
been betrayed by both capitalism and the Christian church
and is a reality only in Socialist society.

The most extensive analogy between social reform
and primitive Christianity occurs in William Allen White's
In the Heart of a Fool (1919). In an overlong novel which
begins with the founding of Harvey (i. e. Emporia), Kansas,
in 1870, White eventually winds his novelistic way to the
contemporary city, rent by a crippling general strike.
The strike leader is Grant Adams, son of Mary and Amos
Adams (Adams for "man, " Mary to recall the mother of
Jesus).   Harvey has been rapidly industrialized during the
early years of the twentieth century and around its cement
and glass factories have grown up squalid working class tenements.   Grant is a carpenter who has worked for years to
organize an effective Wahoo Valley Labor Council.   He has
been driven to the inevitable conclusion that the workers can
find salvation only through Socialism.   White describes Grant
Adams in language reminiscent of the Biblical description of
John the Baptist.   "'I see Grant some way eating the locusts
and wild honey in the wilderness, calling out to a stiff-necked
generation to repent, '"[2] one of the characters says of him.
Grant knows that he must ultimately come into open conflict
with Thomas Van Dorn, the corrupt, worldly, sensuous judge
who speaks for the employers in Harvey.   When the strike

erupts, Grant pleads with the workers to avoid violence. He
is called a "Messiah" and the "Prince of Peace, " in derision
by some and in simple love by those who believe in him.
Grant's secretary is a reformed prostitute whom he has de-
fended against bigoted townspeople.   When there is an explosion in which seven militiamen die, Grant takes the blame
upon himself and gives himself up for trial before Van Dorn.
During the preliminaries Van Dorn says: "'I wash my hands
of the whole business!'" and to a friend: "'Well, George, if
you know so much about the case, what is the truth?'" During his hearing Grant is mocked and reviled and scornfully
asked, "'Do you think you are a God?'" Before the trial
can begin, a lynch mob drags Grant from his cell, whips
and tortures him until he cries out in agony, and finally kills
him. The parallel with the Passion is complete. The Resur-
rection is clearly hinted at when Laura, who is in love with
Grant, declares: "'We know--oh, we do know he's out here--
out here in the dawn.'"

    Analogous to the Socialist tract novels and in many
ways very much like them are the tracts propagandizing for
capitalism.   Badly written, luridly melodramatic, they also
confront capitalist and worker in a strike, but almost invariably the strikers are brutal, stupid, inarticulate and under
the malicious influence of foreign agitators, while the capitalists are brave, clever, self-made men.   There are a few
completely anachronistic novels in this group which perpetuate
stereotypes that were already obsolete at the end of the nineteenth century.   Mabel Farnum's The Cry of the Street (1913),
based on the Lawrence textile strike of 1912, still makes use
of stock melodrama--Ignace Naquet, the strike leader, turns
out to be the long-lost brother of the hero and he is converted from Socialism when he is reunited with his family.   The

argument against Socialism is, for 1913, surprisingly old-
fashioned. Labor and suffering will always exist, warns
saintly Curé Etienne, and Socialists are denying Nature when
they try to do away with poverty and with the resignation of
the poor to their lot. Donn Byrne's novel, The Stranger's
Banquet (1919), the basis for an early silent film, is outrageously outdated. The agitator, Dolan, prophesies:

> 'Red ruin will ride through the streets. The gut-
> ters will be red with blood. There will come a
> night when torches will illuminate the dark corners,
> and the sleek men who have lorded it over us for
> generations will be crucified to their own doors.
> They will dangle from the lamp-posts. Their bod-
> ies will block the sewers. Their women will go
> shrieking through the alleyways in their flimsy
> nightgowns. '

If "red ruin" wasn't enough to stir the sluggish reader's
blood, then the shrieking women in their flimsy nightgowns
certainly would. Byrne frosts the cake with some additional
outworn Gothic elements: a defrocked priest, for example,
who lusts after the pure blonde heroine.

In most of this group of novels, however, there has
been some change. They recognize the necessity for unions
to protect the workers' interests, although union leaders are
generally corrupt, and they grant that capitalists have dealt
harshly with their employees. The really superior man,
however, doesn't need a union to protect him. America has
made it possible for any man who wills it to rise to the top.
Alex Thane, in Garet Garrett's The Cinder Buggy (1929),
starts as a puddler but becomes the head of a great steel
trust. Hyram Bond, in Clarence Budington Kelland's Dynasty
(1929), described in the jacket blurb as "an answer to Babbitt, " begins his career as a mill foreman but quickly becomes the czar of the huge Worthington financial empire.

He brings himself to Amassa P. Worthington's attention by
singlehandedly protecting the financier from striking steel
workers, then proceeds to break the strike by courageous
defiance of the strikers' demands.   Jerry Donohue, in Arthur
Stanwood Pier's Jerry (1917), takes a slightly different route
to success.   From unskilled steel mill worker he moves to
a job on the police force and, by studying in his spare time,
finally passes the bar examination and becomes an Assistant
District Attorney.   Jerry also manages to call attention to
his talents during a bloody steel strike with a display of
manly courage.   David MacNamara, in Donald McGibeny's
Slag (1922), rises to foreman of a steel rolling mill and
confidante of the company president.   John Graham, the
hero of Arthur Train's The Needle's Eye (1924), begins with
a distinct advantage.   He is the heir to a $100,000,000 for-
tune.   But he voluntarily goes to work as manager of one of
the family mines and concludes that strikes would be unnecessary if mineowners lived close to the mines and directed the
operations personally.   These men do not need unions to rise
although they all know how to make use of a strike to further
their interests.

What really confronts us here is the long-standing
myth that any American with gumption invariably attained
economic success.   He either became a skilled worker or a
successful entrepreneur, or he picked up his belongings and
headed west.   The failures, therefore, were lazy or stupid
or both.   The fact that this was already a myth in 1870, and
that certainly by 1890 there was no longer a West to exploit
nor many financial empires lying around to be won, by no
means lessens the prevalence of the idea.   In the pro-capitalist novels, especially in those produced to formula by the
Saturday Evening Post's stable of writers, the myth still

keeps reproducing itself.

One new idea is slowly permeating the capitalist tracts, however.   The capitalists in these novels are entrepreneurs, the bold, dashing buccaneers of the past.   They are personally directing the operations of their mines and factories and are not yet acting out their romances in New York or Chicago executive boardrooms.   But the faceless corporation is just around the corner.   Arthur Train's John Graham, in The Needle's Eye, is fighting a rearguard action when he warns that personal supervision and a visible management can prevent labor unrest.   In the other novels, too, there is a growing recognition that impersonality and diffused management responsibility are exacerbating the labor problem.   "Oh rich man, whoever thou be; thou art, ruler, or master, or body corporate, the keeper of thy brother's life and soul, "[4] apostrophizes Charles Carroll Swafford in The Silent Conflict (1916).   Hugh Corbett, hero of Henry Kitchell Webster's An American Family (1918), determines:

> 'What I'm going to try to find out is what set 'em off; what they think they're trying to do.   If I can manage to get their side of it, I bet I can manage to quiet them down. '[5]

Hugh moves from his family's Chicago mansion into their huge Riverdale factory to set up a "Department of Welfare. " Kelland's Hyram Bond, unlike his boss, Amassa P. Worthington, stays right there in the plant, visible to all and personally on the firing line in Dynasty. He "despises Carnegie as an opportunist, a hypocrite, a poseur and a coward--this Carnegie who ran away to hide from the results of his own written word in the Homestead revolt, and left the putting out of the conflagration to abler and braver and more sincere men than himself. "[6]

The tract-novelists, whether Socialist or capitalist,

were propagandizing for a specific point of view, but many
novelists of the period were examining contemporary society
critically without taking a rigid political position.   More
novelists than ever before were writing about workers and
about strikes, and many were recognizing and exploring the
complexity of working class life.   Most novelists did their
exploring from the outside.   Even in novels dealing with a
working class situation the central characters continued to
be from the middle class.   Jo Hancock in Max Eastman's
Venture is a business executive; Joe Blaine in James Oppenheim's The Nine-Tenths and Victor Dorn in David Graham
Phillips' The Conflict are both labor paper editors; Bill, the
narrator of Ernest Poole's The Harbor, is a journalist; and
these still remain the predominant types.   But in some of
the novels a new kind of character is emerging.   The central characters are workers.   Billy Roberts, the teamster
of Jack London's Valley of the Moon (1913), and his wife
Saxon, a laundry-worker, are as authentically working class
as was London himself.   Yetta Rayefsky in Arthur Bullard's
Comrad Yetta (1913) and Hilda Thorsen in Elias Tobenkin's
The Road (1922) are garment workers.   Idwal Jones' Bram
Dartnell in Steel Chips is a machinist, and William Allen
White's Grant Adams in In the Heart of a Fool is a carpenter.   They are all industrial workers, and they are all the
focal characters of the novels--a new development in Ameri-
can fiction.

     Not only are the characters new but the settings in
which they function have changed, too.   The factories and
mines and sweatshops in some of these novels are real
places, and the authors no longer hesitate to take us directly
inside them.   What was just beginning in the novels before
1910 is now a well-developed characteristic.   More of the

novelists than ever before know the factories from their own observation.   Many of them have learned what goes on in industry as journalists, a few as workers; and now, bursting with their knowledge, they are eager to share it with their readers.   The processes, the languages, the routines of the worker behind the factory wall become the novelists' raw material.

Not only are there now more novels in which strikes are used but some of the strikes are successful.   Even the hack writer aiming at the best-seller lists sometimes includes a strike in his novel, and sometimes the strikers win their demands.   Winston Churchill, who had already made an enormous success with his historical novels, switched to contemporary social themes just before World War I.   He was shrewd enough to gauge the right time to use a strike in a popular novel.   The strike in The Dwelling-Place of Light (1917) is rather remotely based on the Lowell textile strike of 1912.   The heroine, Janet Bumpus, has been seduced and then deserted by the millowner, Claude Ditmar.   Her fury and anger at her betrayer exactly match the fury of the millworkers who have just struck, and Janet joins them, working as a typist at strike headquarters.   Ditmar is killed by a demented striker, and the strike ends with a few concessions to the strikers.   Janet bears Ditmar's daughter and sinks into a convenient decline.   Churchill has used the strike to highlight and complement his heroine's passions.

The strike is especially useful to the western or northwestern novelist.   Since he wants to show us a tough resourceful hero in an outdoor setting, a man capable of handling violence decisively, the strike becomes a perfect vehicle. Zane Grey's hero, Kurt Dorn, in The Desert of Wheat (1919), owner of a wheat ranch in Eastern Washington, has been

plagued by a rash of I. W. W. -inspired strikes among the harvesters.   Kurt joins a vigilante gang which drags an I. W. W.
organizer out of his jail cell and lynches him.   Kurt then
joins the army and continues to exhibit his courage in the
battlefields of France.   He returns to his ranch minus an
arm, marries a banker's daughter and lives happily ever
after.   Hjalmar Rutzeback's My Alaskan Idyll (1922) is something of a surprise.   The novel, a "Western" with an Alaskan locale, uses most of the stock clichês--the strong, outdoor hero who is capable, hardworking, tender and chivalrous
toward women, courageous and incorruptible.   But Rutzeback's
hero, Svend, differs in two ways from the Western stereo-
type.   He is literate (publishes a book), and he becomes a
strike leader.   While working at an Alaskan gold mine, he
organizes a successful strike for an eight-hour working day.

Even the popular love story can find a novelistic use
for a strike.   Margaret Deland shows her headstrong, but
lovable, society girl heroine, Frederica Payton, supporting
a group of striking rubber workers in The Rising Tide (1916).
She joins the picket line and is arrested along with some of
the girl strikers.   But the strike is essentially the device
through which Freddy realizes where her true happiness lies.
When lawyer Arthur Weston bails her out of the House of De-
tention, she gives up her feminist nonsense and agrees to
marry Weston, who has been in love with her all along.
While Freddy has been sympathetic to the strikers but really
aloof from their lives, Lily Cardew, the society girl of
Mary Roberts Rinehart's A Poor Wise Man (1920), allows
herself to be used as a dupe by anarchists planning a general
strike.   Her involvement in the strike is almost disastrous
for Lily.   She marries Louis Akers, one of the anarchists.
Only the decisive (extralegal) action of an armed Vigilance

Committee quells the strike. Akers is killed and Lily falls
into the arms of her true love, William Cameron, one of
the organizers of the Vigilance Committee. Still another society girl, Joyce Bayly, in George Gibbs' The Joyous Conspirator (1927), discovers whom she really loves during a
strike. When strikers plan to dynamite Lord Pembury, the
mine owner, Joyce realizes that beneath his reserved, phleg-
matic exterior beats the passionate heart of a courageous
man, and she throws herself into his waiting arms. The
most saccharine of these popular stories is Helen of the Old
House (1921), by that runaway bestseller writer of the Twenties,
Harold Bell Wright. A syrupy hodgepodge of melodrama and
sentimentality, the novel pictures a strike which is reconciled
by Wallace Gordon, the "Interpreter." Although Wright pictures the strike leader, Jake Vodell, as an utter scoundrel,
he is not entirely unsympathetic to the strikers and they actually win some of their strike demands.

In some of the political novels of the period strikes
are used but they are not usually central to the plot. Very
often the strike becomes a device for revealing collusion between corrupt political machines and corrupt labor leaders.
In Arthur Stanwood Pier's Jerry, for example, the young
steel worker, Jerry Donohue, has a run-in with a Congressional candidate who wants to use the steel union to build a
machine for political patronage. Later, Jerry uncovers a
system of bribery which involves the union, the police force
and the Democratic Party machine. In Junius Jay's bizarre
Open-Air Politics and the Conversion of Governor Soothem
(1914) corrupt unions terrorize the State during a general
strike. When the Governor is shot by one of the union organizers, he stops trying to conciliate the strikers, calls out
the troops and breaks the strike decisively. Florence Con-

verse's The Children of Light and David Graham Phillips'
The Conflict both deal with mayoralty campaigns.   In both
of these novels the strikes bring into the open political deals
between the party machine and the union bosses.   Reginald
Wright Kauffman's The Spider's Web (1913) also deals with
an election campaign.   Luke Huber runs for district attorney
as the candidate of the Municipal Reform League and, once
again, a strike shows up the corruption of the entrenched
political machine.   Despite a street battle between strikers
and strikebreakers the Mayor, the Police Commissioner and
the Governor refuse to interfere.   Luke orders armed security guards to fire on the rioting strikers and is himself
killed by an armed guard.   In Dashiell Hammett's Red Harvest (1929) the strike also has political ramifications.   Hammett, using some of his own experiences as a private detective and a Pinkerton agent, substituted for the formula-
bound detective novel a story of urban crime and racketeering.   In Red Harvest an earlier strike is at the root of Personville's racket-ridden present.   Elihu Willson, with the
connivance of the local police chief, has brought in thugs and
hired gunmen to defeat the strike in his plant.   When the
strike is over, the racketeers continue their hold on the local and state government.   Hammett's Continental Op proceeds to a methodical purge of Personville in which racketeers decimate each other's gangs, much as their real-life
counterparts in Chicago and New York did during the Twenties.
     There is still another type of novel in which strikes
appear in this period--a type quite new to American fiction
and one which produced at least two interesting novels, Valley of the Moon by Jack London and Steel Chips by Idwal
Jones.   In these two novels the strike is neither a microcosm

of the class struggle nor a vehicle to exhibit the sterling
qualities of the hero.   It is simply, and effectively, included
in the novels because strikes are fairly common events in
the lives of most factory workers and because through the
strike the novelist can give us deeper insights into the motivations of working class characters.

Jack London was one of the American pioneers of this
new kind of realistic writing.   He begins The Valley of the
Moon with a vivid and credible description of the lives of
Saxon Brown and Billy Roberts.   Their work, their house-
keeping, their recreations and their family relationships are
as circumstantially detailed as the strike and the violent
clashes into which it erupts.   There is great bitterness as
police, scabs and strikers collide, but exuberance, too.
London understands Billy's sheer physical enjoyment of a
good fight when he thrashes a scab.   London also describes,
with sympathy and understanding, Billy's slow deterioration
under his enforced idleness during the strike and the strain
it imposes on Billy's and Saxon's marriage.

Idwal Jones' Steel Chips is a refreshing, very well
written example of the new realism.   Jones has no ideological axe to grind.   He gives us real descriptions of people
doing real work.   We see them clock in, check out materials
from the tool crib, plan a grinding operation.   We see them
really and credibly at play, too--fishing, cheering a prize-
fight, enjoying a new show at the nickelodeon, wading into a
fist fight, making love.   Bram Dartnell joins the Machinists'
Union because machinists do join unions.   He walks out with
the majority of the other workers in the plant because he
thinks the strike is justified.   He goes back to work when
the strike fizzles out.   Bram wrestles with his life's experiences, learns something from them and looks for physi-

cal and intellectual stimulation in a very human and endear-
ing way.

Another category of realistic novel in which strikes
are an essential ingredient is the group which describes the
organization of Jewish garment workers in New York. There
is a rash of such novels in this period, and some of them
make effective use of actual events in the organization of the
clothing industry--the Triangle fire, the role of the Women's
Trade Union League, the mass arrests of young girl picketers, the virulent prejudice against immigrants and Jews. In
Reginald Wright Kauffman's tendentious novel, The House of
Bondage (1911), the strike is only a convenient peg on which
the author can hang one of his pet theses: that capitalism
drives innocent young girls into prostitution. Carrie Berkowicz, a shirtwaist worker, goes on strike and is arrested
for picketing. Finally, desperate with hunger, she becomes
a streetwalker. The novel is so lurid and so badly written
that neither the strike nor the strikers are very convincing.
James Oppenheim's The Nine-Tenths is not much better.
The novel, a bit more realistic that Kauffman's, makes use
of several actual events--the Triangle fire, the mass-meet-
ing of strikers at Cooper Union and, again, the mass arrests
of girl pickets. Through her participation in the strike,
Myra Craig, a schoolteacher, rids herself of her middle
class snobbishness and is converted to Socialism. The active role of women in the organization of clothing workers
plays an important part in these novels, as it did in reality.
In Comrade Yetta by Arthur Bullard (writing under the pseudonym of Albert Edwards) the central character is a woman union organizer. Yetta Rayefsky, born in Lithuania, goes to
work in a clothing factory when she is fifteen. She becomes
a fiery orator and a clever tactician during several bitter

strikes.   Yetta is also responsible for an uneasy alliance between the women trade unionists and a group of prominent
society women who contribute substantial sums to the strike
fund.   Yetta finally marries Isadore Braun, a Jewish lawyer,
and she and her husband become leaders in the international
Socialist movement.   Hilda Thorsen, the heroine of Elias Tobenkin's The Road, is also a trade union organizer.   She
goes to work as a garment worker to support her son, born
after a brief affair with Raymond Evert, who deserts her
under pressure from his prominent family.   Years later,
Hilda meets Raymond again while Raymond is serving on a
government commission investigating a copper strike.   Hilda
realizes that her working class experiences have made her a
resolute independent woman while Raymond is as weak and
vacillating as ever.   After World War I Hilda joins her
friend and fellow organizer, Frank Hillstrom, in the Soviet
Union, where he has become the superintendent of a Russian
locomotive repair plant.   Yetta and Hilda are both dynamic
women, dedicated to the cause of economic justice and determined to lead useful and independent lives.   Bullard's novel, unfortunately, is clumsily written but Tobenkin's makes
the portrait of Hilda Thorsen both sympathetic and interesting.

Abraham Cahan's The Rise of David Levinsky (1917)
and Samuel Ornitz's Haunch, Paunch and Jowl (1923) are both
thoughtful and well-written novels, the best of those dealing
with the dramatic organizing strikes in the garment industry.
David Levinsky, in Cahan's novel, is born in Russia, arrives
in America in the 1880's and, like thousands of immigrant
Jews, goes to work in a clothing factory.   As a union member he joins in some of the strikes of the period but Levinsky has his heart set on becoming an employer.   With three
hundred dollars of his own and an additional borrowed sum,

he opens a small clothing factory where he works himself
half to death but exploits his employees even more.   Levinsky is no more ethical in his personal relationships than in
his shop.   He makes love to the wife of his friend as cynically as he cheats his workers.   The woman he loves refuses
to marry him and by the time he is middle-aged Levinsky is
a lonely, friendless man still plagued by strikes in his plant.
Ornitz's main character, Meyer Hirsch, is in many ways
similar to David Levinsky.   He is born on a ship which is
bringing his parents to America and grows up on New York's
lower East Side.   Meyer's father is a garment worker who
dies of tuberculosis and overwork.   Meyer helps his uncle,
factory owner Philip Hirsch, deliberately foment strikes
which enrich the Hirsches.   Meyer is the go-between who
bribes dishonest union officials to prolong the garment industry strikes.   Year by year, Meyer grows richer, fatter
and more callous.   At the end, alone, almost a prisoner
within an immense mountain of fat, unloved and unloving, he
can only recall helplessly the words of a musical comedy
song, "Tell me, life, tell me, what's it all about?"   Both
of these novels are moving accounts of the slow moral and
physical deterioration of their central characters.   The
strikes in both novels are realistically described and serve
not only to evoke a historical period but to make Levinsky
and Hirsch unlikeable but memorable and understandable.

        Problems of immigrant labor are important elements
not only in the garment industry novels but in quite a few
others during this period.   The numbers of poor working
class immigrants pouring into the United States continued to
increase up to the beginning of World War I and the impact
of immigration on the American novelist is inescapable.
Some of the novelists continue to depict foreigners ven-

omously as ignorant, dirty, less than human intruders.   The
alien laborer brings with him from his God-forsaken native
land all kinds of strange ideologies and practices: "anarchy
and mob rule, bohemia and vagabondia, sedition and murder,
Latin revolutions and reigns of terror, sex irregularity,...
free love,... atheism, unfamiliarity with soap and water,...
exotic poetry and art... saturated with something indefinable
yet abhorrent, "[7] according to Winston Churchill's catalogue
in The Dwelling-Place of Light.   Churchill's list is significant because it clearly details the two fearful dangers from
the immigrants, their peculiar politics and their peculiar
sexual customs.   The novels which exhibit prejudice against
the foreign-born all show the immigrants subverting American law and order and indulging in loose sexual customs.   In
Donn Byrne's The Stranger's Banquet the foreigners preach
sabotage as well as rape.   A pretty Jewess "dances with
patent wantonness. "   In George Brydges Rodney's Jim Lofton,
American (1920) the strikers plot to dynamite the mine and
take Constance Drake, the mine owner's niece, and Delia
Stratton, the pit boss's daughter, hostage.   Jim Lofton has
already rescued Delia once from the indecent advances of
three I. W. W. miners, so there is no doubt what the miners
have in mind for their pretty hostages.   But the contempt
for foreigners is not always so blatant.

        Even when an author is as sympathetic as Arthur Bul-
lard undoubtedly is in Comrade Yetta toward his fiery immigrant heroine, he cannot quite grant her or the other garment
workers equality with native Americans.   Walter Longman,
an Assyriologist at Columbia University, who is friendly to
the strikers, addresses them during a rally.   "I'm an American, " he begins, and then takes them severely to task for
not having ancestors, like his, who fought in the Revolution

and the Civil War.   The Chosen People, he chastises them,
have not participated in the fight for Liberty.   No matter
that the strikers he addresses weren't in America in 1776
or 1860, no matter even that Longman takes off for an ar-
cheological dig in Central Asia and leaves Yetta and her
comrades to fight it out on the picket lines.   Somehow, the
mere fact that Longman's ancestors were astute enough to
be born Americans makes Longman a superior being.   Yetta
is in love with Longman but she suffers silently until she
can work the disease out of her system, and she finally marries her real equal, a Jewish immigrant lawyer.   Bullard is
a clumsy novelist who is perpetuating an Anglo-Saxon myth
which has had a long history in the novel, the same myth
that forced Scott to mate Ivanhoe with Rowena rather than
with the alien Rebecca, and Cooper to keep his Indians
strictly segregated sexually from his Anglo-Saxons.   Nevertheless, the old convention is cracking slightly.   Immigrants
have become the central characters, even admirable characters, in a few novels.   Thames Williamson's Hunky (1929),
for example, describes sympathetically the lives of a group
of Czech immigrants who win a bakery strike.   The novel is
a poor one, but it represents a change in attitude toward the
foreign-born.   In novels like Ornitz's Haunch, Paunch and
Jowl or Cahan's The Rise of David Levinsky the tables have
been turned.   It is not the immigrant who comes to subvert
the American way of life but the American business ethic
which has corrupted the immigrant.

Occasionally during this period American novelists began to use the strike as a purely literary device, an event
which symbolized something quite apart from the strike, something of deeper human concern.   Sherwood Anderson began as
early as 1916 to experiment with this technique.   In Windy

McPherson's Son (1916) Sam McPherson becomes deeply involved with a group of shirtwaist strikers in Pennsylvania.
He pays for a campaign to educate strikebreakers on the issues of the strike. He persuades rich society women to help
the strikers. He even begins a liaison with one of the striking women but unselfishly renounces her love. The strike,
with its excitements, fears and disappointments, is described
realistically enough, but that is not Anderson's object. What
Sam is desperately trying to do is to make some coherent
sense out of life. Financial success has brought him only a
feeling of disgust for the emptiness of his life and has alienated him from his family. Hard physical work and appease-
ment of his strong sensual appetites have left him exhausted
but still bewildered. His participation in the strike, even
though the strike fails, impresses Sam with two discoveries
which deepen his understanding of American life. One is the
recognition, difficult for Americans, that failure is as essential and positive an experience as success. The other is the
realization that responsibility for others can endow life at
least with form--if not with meaning. At the end of the
novel Sam returns to his wife with two young boys whom
they undertake to rear.

        In Marching Men (1921) Anderson is still probing the
same theme. The ugly, senseless, brutal strikes of the Coal
Creek miners convince Beaut McGregor that life is without
beauty or meaning. He sets out to discover whether there
can be any beauty in the relationships of human beings to
each other. He finds what he has been searching for in his
organization of Marching Men. Order and beauty are implicit in their disciplined unanimity. Anderson's Marching Men
are a rather mindless collective. He never specifies what
they are marching for, and his Marching Men are uncom-

fortably like the marching Brown Shirts in the Germany of
the Thirties.   But for Anderson the orderly ranks of men,
emotionally if not intellectually united, serve as a beautiful
and meaningful contrast to the disorder and conflict of industrial strikes.

Poor White (1920) is less optimistic than either
Windy McPherson's Son or Marching Men. The strikes
in this novel, especially the bitter and violent one with
which the novel ends, are not symbols of mere disorder
but, more profoundly, of the disintegration of a whole way
of life.   In Poor White the series of strikes in an agricultural machinery plant are the workers' last frail resistance
to dehumanization.   Industrialization has destroyed the value
of individual creativity and the strikers fail as society has
already failed.   All of us are being inexorably devoured by
the machine.   In the Thirties Anderson was to continue his
interest in the strike and to move close to the proletarian
novelists of that period.   In the Twenties Anderson was one
of a small group of serious novelists who began to use the
strike as one facet of man's long search for coherence and
meaning.

Ernest Poole in The Harbor and Clement Wood in
Mountain also write about strikes which are at the same
time realistic and symbolic.   While neither novel is a great
work of art, both deal with an interesting set of characters
in believable situations.   In Poole's work, Bill, the narrator,
son of a hard-bitten dock-owner and his idealistic wife, grows
up within sight of New York harbor, but shielded from the
violence of life there.   Poole contrasts the harbor as a symbol of degradation with the stars as a somewhat hackneyed
symbol of aspiration.   When Bill investigates child labor and
the padrone system, he comes into contact, for the first

time, with the harshness of actual life, but this seamy side
of the harbor is quickly counteracted by long lazy hours
aboard Eleanor Dillon's motor launch.   Eleanor keeps Bill's
attention on the beauty and drama of the busy port.   Bill's
marriage to Eleanor and the growing fame of his biographies
of top-flight industrialists keep Bill's life tranquil for a time.
Although he knows that ugliness and violence exist in the
world around him, his life remains uncontaminated.   Little
by little, the ugly truths seep into Bill's consciousness--not
only the incredibly harsh lives of the stokers and longshoremen and the rootless lives of labor organizers but the knowledge that Bill's own comfort is bought at the expense of the
harbor workers' suffering.   Bill is still aloof from the workers, however.   He cannot bring himself to identify with their
brutishness and ignorance.   At last, the strike and his deep
involvement in it bring about a qualitative change in Bill.   He
covers the strike as a reporter.   Then, when his friend Joe
is indicted for "incitement to murder," Bill becomes an active member of a defense committee, and he is transformed
from outsider to participant.   He tries unsuccessfully to explain the change to his father-in-law.

> 'What has the strike given you in return for all it
> has taken away?'
>
> 'A deeper view of life, ' I said.   'I saw something
> in that strike. . . deep down in the people themselves
> that rises up out of each one of them the minute
> they get together.   And I believe that power has
> such possibilities that when it comes to full life
> not all the police and battleships and armies on
> earth can stop it. '[8]

The strike symbolizes both Bill's own metamorphosis from
passive onlooker to dedicated activist and the power inherent
in collective action.

Wood's novel, <u>Mountain,</u> also makes successful use of symbol. The mountain on which the Judson family lives, and from which their fortune is extracted, becomes for Pelham Judson a comfort and a source of security, on the one hand, and a threat on the other. Pelham, the son of a harsh driving Southern mineowner and his gentle, ineffectual wife, grows up close to his mother and out of sympathy with his father's ruthless ambitions. The first time in his life that Pelham receives any praise from his father occurs during a college escapade at Yale when the young student becomes a strikebreaker during a New Haven streetcar strike. As a foreman in his father's mining operation, Pelham is kept busy with engineering problems and an active social life. He gets his first inkling of the existence of a hidden life beneath the surface during an abortive affair with a married woman and several expeditions to the local red-light district, but he is studiously sheltered from any knowledge of the lives of the miners or of the brewing labor situation on the mountain. His ignorance is finally shattered by two pivotal events. He falls in love with Jane Lauderdale, a social worker with a dilettante's interest in Socialism, and he is profoundly shocked by a mine explosion which kills eighteen miners. Pelham is rapidly (too rapidly) converted to Socialism, and he begins to agitate for a strike to enforce safety measures in the mine. When the strike comes, Pelham realizes the full extent of his naiveté. His father's management of the mine is based on the callous sacrifice of the miners' welfare to his own profits. His wife is frigid, both sexually and humanly. Jane is not willing to interest herself in the plight of the miners. The union is also unconcerned with the miners. The State Federation of Labor is quite ready to settle on the company's terms as long as the move will strengthen

the Federation's power.   The miners themselves are not the
idealized worker-heroes Pelham has imagined.   They balk at
any attempt to form an alliance with Negro workers.   Pelham gets an enlightening glimpse into the degraded position
of the Negro woman in the South when he realizes that Diana
Cole, a Tuskegee graduate, will eventually have to make a
tragic choice between marriage to an illiterate, underpaid
Negro worker or concubinage with a white foreman.   At the
end of the novel Pelham leaves his home with several bitter
realizations.   The union has been destroyed.   His marriage,
patched up for the moment, has been wrecked.   His chances
for rewarding work are very slim since his name has been
posted on the industry's blacklist.   Wood has made the strike
the instrument for Pelham's education in reality and the symbol for the growing suspicion, hostility and betrayal under-
mining American life.

The strike in Sinclair Lewis' Babbitt is the external
event which signals the loss of a man's integrity.   George
Babbitt, for all his hypocrisy and self-deception, is in sympathy with the workers when telephone girls and linemen,
dairy workers and truck drivers in Zenith strike against a
wage cut.   When the Reverend Drew preaches against the
strike, arguing that '"the boss goes among them (the workers)
smiling, and they smile back, the elder brother and the
younger, '"[9] Babbitt reacts with a healthy, "oh, rot!"   But
he is too cowardly to express his sympathy openly.   The
best he can hope for is that he can remain silent and still
preserve his own position in the business community of Zenith.   The ruling clique in the town is not satisfied with neu-
trality, however, and Babbitt's cronies at the Athletic Club
insist he must publicly join the Good Citizens League which
will "keep the reds in their place" and guarantee the open

shop in Zenith.   Babbitt's brief struggle with his conscience
soon comes to an end.   He joins the Good Citizens League
and then can only wail impotently: "I've never done a single
thing I wanted to in my whole life. "

A strike is also used imaginatively in Louis Bromfield's The Green Bay Tree (1926) and its sequel, A Good
Woman (1927).   Bromfield sees the city and industrialism
as a corruption of the ideal agrarian society.   The mills
surrounding palatial Cypress Hill have wrecked the beauty
of an earlier idyllic rural world.   Cinders from the mill
have already blighted Cypress Hill's beautiful gardens.   The
strike allows the beauty of the past to flower for one last
time.   With the mills shut down, the sun shines clearly, an
eloquent silence descends on the district and the garden
blooms briefly once more.   On the night the strike begins,
Naomi Downes gives birth to twins, and Philip Downes, dying of typhoid fever, begins to recover.   The strike thus
marks a pause just before a way of life dies forever, but,
more than that, the strike also marks the beginning of a new
life.   Bromfield's novels are trite and badly overwritten, but
the author has found a way to use the strike significantly.

With the end of the Nineteen Twenties America enters
a new period with unprecedented problems.   The American
novel is entering a new period, too, one in which the strike
will assume unprecedented importance.

Notes

1.   Daniel Poling, The Furnace (New York: George H.
        Doran Co. , 1925), p. 240.

2.   William Allen White, In the Heart of a Fool (New York:
        Macmillan Co. , 1919), p. 433.

3. Donn Byrne, The Stranger's Banquet (New York: Harper and Bros., 1919), p. 51.

4. Charles Carroll Swafford, The Silent Conflict (Boston: Roxburgh Publishing Co., 1916), p. 291.

5. Henry Kitchell Webster, An American Family (Indianapolis: Bobbs-Merrill Co., 1918), p. 72.

6. Clarence Budington Kelland, Dynasty (New York: Harper and Bros., 1929), p. 178.

7. Winston Churchill, The Dwelling-Place of Light (New York: Macmillan Co., 1917), p. 304.

8. Ernest Poole, The Harbor (New York: Macmillan Co., 1916), p. 368.

9. Sinclair Lewis, Babbitt, in Lewis at Zenith (New York: Harcourt, Brace and World, Inc., 1961), p. 531.

Chapter 5

THE PROLETARIAT IN REVOLT: 1930-1945

The Nineteen Thirties opened in the gloom of the
greatest depression the country had ever known and closed
in the fear of spreading Fascism.   These two phenomena--
the Great Depression and European Fascism--pervaded the
life and the literature of the decade.   The Depression, sig-
nalled by the stock market crash in October, 1929, affected
millions of Americans.   By 1933 there were thirteen million
unemployed in the country, twenty-five percent of the total
working force.   Between 1932 and 1939 there were never
less than seven million out of work.   Benito Mussolini's
Italian Fascism had seemed a distant and rather laughable
system, hardly threatening to a bumptious, prosperous United
States.   But after 1933 Adolf Hitler's steady successes at international diplomatic bargaining tables began to loom as a
serious challenge to democracy.   The Civil War in Spain, in
which Hitler and Mussolini tested the strength of Fascist
armament, gave rise to the fear that the totalitarian state
was invincible.

Both the Depression and the growing power of Fascism
shook the confidence of a great many Americans, by no
means only Marxists or Communists, in the capitalist system.   Economically and politically, it no longer seemed a
system capable of providing the minimum necessities of life.
It was a relatively easy step from disenchantment with capitalism to an acceptance of Marxist theory, which had always

117

insisted that capitalism was doomed and would ultimately give
way to a new and more equitable system.   By 1932 many intellectuals were ready to accept leadership from the Communist Party, to vote for its national candidates and to agree
that inequity was inherent in capitalism and ineradicable from
it.

The intensity of the economic and political experience
of the Thirties had a deep impact on the novels of the period.
Many of the writers to whom capitalism seemed a moribund
system translated into fictional terms the confrontation between capitalist and proletariat predicted by Marx.   The use
of strikes in the novels of the time multiplied dramatically.

With the outbreak of World War II the primary concerns of the nation--and of the novelists--shifted to new interests.   After 1945, strikes almost disappeared from the
novel, although there was an overlap of the class war concept which lasted until the early Fifties.   Many of the young
novelists beginning to write in the Forties were substituting
their war experiences for the Depression but many of them
continued to see society as a confrontation between exploiter
and exploited.   The bosses of the Thirties became the army
officers and the workers the enlisted men in a number of
post-war novels.

The novels written between 1930 and 1945 in which
strikes appear are significantly different from those written
earlier.   Although many are still poorly written, a far greater proportion are technically competent and a few are even
better than competent.   Josephine Johnson's poetic style in
Jordanstown (1937), Tom Tippett's credible and moving characterizations in Horse Shoe Bottoms (1935), Sherwood Anderson's creation of an interesting heroine in Kit Brandon (1936),
Benjamin's Appel's tight plotting in The Power-House (1939)

and Charles Givens' genuine humor and charming fantasy in
The Devil Takes a Hill Town (1939) are no longer glaring
exceptions.   This group of writers includes a number who
have mastered their art well enough to experiment.   They
are influenced by the innovators of the Twenties and although
much of their experimentation is imitative, they advance the
novel by their willingness to try new techniques.   Joyce's
interior monologue reappears in William Blake's The Painter
and the Lady (1939); Hammett's use of the tough detective
story to make a social comment is echoed in Joseph Francis
Delany's The Christmas Tree Murders (1938) and Rudolf Kagey's Judas, Incorporated (1939); Hemingway's taut repetitive
style is imitated (badly) in Fred Rothermell's The Ghostland
(1940).

   This group of novelists has made another significant
breakaway from its literary predecessors.   These writers
are no longer using the strike for the very limited purposes
of the past.   Their novels use the strike with tremendous
variety.   It can symbolize hope, despair, death, redemption,
salvation, love, brotherhood, betrayal.   These novels show
us strikes of lumber workers, steel workers, cotton mill
workers, coal miners, cannery workers, fruit pickers, fishermen, auto assemblers and many, many more.   We see the
strikes through the eyes of workers, labor organizers, re-
porters, capitalists, artists.   Strikes are won, lost, unresolved, won only to be lost in the long view, lost only
to be ultimately won.

   The background of many of the novelists differs from
those of earlier novelists who made use of strikes.   Many
more than in the past have personally experienced strikes
as workers in industry and they describe in their novels
many of the hundreds of actual strikes of the Thirties.

Many of the writers have consciously and deliberately sought
work experience in a factory or mine and have tried in their
own lives as well as in their novels to identify the artist
with the worker.   Because of their first-hand knowledge these
novelists write of strikes with authenticity and with passion.
Because they know their material intimately and because they
feel it so closely, almost all of them take us inside the factories and mines.   In the past only the exceptional writer
showed his working class characters actually at work.   Now
Granville Hicks, writing in the New Masses in 1934, says:
"It would be inconceivable to write a novel about an automobile worker without showing him inside the factory."[1]   During the Thirties the novelists writing on proletarian themes
invariably show us, often in great and knowledgeable detail,
the actual work in the factories and mills.

Not that the factory scenes were introduced solely
through the novelists' own inclinations.   The proletarian
novelists, schooled by Marxist critics, were under some
compulsion to introduce detailed descriptions of factory life.
Mike Gold, Granville Hicks, Philip Rahv, influential Marxist
critics of the period, were hammering away at the novelist
to "proletarianize" his work.   If the young novelist wanted
good reviews--or any review at all--in the journals of the
Left, he had to include some very explicit descriptions of
work.   What the Marxist critics really wanted were novels
about working class life written by workers and read by
workers.   They never got all they wanted.   More workers
than ever before were writing novels but the total number
who did was still a minority.   For every Thomas Bell or
Jack Conroy who actually started in the mines or on the assembly lines there were dozens of "proletarian novelists"
who wrote about workers but themselves stemmed from mid-

dle class origins.   As for working class readers, the Marxists never influenced very many.   At best, most proletarian
novels never sold more than fifteen hundred copies, and most
novel readers in the Thirties, as before and since, were of
the middle class.   Unable to make the proletarian impact
they hoped for, Marxist critics reluctantly settled for novels
about the working class, written by and for the middle class.
All the more reason, then, for their strident insistence that
the proletarian novel must take the reader inside the factory.
The middle class reader was not to be let off lightly.   He
was expected to learn a great deal about factory life from
the proletarian novel.

In many of the novels the writer goes somewhat beyond
a naturalistic description of the factory.   He attempts to portray the reverence the worker has for work and the creativity
he displays in doing his job well.   The proletarian writer is
anxious to prove not only that the worker is a sensitive and
creative human being but that it is the worker who cares
about the end-products of the industrial process.   The capitalist is concerned only with extracting high profits; the worker wants to produce high quality steel or unadulterated to-
matoes or long-lasting automobiles.   Even though the plant
and its products do not belong to him, he is concerned with
production for use.   If all he produced did belong to him,
how much greater his incentives to quality would be.   The
novelists do not question the value of industrialism.   They
assume that the goods produced by a highly developed industrial system will help make life richer and more comfortable.   Capitalists, however, in their competitive, indivi-
dualistic drive for profits are perfectly willing to produce
shoddy goods.   Under the pressure to produce descriptions
of factory processes, the novelists often include descriptions

which are so detailed and so extended that they become tedious and dull despite their authenticity. Too often, this authenticity turns out to be the only virtue of the novel.

   Strikes are now almost invariably viewed, at some point in the novel, from the inside and through the eyes of strikers and participants. This viewpoint leads to the use of a new vocabulary--the workers' vocabulary--and to a new awareness of the rhythms of a strike. At its worst, the viewpoint also leads to such a literal transcription of the strikes that some of the novels sound like manuals for the instruction of strike organizers or like a series of strike bulletins strung together. But in many cases the novelists catch the excitement and high hopes as the strikes begin, the tedium as they proceed, the fear and desperation as hunger and want set in, the sense of brotherhood and love as strikers overcome difficult crises together. Sherwood Anderson describes some of these rhythms in a New Masses article:

> Occasionally something breaks out--a strike.
> Were you ever in one? The experience is something never to be forgotten.
>
> A kind of tremor runs through a plant, or mine.
> There are cries and shouts. The workers pour
> out. Meetings are held. Something happens.
> These little individual units, the individual workers,
> lost down there in that amazingly beautiful and
> terrible thing--the modern world of the machine--
> these units, so tied, so bound to the machines,
> suddenly fly off the machines. . . .
>
> Light coming into dull eyes, hope into brains dulled
> by long years of toil. Men are marching now.
> They are singing. The strike is a marvelous
> thing.
>
> There is this sense of brotherhood come back,
> shoulder touching shoulder, at last in these lives
> a period of aliveness and of hope, of warmth, of
> brotherhood in struggle. [2]

He uses the experience again in his novel, Kit Brandon:
"The feeling workers get in the great factories of America...
no poets among them yet to sing of it... the song coming
some day to be a part of the coming revolution too... the end
of the glory of the day of the buyers and sellers, of the
money men.... "[3]

Another significant change to be found in the novels
of the Nineteen Thirties is the sense of insecurity and fear
in many of them.   Confidence in the relatively stable economy
of the past, the unthinking reliance on democratic institutions,
the easy belief in the military superiority of the United States
have all been deeply shaken.   The novelists seem to be seeking desperately for something in which to believe, for some
stable institution on which to depend.   Some of them look to
the family with hope, and several of the novels in this group
develop a strike situation within a family chronicle.   The
novelist may trace a family history through several generations, seeking comfort in the continuum and solidarity of a
united family as the outside world begins to crumble.   The
theme is explored in Sarah Atherton's Mark's Own (1941),
Marcia Davenport's The Valley of Decision (1943), Louis
Adamic's Grandsons (1935) and Louis Zara's Give Us This
Day (1936).   In a variation of the family theme the novelist
may depict one generation of a large family with complex
relationships among its members--relationships which are
strained or cemented under the stress of a strike.   Ruth
Comfort Mitchell's Of Human Kindness (1940), Elmer Rice's
Imperial City (1937) and Charles G. Norris' Flint (1944) all
develop intricate family relationships around explosive strike
situations.

Other novelists seek comfort and stability in a millenial approach.   Shaky the world may be, but take heart: the

revolution is at hand, and it will solve all of today's diffi-
culties.   Since the revolution is so close, personal problems
can wait until the great millenial day when the revolution has
been won.   Those characters in the novels who have the conviction that the great day is upon them sometimes develop an
engaging insouciance.   They no longer have to worry about
jobs or unpaid bills or the mean little problems that beset a
depression-ridden America.   Thomas Bell's Striker Godown
in The Second Prince (1935) is one example.

> 'You said you would tell him America owed every
> man a living and a damned good one.   You said
> you would tell him to punch his boss on the nose
> and refuse to work.   You said you would tell him
> to get drunk and chase after women and gamble
> away his mother's rent money and not to worry
> about saving for the future because a revolution
> was due any day and by the time he was fifty
> everybody would be taken care of by unemployment
> insurance and old-age pensions.   That's what you
> said, wasn't it?'[4]

The novelist seems to be exorcising his own fear of the uncertain present by creating a hero so sure of the future that
he can be outrageously improvident.

Still other novelists find a measure of comfort in the
belief that the individual can find salvation only by submerg-
ing himself in the collective.   By losing himself in the group
he finds a more potent and effective self.   Louis Flood, one
of the characters in R. L. Duffus' Night between the Rivers
(1937), wishes wistfully that he could be an active participant
in the general strike raging in New York.   He believes that
becoming "one drop in that ocean" could bring him a feeling
of exaltation.   One of Louis Gollomb's characters in Unquiet
(1935) finds fulfillment when she joins other strikers: "Life
generous with meaning and comradeship was hers again."[5]
Even when the novelist cannot quite bring himself to believe

that the individual must lose himself in the crowd, he often
seeks solace in the faith that a better and more just world
is possible, even inevitable, under the leadership of the
Marxists.

The most far-reaching change evident in many of the
novels in this group is a completely new attitude toward the
middle class.   Most novels of the past, including those which
made use of the strike, found in the middle class dependable
virtues of moderation, rationality and sturdy independence.
The middle class hero was able to stand away from both the
grubby, grinding life of the mechanic and the idle, pointless
life of the very rich.   Suddenly, during the Thirties, the
middle class becomes the symbol for vacillation, indecisive-
ness and helplessness.   What is perhaps surprising is that
the middle class characters themselves so often condemn
their own class vehemently.   One might expect an actively
class-conscious worker to express such an attitude, as does
Thomas Bell's Mike Strovenik, the strike leader in The Second Prince: '"It's the liberals, the intellectuals who make
me vomit.'"[6]   But when self-hatred has developed as viru-
lently as many of the passages in the novels indicate, we
can only conclude that a deep malaise had taken hold of the
intellectuals of the period.   Enamored of Marxist theory as
the solution to seemingly insuperable problems, the novelist
swallowed whole the concept of the workers as the only revolutionary class in society.   Many out-Marxed Marx in denying to the middle class any role at all in the coming struggle
for power.

Along with all these innovations in technique, emphasis
and attitudes there remain among this group of novels some
curiously anachronistic remnants of the past.   The American
Dream, that once potent confidence in the possibility for any

man with grit and determination to make it to the top, has
almost disappeared. Edmund Wilson writes its obituary in
1931:

> The old American ideal and legend of the poor boy
> who gets to be a millionaire, which gradually came
> to take the place of the poor boy who got to be
> President, has today lost almost all its glamor....
> The romance of the legend of the poor boy was the
> romance of the old democratic chance, of the car-
> eer open to the talents--but the realities of a mil-
> lionaire society have turned out to be the monstrosi-
> ties of capitalism. 7

But here and there, even in novels dealing with labor unrest,
where its appearance is least likely, the idea persists.
Thomas Rowan tells us in Black Earth (1935) that "... it was
a matter of record that miners had been known to save their
money, watch their opportunities, and become American millionaires and powerful figures in the world of industry. "8

The old hatred and contempt for foreigners have almost died out in the novels. The drastic curtailment of immigration during the Nineteen Twenties had limited the number of foreigners coming into the country. Those who had
arrived before World War I were by this time mostly absorbed into the native culture. The Palmer Raids of the
Twenties had led to the deportation of many of the most vo-
cal dissidents and to the intimidation of those remaining in
the United States. The "foreign" ideologies of the Thirties
were being advanced, for the most part, by native-born
Americans. By the Thirties the wholesale deportations of
the earlier decade sat heavily on many consciences. There
were many misgivings about the blatant disregard for civil
rights during the Palmer period, and attitudes toward the
foreigners had softened considerably. Not that the latent
hostilities had disappeared entirely. Among workers compet-

ing desperately for the few available jobs the malice and suspicion persisted.   But in the novels it has given way to a
new consciousness of the contributions foreigners have made
to American culture and of the internationalism of the workers' movements.   Workers of many nationalities are apt to
be shown cooperating during a strike.

The Haymarket Affair, once an extremely popular
theme for novelists dealing with strikes, has been relegated
to the history books, but in Ruth Russell's <u>Lake Front</u> (1931)
it returns once more as an important part of the plot.   Young
James O'Mara observes the McCormick Reaper strike at
first hand as a reporter, and participates directly when he
tries to get a message to one of the Haymarket anarchists.
There is, as a matter of fact, remarkably little use made
in the novels of the Thirties of the tempestuous history of
American labor.   Partly, this is because the novelists are
caught up in the immediacy of current labor struggles and
partly, because the proletarian novelists are contemptuous
of the existing trade unions, especially the American Federation of Labor.   They see the A. F. L. as a reactionary force,
opposed to Socialism and dedicated only to the protection of
the "labor aristocracy," the skilled craftsmen.   The history
of past strikes will not drive home the lesson that workers'
solidarity must go beyond the immediate strike demands--to
the overthrow of the whole capitalist system.

A few of the entrepreneurs in these novels still stand
firmly on their right to run their businesses without interference from unions, but such stances are now rare.   Peter
Mahoney, the self-made man in Ray W. Sherman's <u>The Other
Mahoney</u> (1944) says: "'If the time ever comes when we put
hobbles on the builders of business, the America you and I
have known would vanish from the earth.'"[9]   But most of the

capitalists in these novels, more often than not wooden and
unrealized characters, are not quite that unreal. The America of uncontrolled capitalism that Mahoney is talking about
has vanished from the earth. Capitalists have recognized
and accepted the inevitable--but now anti-union activities have
become far more subtle and sophisticated. Federal legislation had finally recognized the right of workers to organize
but labor spies, provocateurs within the unions, pitting the
American Federation of Labor against the newly organized
Congress for Industrial Organization, became highly developed
techniques, and outright terror against organizers--in the
South, in the coal regions, in California--was widespread.

     The dislike for union organizers persists and when
the organizers happen to be Communists as well the novelists can be moved to venom. Ruth Comfort Mitchell cannot
even bear to give the Communist organizer in Of Human Kindness a name. She is referred to throughout the book as the
Black Widow. Dorothy Meyersburg shows the union organizers in Seventh Avenue (1941) as venal, corrupt trouble-
makers who use intimidation and sabotage to force the har-
ried dress manufacturer to agree to the unionization of his
shop. Their tactics finally drive him to suicide.

     One of the central themes dominating many of these
novels is the chasm which has developed between classes.
In many of the novels the division is described in Marxist
terms: the inevitably emerging historic struggle between the
ruling capitalist class and the proletariat which will eventually take power. It is a struggle which divides the two classes decisively. Immediate benefits, no matter how liberal,
will not be enough. The two opposing classes are locked in
a battle for supremacy in which only one class can be victorious. In the course of this "final conflict" the two classes

become unalterably differentiated, not only in their aims but
in their ideals, their cultures, their pleasures and even their
language. Sometimes this concept was so rigidly applied
that the class struggle took precedence over literary skill.
All a would-be novelist needed to do was to recognize the
existence of the class struggle and align himself with the
right (that is, the workers') side. A good novel would flow
from his typewriter automatically, as it were. Thoughtful
critics, even Marxist critics, argued against such oversim-
plification. But they also insisted that no good proletarian
art could be produced without recognition of the class struggle as a necessary prerequisite. Hamilton Basso is one of
the novelists who comments on the unbridgeable gap between
worker and capitalist. He says, in In Their Own Image
(1935): "It was as if the fact that he had gone out on strike
accentuated the difference between him and the rich people
who live in the houses, bringing into sharper relief all the
conflicts that were between them. "10 William J. Blake
translates the class struggle into a somewhat anatomical
metaphor in The Painter and the Lady: "The class struggle,
that surgeon's knife, cut through the physiological mess of
society, tore its ligaments of speech and legend, color and
song, and revealed the gangrene. "11

Acceptance of the necessity of the class struggle is
not universal. There are several novelists who view the
warfare between worker and capitalist as a tragic misunder-
standing which only serves to destroy both. Charles Norris'
Flint describes a deadly war between Rory O'Brien, the longshoremen's strike leader, and Stanley Rutherford, the ship-
owner, played out against the background of San Francisco's
general strike in 1934. With both men dead at the end of
the novel, a survivor sadly comments: "'Rory was labor;

Stan was capital--employee and employer, the worker and
the businessman. When they fight, see what happens? They
destroy each other! If they could be friends. '"[12] Humphrey
Pastor, President of the Associated Farmers in Ruth Mitchell's Of Human Kindness, makes an impassioned plea for
classlessness: "'... we're going to clean house of the rats
and the termites. America needs more than defenders of
her liberties: she needs crusaders to reaffirm an American
classless society. The great American need at this moment
is for right thinking. '"[13] Pastor (because he is the good
shepherd of his flock) convinces the other ranch owners that
his view of a classless America is correct. When the Communists have been discredited and driven out of the community, the striking fruit pickers come to their senses and
peace returns to the embattled valley.

Closely related to the theme of the class war is the
emphasis in several of the novels on the stiff-necked intransigence of both sides. In Marcia Davenport's The Valley of
Decision, Jim Rafferty, the union organizer, and William
Scott, owner of a Pennsylvania steel mill, confront each other during a strike in 1883. Rafferty refuses to budge from
his demands for an eight-hour day and union recognition even
when his union members are willing to compromise. Scott
absolutely refuses to negotiate and hires armed private police
to escort scabs into the mill, although his son is urging him
to talk to Rafferty. Scott is eventually shot by Rafferty, who
is in turn killed by Scott's armed guards--a tragedy which
might have been averted if both opponents had been willing
to give a bit. William Bradford Huie makes the same point
in Mud on the Stars (1942). Buck Delancey runs his mining
empire like a feudal kingdom. When the United Mine Workers call a strike in 1934 both camps arrive at an impasse.

Neither side will give an inch and both suffer unnecessarily
in consequence.

The class differentiation in most of this group of novels is deeply affected by Marxian economic theory.   The rigid Marxist definition of economic classes is very different
from the rather loose use of the term "class" by earlier
novelists.   Classes are not differentiated primarily by wealth
or educational level, or even by the kind of work performed
by class members.   Capitalist society is divided into economic classes determined by their relationship to the means
of production--the factories, the mines, the utilities, the
transport system and the land.   Those who own the means
of production are capitalists even if the individuals are not
rich and even if they work longer hours than their employees.
Those who do not own any of the productive resources and
who earn their livelihood by working for the capitalists con-
stitute the working class or the proletariat.   All the rest--
those who are self-employed or in the professions or in the
arts--make up the middle class, whose loyalties shift back
and forth between the two contending forces as circumstances
change.   Ultimately, the clash between capitalist and worker
explodes into a socialist revolution in which the working class
will take power from the capitalists.

To most of the novelists who have accepted this description of class antagonism, individual capitalists may be
pleasant, cultivated, urbane, even humanitarian, but as members of an exploiting class they must inevitably become reactionary as they try to retain an anachronistic system.   Some
of the critics of the time warned against such an inflexible
and mechanical application of Marxism to literature but their
injunctions had little impact on most of the proletarian novelists of the Thirties.   When they do portray a capitalist, he

is almost always a two-dimensional villainous exponent of exploitation and dehumanization.   The capitalist, a parasite living off the labor of others, finds rationalizations to prove he is entitled to his favored position.   Ruth Russell's James O' Mara, the journalist who has become a railroad magnate, in Lake Front, gradually deserts his ideals and by the end of the novel he is hard, ruthless and inhuman.   His employees are "part of the machine. "   Even in such a sensitive novel as Josephine Johnson's Jordanstown the capitalist, John Chapman, sacrifices all humane values to his love of power and luxury.   John Hyde Preston's capitalist, Marston, in The Liberals (1938), has convinced himself that he is starving out his striking employees for their good.   He is embittered when he discovers that his solicitude is not appreciated by the workers.

John Chamberlain, reviewing some of the proletarian novels in 1948, accuses the writers of depicting all the businessmen in clichés.   He believes that their inability to create credible capitalist characters is the result of their mistaken belief in socialism.

> The modern novelist is emotional and subjective when he approaches the theme of U.S. industry....
> The... tradition, which... reached noisy fruition in the books of the 'proletarian' 1930's was that of literary socialism....   As things stand, their own caricatures of the businessman do not derive from living examples but from a dry and doctrinaire attitude.   Their businessman characters are all clichés; their plots have no creative originality. [14]

Chamberlain's thesis does not explain why the capitalists in the novels of the period which do not derive from "literary socialism" are no more successful.   While many of the proletarian novelists are guilty of doctrinaire attitudes, most of the novelists of the Thirties had difficulty portraying capitalist characters. Since most of them had themselves come from the working class or the lower middle class, their opportunities for first-hand observation of capitalists had necessarily been limited. In addition, something had happened to the capitalist structure which made the novelists' job infinitely harder. There were no capitalists any longer, in the old sense of the robber baron or the millowner or the mine superintendent. The capitalist of the Thirties was no longer the captain of industry but something remote and faceless, a corporation board or a stockholders' group or an international cartel which the novelist could not capture in human and personal terms. The lack of real knowledge about the lives of capitalists and the elusiveness of the new capitalism, added to the proletarian novelist's rigid ideological framework, made it even more difficult for him to portray a capitalist, but fully realized businessmen are rare in all the novels of the period.

Contrasted with the capitalist is the working class character. At the worst he is also a cliché--heroic, revolutionary, untroubled by doubt, willing to endure martyrdom for his cause--because he is not individualized but a representative of his class. Many of the middle class characters in the novels are sentimental and romantic about workers, endowing them with inherent strength and sensitivity. Or, if they take a tougher stance, they still attribute to the working class as a whole an inherent superiority because they, and they alone, are equipped by their historical position as workers to bring about the coming revolution.

At the first American Writers' Congress in 1935, Joseph Freeman, the critic and novelist, contributed to the discussions an uncompromising analysis of the relative value of worker and intellectual to the revolution:

> Even the most proletarian of writers and intellectu-
> als cannot call a general strike. They cannot
> switch off the electric lights, halt the street-cars,
> stop the factories, tie up the ships; they can't go
> out into the streets and take rifles and fight....
> Under the bloody repression of fascism, the intel-
> lectuals recognized this tremendously significant
> fact, that the workers alone are socially, industri-
> ally, politically in a position to shut off industry
> under capitalism, to take it over under socialism.[15]

The would-be proletarian novelist had better be clear what
role his worker characters are expected to play in his novel.

Buffeted between proletariat and capitalist stand the
generally contemptible middle class characters. Vacillating,
wavering in their loyalties, parasitically living off crumbs
dispensed by the capitalists, they have only one real function.
They come to life only as they align themselves with the as-
pirations of the working class. What is true for the middle
class character is also true for his creator. He cannot develop fully as a creative artist, proletarian critics admonish
him, unless he learns to look at life through a worker's
eyes. When the middle class character remains uncommitted
on the sidelines he is ineffective, a useless appendage to a
society in upheaval. The contempt for the intellectual unwill-
ing to dedicate himself fully to working class goals is expressed by the union organizer in Thomas Bell's The Second
Prince. "'All they do is talk', " he says. His disgust seems
to be justified when the main character decides at the end of
the novel to retreat to an isolated country house to write a
historical novel. Striker Godown is contemptuous of himself
for his decision. He admits that his retreat is an act of
cowardice. "'Tonight I know I'm running away because I
haven't the guts to stay and fight, to do what my head tells
me I should do if I were true to my principles and logic. '"[16]

When this dislike for the role of the middle class, and

particularly of the intellectual, is carried to the ultimate ex-
treme, it becomes a suspicion of all cerebral activity, a
virulent anti-intellectualism. Sometimes this takes the ludi-
crous form of trying to act like a worker or acting the way
an intellectual thinks a worker acts. Joseph Freeman and
Floyd Dell have both written of their recollection of Mike
Gold affecting dirty shirts and stinking three-cent cigars,
spitting on the floor because he wanted to be regarded as a
proletarian. The novels in this group which cling most desperately to the myth of superhuman workers and despicable
intellectuals fail not so much because they portray reality
more or less inaccurately. They fail because the novelists
have so rigidly limited their artistic range that they are unable to give us anything deeper than novelized slogans. There
is some fine journalism in some of these novels but very little art.

Capitalist and worker ranged inexorably against each
other are common situations in most of the novels in this
group. The confrontation most often culminates in a strike.
In many of the novels the drama of the confrontation is also
heightened through a head-on collision between Communist
and Fascist. In the literary shorthand of the proletarian
novel of the Thirties, the Communist stood for the worker
at the highest level of consciousness--aware of his revolutionary role and prepared to fight for his convictions. At
the other end of the scale, the Fascist represents the capitalist so desperate at the realization that his system is doomed
that he will use any means to forestall the inevitable--chi-
canery, violence, murder or war. There is a steady parade
of vigilantes in many of the novels. They murder two organizers in Louis Adamic's Grandsons, load I. W. W. strikers
on freight cars and ship them to Idaho in Louis Colman's

Lumber (1931), murder a picket in Joseph Delany's The
Christmas Tree Murders, lynch Butte miners in Norman
McLeod's The Bitter Roots (1941), kidnap an investigating
delegation in Leane Zugsmith's The Summer Soldier (1938).
They are organized as the Green Legion in Charles Givens'
The Devil Takes a Hill Town, as the American Legion in
Daniel Mainwaring's The Doctor Died at Dusk (1936), as the
Gold Shirts in Mari Sandoz's Capital City (1939) and as the
Order of the Royal Knights in Fred Rothermell's The Ghost-
land. All of these groups are nongovernmental, work extra-
legally (although often with the tacit support of legal agencies), and go into action when the democratic process seems
to be favoring the strikers.   The vigilantes have their genesis in some actual organizations of the period like the Black
Legion and the Silver Shirts as well as the activities of some
American Legion chapters, but their literary purposes are
not merely to anchor the novels in reality.   The vigilante
groups point up the growing threat of Fascism, the repres-
sive form to which a dying capitalism resorts.   The lesson
of Hitler's Brown Shirts has not been lost on the novelists.

        The violence, repression and illegal methods of the
Fascists takes another form in several of the novels.   The
capitalists make extensive use of illegal labor spies and
strikebreaking agencies to destroy the rising power of the
workers' organizations.   These techniques also have their
real counterparts, as the LaFollette Committee revealed
with abundant evidence in its report in 1937.   Again, the
novelists make literary use of labor spy activities in order
to dramatize the extremes to which capitalism will go in order to retain power.   Benjamin Appel's The Power-House
gives a detailed account of strikebreaking activities and their
intimate connection with criminal rackets.   John T. McIn-

tyre's Ferment (1937) also deals extensively with the techniques of strikebreakers.   One of the agency heads explains
his work:

> 'I've been breaking strikes for twenty years,' said
> Cavo, 'and my experience has shown me that if
> you can bring three things together at the same
> time--and the right time--you take your money,
> pack up and go home.   And those three things are:
> the police, the appearance of violence on the part
> of the strikers, the feeling among them that their
> jobs are lost.   Those things, when they come to-
> gether, slacken all their guts, and from then on
> they aren't much good.'[17]

Cavo's matter-of-fact analysis, which might as well be that
of a sales manager analyzing a sales campaign, is no accident.   McIntyre intends Cavo to sound like a typical businessman.

None of the novels presents Fascist activity--either
of the vigilante or the labor spy variety--in a sympathetic
light.   Attitudes toward Communists vary widely, however.
On the one hand, Communists are shown as the saviors of
mankind, selflessly dedicated to creating a better world for
all.   Many writers of the period joined the Communist Party
or came very close to it because it seemed to know the answers in a chaotic and bewildering world.   A troubled Howard
Fast, resigning from the Communist Party in 1957, states
his reasons for joining the Party many years before:

> I joined the Communist movement for two reasons.
> I believed that in the Communist Party was the
> beginning of a true brotherhood of man, working
> with devotion for socialism, peace and democracy.
> Secondly, I believed that a Communist Party offer-
> ed the most effective resistance to fascism.[18]

The great promise which the Communists seemed about to
fulfill was a liberating inspiration, the release of all mankind from the constricting incomprehensible present.

To the writer the Communist Party of the Thirties
was especially attractive because it appeared to offer him an
artistic shortcut. It seemed possible to bypass the long lonely process during which a writer learns his craft, develops
a philosophy, and begins to translate his observations into a
work of art. Guided by the ready-made philosophy offered by
the Communists and bolstered by illusory and frenzied activity
on behalf of the workers, the young writer could easily delude
himself that all he needed to do was to pour his passion into
a manuscript and--presto!--a great novel was born. Communist critics of the time helped to foster the illusion by
praising extravagantly any novel with the accepted political
viewpoint, no matter how ineptly written.

Participation in left-wing writers' groups like the John
Reed Clubs and the League of American Writers gave the
young writer a sense of fellowship, but it could also be an
instrument of self-deception ultimately injurious to many
fledgling writers. The peripheral cultural activity of the
associations could easily be mistaken for creative activity.
The time the writer devoted to demonstrations, picketing,
electioneering and producing manifestoes and strike bulletins
was time he took from creative writing, and, possibly more
harmful, time he took from learning his craft. The bustling
activity of the clubs also helped to delude those without talent
into prolonged self-deception about their lack of creative
ability. But it would be a mistake to deny some of the positive effects of the writers' clubs. Young writers needed the
sense of comradeship the clubs gave them, and benefited
from the discussions and activities there. The writer learns
his craft from writing and even a strike bulletin or a leaflet
can teach the writer something he needs. Many writers,
even if they did not produce great novels, become competent

craftsmen.

Once convinced that the Communist knew more and
did more than ordinary human beings, the novelist was often
tempted to picture his Communist characters as superhuman
saints.   Even when he did not succumb to that temptation, he
frequently portrayed middle class characters who confessed to
admiration and envy of Communists for their omniscience,
their utter commitment and their singlemindedness.   Ann
Marston cries out, in Preston's The Liberals: "'Sometimes
I wish I could be a Communist like Greg.   I wish I could be
absolutely one thing fiercely.'"[19]   Rhoda Townsend, in Adriana Spadoni's Not All Rivers (1937), also envies the Communist commitment when she says: "'It must be lovely to
believe in anything so much that you don't care what happens
to you.'"[20]

By no means all novelists in this group look upon Communists as saviors.   To many the Communists are a self-
seeking destructive force willing to sacrifice any number of
careers--or lives, for that matter--to their abstraction about
a coming revolution, or to a passion for power.   Dorothy
Meyersburg in Seventh Avenue accuses Communists of vicious
mischief in their organizing tactics.   In Darwin L. Teilhet's
Journey to the West (1938), Communists coldbloodedly arrange
for Rufus Cobb to be severely beaten when he saves a struck
ship from a Communist dynamite plot.   Lauren Gilfillan portrays the Communists in I Went to Pit College (1934) as do-
nothing talkers who impede the progress of the miners'
strike.   When her heroine tries to expose their role, they
spread a malicious report that she is a company spy.

Critics, remembering the Thirties, are as divided as
the novelists in their assessment of the role of the Communists and radicals.   Louis Filler denounces them roundly:

> It is rarely realized that the economic depression
> was not only a human and social tragedy, but also
> an opportunity. It provided jobs for administering
> the jobless. It created writing jobs. There were
> jobs for enterprising comrades in the unions and
> unemployment councils, on the government projects,
> in the government itself, in the various levels of
> the radical groups--startingly good jobs, in many
> cases. [21]

Malcolm Cowley, on the other hand, remembers their effect
fondly:

> It was the great dream that men would cease to be
> slaves of history; that instead they would study its
> laws, as Marx had already done, and would shape
> the history of the future by their joint efforts. We
> had the feeling in those days that history and the
> future and the Russian Revolution were all on our
> side, and that the little assignments we carried
> out were bathed in a supernal light. [22]

The truth lies probably somewhere in between. Not all Communists were always highminded. Some had personal and ig-
noble motivations. But Filler's "startlingly good jobs" are
mostly a trick of his memory. The writing jobs, where they
existed at all, were often grubby, dull and underpaid assign-
ments. Those who worked for the Federal Writers' Project
earned something like $100 a month. More often than not,
jobs in the unions and the unemployment councils and the
radical groups paid startingly low wages and involved real
physical danger. The mortality rate for organizers was very
high, not only in the proletarian novels but in real life as
well.

Cowley's memory is probably a bit more accurate.
Political activity on the Left was not only frenzied but surrounded by an illusion of immediacy and importance. But
Cowley is probably generalizing too broadly. Not all Communists and radicals were always convinced that they were
making history.

The difference between what Filler remembers and
what Cowley does can be attributed in part to the periods in
which they were recalling the Thirties. In 1954, when Filler
wrote his article, the political atmosphere made it all too
easy to see Communists as evil conspiratorial monsters.
Ten years later, when Cowley's article appeared, not only
had the wave of anti-Communism begun to ebb but, as the
Thirties receded farther into history, it was easier to remember them less bitterly and more nostalgically.

The strikes in this group of novels serve many purposes. They can represent the beginning and, just as often,
the end of an action or a mood or a characterization. The
strike can serve to lift men out of themselves and sweep
them to heights they could never otherwise have attained.
Meek unheroic little Aaron Traum in Hyman and Lester Cohen's Aaron Traum (1930) becomes an impassioned orator
and indefatigable organizer when his garment shop goes out
on strike. Tom Tippett's John Stafford in Horse Shoe Bottoms is a stolid hard-working miner with limited horizons
until his participation in a series of strikes turns him into
a thoughtful, persistent and clever fighter.

The strike can raise a man from an ignorant beast
responding only to the needs of his belly into a conscious
revolutionary with long-range goals and deep convictions.
Carleton Beals' heroine, Esperanza Huitron, in The Stones
Awake (1936), begins life as an illiterate, hungry peasant
and learns through her active participation in a soap factory
strike and later in a miners' strike that she can play an important role in Mexico's revolutionary struggles. Katherine
Marling in Constance Cassady's This Magic Dust (1937) enters
a tragically doomed steel strike as a rather naive artist, anxious to help but ineffective, but in the course of the strike

she becomes a dedicated and resourceful organizer. Ward
Moore's Simon Epstein learns from his strike experiences,
in Breathe the Air Again (1942), that no strike is ever completely lost.   All strikes teach the workers important lessons
in strategy.   Stéphane Sabatier in William J. Blake's The
Painter and the Lady becomes not only a better painter but
a dedicated revolutionary through his participation in a vine-
yard workers' strike.

The strike can be an instrument for spiritual redemption.   In Royal Wilbur France's Compromise (1936), attorney
Emory Young is well on his way to becoming a dehumanized
machine.   During a court trial he is willing to sacrifice a
man he knows to be innocent, in order to bolster his own
career.   When his first love, Justine Bartlett, is killed in
a West Virginia miners' strike, he sees the light and wrecks
his chances for nomination to the presidency by his public attack on the coal mine owners.

The strike can become a source of fun and excitement,
as it is to a striker's child in Lauren Gilfillan's I Went to
Pit College:

> 'I like the strike.   It's more excitin' than before.
> I like to sing songs to the meetings, and there's
> speakers to the mass meetings, and then there's
> more to eat, too, for we git food off the relief and
> Mamma and Papa didn't go bummin' afore the
> strike.   And we got dresses off the relief. '23

The hero of Elizabeth Corbett's Charley Manning (1939) has
the time of his life running a street-car when the drivers
strike, and he sums up the strike as "fun, while it lasts. "

The strike can symbolize hope for the future.   Louis
Flood, the martyred hero of R. L. Duffus' Night between the
the Rivers, predicts a better world even if the strike is lost
--as it eventually is.   The strike can bring about a renewed

spirit of comradeship and brotherhood.   Irving Howe quotes
one of Sherwood Anderson's letters, written after he had
spoken at various mill town strike rallies in the South during
the early Thirties:

> 'There is a way in which people, workers, when
> they go on strike, even when they are pretty sure
> to lose, get something. ...   In the mill they are
> dominated by a big, tightly organized thing.   It
> makes them feel small.   They lose the sense of
> each other.   But then a strike comes and for a
> time at least, they get a rather fine feeling of
> each other. ...   Why, they are people in love
> with each other. '[24]

The strike is not uniformly an instrument for progress
or good.   It can be used as a stepping-stone for indolent or
ignorant men to move into positions of leadership or power,
as in Huie's Mud on the Stars.   It can be used as a cover
for murder, as in Daniel Mainwaring's The Doctor Died at
Dusk (1936).   It can become a profitable gold mine for crook-
ed or lazy organizers, as in William Carlos Williams' White
Mule (1937) or in Thomas Rowan's Black Earth.   The strike
can symbolize death--of an era, as in Rachel Field's And
Now Tomorrow (1942); of a town, as in Philip Wiener's And
So Dedicated (1940); or of a political system, as in Joseph
Freeman's Never Call Retreat (1943).

William Carlos Williams' White Mule and Tom Tippett's Horse Shoe Bottoms are about as different from each
other as two novels can be, yet both make important and
serious use of strikes.   The two novels show how varied the
literary strike had become by the middle of the Thirties and
how different the purposes it served could be.   In White Mule
Williams was attempting to translate to the novel the objectivism with which he had already experimented in his poetry.
The novel, describing Joe and Gurlie Stecher's life in New

York in 1893, attempts to communicate actions, events and
emotions strictly "objectively"--through the use of concrete
specific details seen externally and described in simple un-
metaphorical language.   Joe, a foreman in a printshop, has
devoted himself singlemindedly to supporting his wife and
family.   An immigrant from Germany, he has adapted himself to life in America but is never really comfortable with
American mores.   Joe, trained in the stern German traditions of hard work, long apprenticeship, strict class divisions
and absolute criteria of honesty, is alienated from both his
employers and his fellow-workers.   The bosses are not above
manipulating bids to obtain an important government contract
and the pressmen shirk their duties, complain constantly and
mishandle the presses.   When the strike begins, Joe keeps
the presses going with strikebreakers.   Despite his contempt
for his employers, Joe is unshakeably loyal to them.   He
suffers stoically the threats, insults and physical manhandling
to which he is subjected by the strikers, and just as stoically,
accepts the ingratitude of his bosses.   When the strike is settled, the strikers return to work with small pay raises.   Joe
continues to work for the same pay and is not given even a
word of praise for his efforts.

        Joe's attitude toward strikers and employers is de-
scribed entirely in objective terms: conversations with the
union agent, the boss' outbursts of temper, Joe's monosyllabic
and reluctant descriptions of the day's events to his wife,
Gurlie.   There are no interior monologues, no auctorial in-
trusions and no attempts to analyze how the characters are
affected by events.   Joe advises his boss to compromise with
the employees and avoid a strike.   The boss damns the strikers as disloyal ingrates.   Joe accuses him of making profit
out of their labor.   The whole scene takes a single succinct

paragraph. Williams makes effective use of indirection, too.
As Gurlie waits for Joe to come home, she imagines him
being kicked and beaten by the strikers. The scene she imagines is not real, never really takes place, but, again, in
one brief paragraph and without emotional histrionics, Williams concentrates the essence of the fear and uncertainty a
strike can evoke in a working class family.

The strike in White Mule is only one of the events in
the Stecher family life, and not the most important. The
birth of their younger daughter, a family Christmas party,
a drunken neighbor's terrifying attack on his wife are just
as essential to Williams' description of the Stechers. All
of these events, including the strike, are presented in language and style natural to the kind of people Williams wants
us to know. He keeps his own reactions entirely out of the
novel. He is writing about proletarians but he is not writing
a "proletarian novel. "

Tom Tippett, on the other hand, is very much concerned with producing a proletarian novel. Horse Shoe Bottoms tells the story of John Stafford, who leaves England in the
1870's with his young bride Ellen to work in the Wantling
coal mine in Illinois. Tippett tells, in great detail, of the
severe life of the nineteenth century miner--long hours of
work, accidents, wage cuts. The drive for organization of
the miners into a trade union begins soon after John's arrival
in the United States, but it is a long slow process, carried
on in secret, with many setbacks. John becomes active in
the union movement and is soon recognized as a leader. He
is elected to represent his fellow miners at a union convention and there, under the influence of the eloquent older miner, John Siney, he becomes convinced of the need for a
national miners' union. John learns slowly and painfully

how to appeal to the other miners and how to present their
demands to the mine owners.   Despite poverty and deprivation, his relationship to Ellen grows more tender and understanding.   There are a series of strikes in the novel, the
miners' desperate and pathetic attempts to better their conditions, and, more basically, their groping efforts to attain a
life of dignity.   The strikes generally fail.   Even when the
miners win a demand or two, the next economic slump wipes
out their gains.   But the strikers win something, too.   Each
time they strike they learn a bit more about organization and
cooperation.   Each time a few more miners, especially
among the younger ones (they enter the mines at twelve),
aspire to a more ambitious dream--a fulfilled and dignified
life.   Through all of the picketing, hunger, violence and suffering, John Stafford changes from a brutish ignorant creature
knowing only animal desires to a sensitive strong human
being.   His sufferings teach him compassion for his wife
and children as well as for the other miners.   He begins
to read so that he can understand the workers' struggles
better.   The novel ends with John's death from tuberculosis.
He has gained few of the goals to which he had dedicated his
life.   He dies poor, his young sons are doomed to become
miners too, the miners are still struggling to organize, and
a life of dignity for the miners is still a distant dream, but
John Stafford has found a meaning in his life.   His family
and the miners in his pit recognize, although inarticulately,
that John Stafford's humble inconspicuous life has deeply affected all of them.   Tippett sentimentalizes some of the
scenes in his novel, especially John's funeral, but he keeps
his style simple, unornamented and effective.   He presents
convincingly and movingly the strong loving relationship between John and Ellen, and John's stubborn persistence in

building the union.   To Tippett the strikes are of central importance in the novel.   Their cumulative effect is one of slow
growth and development--in John Stafford as a man and among
the miners as a collective.   One of the best of the proletarian novels of the period, Horse Shoe Bottoms uses the strike
effectively to deepen the intellectual and emotional impact of
the miners' lives it portrays.

Another novel which uses a strike effectively, while
breaking away from the proletarian formula, is Erskine Caldwell's God's Little Acre (1933).   Caldwell's strike leader,
Will Thompson, is a character of great depth and power.
Will is strong, lusty, virile, but his experiences in Southern
textile mills have created in him a doubt whether he is really a man.   His desperate struggle to conquer that doubt eventually kills him.   On his father-in-law's farm in Georgia he
feels himself "nothing but a dead sapling sticking up in the
ground. "   In his shabby company house he is "nothing but a
piece of company property. "   He needs to keep proving his
virility--in bed, at the machine, on the picket-line, and finally in a direct confrontation with the machinery which is destroying his manhood.   Will leads the strikers into the struck
mill and pulls the switch which turns on the power.   Just before the mill guards shoot him, Will has one glorious moment
when he knows he is a real man and when he is at last sure
that his wife, the strikers and the company also realize Will
Thompson's strength and humanity.   Caldwell brought a storm
of indignant disapproval down on himself with God's Little
Acre.   The strait-laced objected to his explicit sexual scenes.
Conventional-minded critics found his characters too crude,
his situations too raw, his descriptions too surrealistic.
Marxist critics took Caldwell's novel too literally and chided
him severely for not producing an orthodox proletarian novel.

He omitted the prescribed description of every dreary strike
detail, he showed his hero in bed instead of at the union hall,
he described workers humorously and ironically instead of
solemnly.   But it is precisely Caldwell's departures from
conventional formulas which make God's Little Acre a strong
work, well worth re-reading more than thirty-five years after
its first appearance.

A good many, perhaps most, of the proletarian novels
of the Thirties failed to overcome some of the deadening influences of the period.   Young, unskilled novelists, encouraged
by critics of the Left to ignore technique, never learned how
to write a novel.   The authors were often more interested in
producing truthful reportage than a work of art, and ration-
alized their contempt for their craft by assuming that bourgeois artistic standards of the past were no longer valid,
having been superseded by new proletarian concepts of art.
But the new criteria were never precisely defined and by
bourgeois standards many of the proletarian novels are technically poor.   Even more serious than the technical faults,
however, is a narrowness of vision which is characteristic
of most of the novels in this group.   Those novelists who
have accepted Marxist theory are so sure that they, and they
alone, know the right road to salvation that they fall into a
stuffy self-righteous pose which is fatal to the production of
great art.   The same self-righteousness affects both Marxist
and anti-Marxist novelists, however.   In their earnest efforts
to prove their opponents wrong, both groups use the same
methods.   But although most of the novels can be faulted,
the period itself is full of a sense of excitement.   The novelists are engaged with their materials, conscious that they
are dealing with important human concerns.   Most of the
novels are much more interesting than earlier novels which

had used the strike.   They are concerned with human motivation, with man's relation to society, with broad social issues.
The monopoly of the genteel middle class on the American
novel has been decisively broken.   Poverty, ugliness, brutality, violence and conflict and their causes are now just as
much the novelists' concern as love, romance and adventure,
and better technicians and more profound thinkers are now
free to explore these themes in depth.   The American novel
using the strike has come of age.   It spins off into a distinctive genre, the "strike novel. "

Notes

1.   Granville Hicks, "Revolution and the Novel, " New Mass-
      es, " XI:6 (May 8, 1934), p. 22.

2.   Sherwood Anderson, "Let's Have More Criminal Syndi-
      calism, " New Masses, VII:9 (February, 1932), p. 3-4.

3.   Sherwood Anderson, Kit Brandon (New York: Charles
      Scribner's Sons, 1936), p. 64.

4.   Thomas Bell, The Second Prince (New York: G. P. Put-
      nam's Son, 1935), pp. 106-107.

5.   Joseph Gollomb, Unquiet (New York: Dodd, Mead and
      Co. , 1935), p. 173.

6.   Bell, op. cit. , p. 191.

7.   Edmund Wilson, The Shores of Light (New York: Farrar,
      Straus and Young, Inc. , 1952), p. 526.

8.   Thomas Rowan, Black Earth (New York: Hillman-Curl,
      Inc. , 1935), p. 237.

9.   Ray W. Sherman, The Other Mahoney (New York: Ives,
      Washburn, Inc. , 1944), p. 328.

10.   Hamilton Basso, In Their Own Image (New York: Charles
       Scribner's Sons, 1935), p. 233.

11. William J. Blake, The Painter and the Lady (New York: Simon and Shuster, 1939), p. 214.

12. Charles G. Norris, Flint (Garden City, N.Y.: Doubleday, Doran and Co., Inc., 1944), p. 353.

13. Ruth Comfort Mitchell, Of Human Kindness (New York: D. Appleton-Century Co., 1940), p. 295.

14. John Chamberlain, "The Businessman in Fiction," Fortune, XXXVIII:5 (November, 1948), p. 144.

15. Henry Hart, ed., American Writers' Congress (New York: International Publishers, 1935), p. 169.

16. Bell, op. cit., p. 287.

17. John T. McIntyre, Ferment (New York: Farrar and Rinehart, Inc., 1937), p. 171.

18. Howard Fast, "My Decision," Mainstream, X:3 (March, 1957), p. 30.

19. John Hyde Preston, The Liberals (New York: John Day Co., 1938), p. 97.

20. Adriana Spadoni, Not All Rivers (New York: Book League of America, 1937), p. 173.

21. Louis Filler, "Political Literature: A Post-Mortem," Southwest Review, XXXIX:3 (Summer, 1954), p. 189.

22. Malcolm Cowley, "A Remembrance of the Red Romance," Esquire, LXI:3 (March, 1964), p. 124.

23. Lauren Gilfillan, I Went to Pit College (New York: Viking Press, 1934), p. 111.

24. Irving Howe, Sherwood Anderson (n.p.: William Sloane Associates, 1951), p. 217.

Chapter 6

THE "STRIKE NOVEL": 1930-1945

From the novel of social protest, a characteristic form during the decade of the Thirties, a completely new and distinctive genre evolved: the strike novel. The period between the rise and the decline of the strike novel was extremely brief--fifteen years at the most--but within that time a new form with its own highly specialized conventions developed. The strike novel, which does not merely <u>use</u> the strike but is essentially <u>about</u> a strike, has its genesis in the proletarian novel. It is not easy to define the proletarian novel, since even the briefest survey of the critical literature of the Thirties reveals a wide difference of opinion among the critics of the Left.

One of the more perceptive analysts of the time, V. F. Calverton, attempted as early as 1925, in his <u>The Newer Spirit,</u> to define proletarian art. Calverton maintained that proletarian art differed radically from bourgeois art because it was based on a new concept of morality. Virtue, as defined by the capitalist ethic, equates goodness with property values. Honesty (or respect for the other man's material possessions) and chastity (or respect for the other man's chattel property) are highly regarded virtues. The proletarian ethic discards the bourgeois concept of the innate wickedness of human nature and sees instead that crime is the result of conditions. Proletarian art, then, would not need to be sermonical. You don't preach at people to be good when

it is an unjust social system which has made them bad.
Proletarian art would boldly and objectively explore crime,
violence and sex instead of hiding them behind the circumlo-
cutions of bourgeois prejudice.   "Evil in characters, " Calverton says, "is pictured without the attempt to make them
hideous"[1] by the proletarian artist.   Only the system which
creates evil can be hideous.

There was not much dissension about the philosophical
base of proletarian art.   Most left-wing critics agreed that
sympathy for, or actual identification with, the working class
and belief in the eventual triumph of Socialism were essential elements of proletarian art.   The necessary degree of
commitment of the artist, however, gave rise to furious disagreement among the critics.   Was it necessary for the proletarian artist himself to be a worker, did he need to write
about the workers, or could he be from the middle class and
write about the middle class but from a class-conscious point
of view?[2]

The most extended discussion of the subject--and a
remarkably bitter one--occurred during the first American
Writers' Congress, convened in 1935.   Joseph Freeman,
speaking on "The Tradition of American Revolutionary Literature, " was willing to grant full status as a proletarian artist
to any writer who opposed capitalism and supported the aims
of the revolutionary working class.   The writer need only be
against capitalism on "fundamental questions. "   His political
function is properly among other writers as an ally of the
workers.   Malcolm Cowley, at the same Congress, defined
the proletarian novel much more rigidly.   A proletarian novelist has to write about the proletariat, and Cowley was very
doubtful whether middle-class novelists were really capable
of writing about the working class from a revolutionary point

of view. Edwin Seaver disagreed. His position, somewhat
closer to Freeman's, was a very broad one. All the proletarian artist needed to earn his membership was a point of
view. He did not need to limit the class he wrote about; he
did not need to be a proletarian himself; he needed only to
have a loyalty toward the working class and a belief in dialectical materialism. But Martin Russak fiercely disagreed
with Seaver during the discussion and supported Cowley's
contention that the novel could only be proletarian if it portrayed proletarians. "I don't think our novels should be concerned with the emotions and reactions and values of the upper or middle classes or the lumpenproletariat, "[3] Russak
said.

Granville Hicks, writing on the subject in The Great
Tradition (1935), proposed a kind of compromise definition.
At the moment, proletarian literature need only speak for
the worker to deserve the title. As the working class comes
closer to taking over political power it will produce its own
spokesmen. At that point proletarian literature will come
from the proletariat and be "truly and fully proletarian. "
Melvin Levy, in an early article (1931) on the subject in
New Masses, advocates a kind of mystical proletarianism.
The really significant proletarian art will be produced neither
by the class-conscious worker nor the worker-oriented intellectual but by the writer so imbued with the sense of the
proletariat triumphant that he will write about and for the
worker despite himself "because the powerful stirring of the
proletariat has forced itself upon him without his will. "[4]

In a long article in the April/May, 1935 issue of
Partisan Review, Edwin Seaver expands the position he took
at the Writers' Congress. The proletarian novel, he insists,
cannot be limited to novels produced by the proletarian writ-

ers, nor to the work of middle class writers loyal to the
working class, nor to fiction dealing with workers' lives.
The proletarian writer must have a revolutionary purpose.
The aim of the writer must be "not merely to understand the
world and not merely to explain it, but to change it."[5] It
comes as something of a shock to discover that Leon Trotsky,
the brilliant, erratic theorist of Communism, denied even the
possibility of a proletarian art in <u>Literature and Revolution,</u>
published in an American edition in 1925.

> It is fundamentally incorrect to contrast bourgeois
> culture and bourgeois art with proletarian culture
> and proletarian art.   The latter will never exist,
> because the proletarian regime is temporary and
> transient.

Once a truly classless society is established--and that would
be soon after the victory of the Socialist revolution--it is
pointless to talk about either bourgeois or proletarian art.

The argument raged, then died down as revolutionary
literature gave way to new themes.   It sputtered here and
there for another decade but was never resolved.   As late
as 1950 Howard Fast, in <u>Literature and Reality</u>, was still
making a stab at defining proletarian art.   He was content to
bestow the accolade on the artist who chose his side, the
side being, necessarily, that of the worker.

> To become art, the strike must be related to his-
> torical process, and that relationship can hardly
> be neutral.
>
> The strike is not just a strike; it is many, many
> things, and since most of these things are quite
> unlike, they cannot all be the truth....
>
> The truth is on one side or another, and before
> the writer can ascertain the nature of the truth,
> he must choose sides.   The truth is partisan, not
> neutral. [7]

With this plea for a partisan truth, we can conclude

the pros and cons. Whether the proletarian novel ought to
be by, for, to or about the working class, we can recognize
as a distinctive development of the Thirties the realistic novel protesting social conditions under capitalism and advocating a political-economic-social transformation to Socialism.
Within this broad category there are subclasses carefully
distinguished by Walter Rideout in The Radical Novel in the
United States. He isolates four different types of proletarian
novels.

> ... most of the novels can be fitted fairly easily on
> the basis of content or subject matter into four
> main groups: (1) those centered about a strike;
> (2) those concerned with the development of an in-
> dividual's class-consciousness and his conversion
> to Communism; (3) those dealing with the 'bottom
> dogs, ' the lowest layers of society; and (4) those
> describing the decay of the middle class.

One of the subdivisions of the proletarian novel which is a
kind of precursor of the strike novel is that whole group of
novels in the Thirties in which the central figure is shown
developing specifically into a labor official or a radical political organizer. Because the novel describes the educational
process which turns him into a professional organizer, the
novels in this group naturally include a number of strikes as
part of their protagonists' life experiences.

The novels portraying lives of organizers have elements in common. In all of them the novelists show in me-
ticulous detail precisely why the characters chose lives as
working class leaders. In each case participation in a lost
strike plays an important part in the decision. Only Ruth Mc-
Kenney's Jake, in her Jake Home (1943), is born into the
working class. He is the son of a Pennsylvania coal miner
who goes into the mine himself at eleven when his father is
killed in a cave-in. Jake marries the daughter of a tool

superintendent and reluctantly adopts the petit bourgeois goals
of his wife and her family.   Before long he is a section foreman regarded with suspicion by the miners who had been his
comrades.   Their feeble strike, attacked by company police,
brings Jake to his senses.   He joins the strikers, is badly
beaten up and starts on his long arduous route toward a career as a full-time organizer.   In the other novels in the
group the protagonists all stem from middle class backgrounds.   Glenn Spottswood, in John Dos Passos' Adventures
of a Young Man (1938), is the son of a Columbia University
professor.   Jack Conroy's Robert Hurley, in A World to Win
(1935), is the offspring of a peculiar liaison between Terry
Hurley, a rough uncouth sawmill worker, and Martha Darrell,
a genteel sex-starved poetaster, who impresses upon Robert
her own snobbish pseudo-intellectualism.   David Markand, the
confused hero of Waldo Frank's The Death and Birth of David
Markand (1934), is a rising young executive in his family's
tobacco business when he abruptly leaves his job and family
in order to find himself through experience among the workers.   Josephine Herbst's contribution to this group of novels
is a trilogy consisting of Pity Is Not Enough (1933), The Executioner Waits (1934) and Rope of Gold (1939).   In a long
letter to David Madden, editor of Proletarian Writers of the
Thirties (1968), Miss Herbst claimed that she was trying to
show the powerful effect of America's history on a pioneer
family, the gradual disintegration of old traditions as World
War I and the Depression made isolation of the United States
from European political currents impossible and, finally, the
breakdown of international hope as another World War became
inevitable.   Perhaps.   All the elements Miss Herbst talks
about are certainly to be found in the three novels.   But
looking at them thirty years later, the reader finds them

much less panoramic in scope than their author claims, and
much more an attempt to translate into novelistic terms a
common theme of the Thirties--the disintegration of capitalism and the imminent triumph of Socialism.   At any rate, an
important theme of the final volume, Rope of Gold, is the
development of Steve Carson and Jonathan Chance into dedicated organizers.   Chance rises above his origins as a banker's son and dilettante writer, and Carson overcomes the
temptations to middle class delusions inherent in his marriage
to the daughter of a well-to-do farmer.   The novelists stress
the middle class connections or origins of all the protagonists
in this group of novels not only to add drama and conflict but
also to embody a theorem very important to the proletarian
novelist.   Communist conviction, innate to those born and
brought up as workers, was not unattainable for those of the
middle class who were strong enough and willing enough to
throw off the false "American Dream" and hitch their wagons
to the working class star.   Even the born and bred worker
needed to renew his faith periodically to guard against insidi-
ous middle class notions.   It is precisely the role of the Communist Party organizer to remind workers when they stray
from working class goals and it is precisely the Communist
Party's understanding of working class goals that constitutes
its "vanguard role. "

John Dos Passos is scornful of the Communists' arrogance in assuming a "vanguard role. "   In Adventures of a
Young Man his Communist characters are without exception
despicable, weak, double-dealing and contemptible.   Irving
Silverstone, the Communist organizer who is sent to give political direction to the striking miners, is a parlor orator,
who spouts slogans and runs for cover when the going gets
tough.   Neither he nor the Party is at all concerned with

the workers for whom they pretend to speak. Silverstone is willing to use any means--blackmail, violence, betrayal--for his ends, and his ends do not include the welfare of the working class. The Party is concerned only with maintaining itself and its members and ultimately, but quite hypothetically, bringing about a Marxist revolution in America. Dos Passos tells the story of Glenn Spottswood, who becomes a Communist Party organizer. His first strike experience is among a group of Texas pecan-shellers. The strikers remain shadowy characters. With the exception of Frankie Perez, who turns up later as a Trotskyite fighting in Spain, and Guadalupe, who helps on the strikers' defense committee, the strikers have neither names nor personalities. Glenn's second strike assignment, among hill-country miners, also leaves the strikers undifferentiated. Except for the miner, Pearl Napier, whose sturdy independence and courage are betrayed by the Communists, and Pearl's sister Wheatly, with whom Glenn has a brief, fierce sexual encounter, the miners are all subordinated to Glenn and Silverstone and the growing intellectual antagonism between them. Finally, Glenn openly defies Silverstone and tries to wrest the defense of the miners accused of murder from the cynical control of the Party. He is isolated, expelled and hounded until he decides to join the Loyalists in Spain, where the Communists cold-bloodedly arrange for Glenn to be killed.

The biggest difference between the novel about the labor organizer and the strike novel lies in the function of the strike in the novels. In the novels about labor organizers the emphasis is still on the individual--his motivations, his reactions, his development or disintegration. Waldo Frank wants to show us how David Markand reacts to injustice against workers on strike and why he concludes to devote

his life to bringing Socialism to power.   Ruth McKenney
wants to let us know how Jake Home moves from miner to
middle class foreman and, finally, to leader of working class
struggles.   John Dos Passos tells us Glenn Spottswood's
story from boyhood through death in Spain.   As the main
character in each of the novels moves from job to job, from
area to area, sometimes from industry to industry, he experiences several strikes as part of his professional involvement in labor organization.   In the strike novel the individual
has lost importance.   The real protagonist has become the
strike itself, and the novelist is primarily concerned with
its genesis, development and resolution.   The strike novel
develops in the Thirties as the fictional counterpart of the
growing number of books of reportage which describe strikes
in extensive detail.   Ruth McKenney's Industrial Valley (1939),
describing the Akron rubber strike of 1934, and Lallah Davidson's South of Joplin (1939), detailing the 1935 and 1937 lead
mine strikes in Picker, Oklahoma, are two examples of this
type of documentary literature.   Both of these volumes attempt to show not only the incidents of the strikes but the
everyday lives of the strikers, the issues which led to the
strike decision and the larger economic and social problems
facing the whole country--all important elements of the strike
novel.

Strike novels, at the height of the development of the
genre, are characterized by an extraordinary homogeneity.
All the examples of the type show the same qualities and
differ from each other only in details.   This similarity
among the novels is not, to begin with, the result of external demands imposed on the novelists by critical or political pressure.   It seems to grow out of the novelists' own
desire to equate the strike with a sweeping revolutionary

change which is about to bring justice to America.   In time,
a rigid interpretation of the strike novel was demanded by
the authoritative--and authoritarian--critics.   It is partly because of their insistence on a strict formula that the strike
novel disappears from the American literary scene.

The strike in the strike novel is invariably utilized at
two levels: the literary and the political.   The strike must
be crucial to the plot, must in fact be the plot.   The strike
must be described in lavish and authentic detail and, where-
ever possible, specific incidents from actual strikes of the
time are incorporated into the novel.   The strike must develop from an emotional action by the workers into a militant,
highly organized activity.   But, in addition to all these elements, the strike must serve a symbolic political function:
it must become in the novel an explicit microcosm of political revolution.

In Sherwood Anderson's Beyond Desire (1932) the
strike is the vehicle which brings to the surface the corruption seething beneath the surface of America.   In a community mouthing ideals of brotherhood and justice, vigilantes and
corrupt police actually inflict violence and suffering.   The
collective power which organizes a strike will someday organize a successful revolution.   In Arnold Armstrong's
Parched Earth (1934) the strike precipitates the dynamiting
of the dam and the destruction of the whole town of Caldwell.
Someday, the whole system of capitalism will also be destroyed.   In Thomas Bell's Out of This Furnace (1941) the
strikes ultimately bring about the organization of the C. I. O.
and an industry-wide steel contract.   Someday, the whole
working class will organize and take over the steel industry.
Although the fruit tramps' strike in John Steinbeck's In Dubious Battle (1936) is unresolved at the end of the novel,

there is a distinct implication that more strikes and further organization of the workers will follow in the cotton fields and other California agricultural areas. The strike in Clara Weatherwax's Marching! Marching! (1935) is also still in progress at the end of the novel but, again, a continuing revolutionary process is suggested.

The strike novel must also show the effects of the strike on the characters--not merely, as in the novels of the past, as one of a number of influences on them or as just another in a series of incidents in their lives. In the strike novel, at least one of the major characters must be shown to progress from political unawareness to class-conscious identification as a worker and a revolutionary, directly because of his experiences during the strike. His thinking is transformed as his experiences educate him politically. This development is an important fictional version of the Marxist dictum that re-education from bourgeois thinking occurs only during struggle. The character in the strike novel realizes in the course of the strike that salvation for the worker lies not in a better job nor in moving out of the working class but in changing society into a new classless form. Robert Cantwell calls the second part of The Land of Plenty (1934) "The Education of a Worker. " In it Johnny Hagen matures both politically and physically and discovers that rising in the world is "rising in the way a corpse rises when it has lain for a long time under water. "[9] Real success comes only from identification with the workers' collective struggles. In William Attaway's Blood on the Forge (1941), Mat Moss, a Negro Kentucky sharecropper, comes north to work in Chicago's steel mills. Just before he is killed he realizes that equality for the Negro lies in working class unity against the bosses, the kind of unity he has experienced during his participation in a strike. The strike is the educational vehicle for Johnny Dobie in Thom-

as Bell's Out of This Furnace, for Dave Houston in McAlister
Coleman and Stephen Rauschenbush's Red Neck (1936), for Larry Donovan in Jack Conroy's The Disinherited (1933), for Ishma
Hensley in Olive Tilford Dargan's Call Home the Heart (1932),
for Bill Bradley in Charlie May Simon's The Share-Cropper
(1937), for Jim Nolan in John Steinbeck's In Dubious Battle and
for Aline Weinman in Leane Zugsmith's A Time to Remember
(1936).   They all graduate with honors from their revolutionary
strike universities.   Even though the strike in Olive Tilford
Dargan's A Stone Came Rolling (1934) is broken, the textile
workers learn during the strike to value their own importance
and to look forward to the happy day when they would be "marching...not merely to free themselves from hunger, but to free a
world from the dark age of poverty."[10]   Mary Heaton Vorse's
strikers, by the end of her novel, Strike! (1930), have also advanced to social consciousness, even if not all the way to Socialist consciousness.

    Jack Conroy's Larry Donovan, in The Disinherited, con-
cludes that he has been deluding himself in expecting to better
his life as long as capitalism continues to exist.   Work--and
strikes--have taught him that one job is really much like any
other job, one factory much like all the others.   The whole industrial system under capitalism exists only "for extracting the
last ounce of energy" from the workers.   Conroy earned high
praise from an influential Soviet critic, Anna Elistratova, for
his account of Larry Donovan's political education.   Larry
learns finally to discard his "dreams of bourgeois comfort"
and "illusions about American democracy" and it is to Conroy's
credit that he knows Larry "has to travel a long road before he
finally begins to awaken to revolutionary consciousness."[11]
Larry's intellectual progress must, of course, culminate in
"revolutionary consciousness."   Nothing short of complete con-

version would have satisfied Mme. Elistratova.

The strike novels are always sympathetic to the strikes, and they always describe them from the inside. The novelists take us into the homes of the strikers, into the factories where we can see them at work, into the union halls where the strike is planned, into the bars and pool halls and movie houses, into the soup kitchens and on the picket lines. All of the descriptions of the strikes in these novels ring true. There is no doubt that the novelists know their subject from close personal experience.

Left-wing critics made sure that the novelist thoroughly learned his subject by the judicious use of praise, censure and exhortation. Granville Hicks, for example, discusses "The Problem of Documentation" at length in his long series on "Revolution and the Novel" in New Masses. He says:

> When, however, the documentation of a novel consists in a record of the events of a strike, let us say, the comparison between the strike in the novel and strikes in real life, though there is still room for differences of interpretation and evaluation, offers much more opportunity for impersonal exactness. Authenticity is always essential, but in the novel that portrays social forces one can tell much more easily when authenticity is lacking. [12]

Sherwood Anderson, probing for a way to present the mill workers in Beyond Desire to readers who did not understand their way of life, is forced to the conclusion that the task is almost impossible. Only those who themselves have experienced factory life can really understand. "People from the outside don't know how you feel. You have got to work in a place to know. You have got to be there through long hours, day after day, year after year."[13] There can be no substitute for experience if the writer wants to produce an authentic strike novel. By the end of the decade some of the critics had begun to wonder whether they had overemphasized experience as an essential prerequisite. Philip Rahv, writing in 1940, says: "Experience

is the main but by no means the total substance of literature."[14]
Unless experience is transmuted by values, ideas and judgments
it has not been turned into literature, he suggests.

In novel after novel, long, dreary pages describe exactly
what workers do at work: dockers and seamen in Walter Havighurst's Pier 17 (1935), chocolate factory workers in John Klempner's Once Around the Block (1939), textile workers in Grace
Lumpkin's To Make My Bread (1932), spray painters on an automobile assembly line in Sterling North's Seven Against the Years
(1939), salesgirls and stock clerks in a department store in Leane Zugsmith's A Time to Remember. These exhaustive descriptions are included for a number of reasons. To the strike novelist work itself has a kind of mystical importance. Marx's economic theory stressed that all value is created by labor, so the
worker at work is the foundation on which all of society rests.
The complex organization of modern industry is also important
to the strike novelist. The cooperation and collective planning
required in industry presages the collective organization of Socialist society. The strike novelist also is conscious that he is
dealing with a subject relatively new to the American novel and
that he is dealing with it in a new way and from a new standpoint.
He is careful to include, as a point of pride, the grubby details
his genteel middle class predecessors were careful to omit.
Finally, the strike novelist hopes he can attract a new kind of
mass reader--the workingman himself, who would presumably
be fascinated by authentic descriptions of what he did every day
on his job.

The strike novels are just as detailed in their descriptions of strikes as of the work inside mine or factory. Robert
Cantwell's strikers in The Land of Plenty go out in protest when
twenty militant workers are fired. Clifton Cuthbert's textile
workers in Another Such Victory (1936) join the union and go

out on strike because they are earning only eight dollars a week
and have been subjected to intolerable speedup. Sterling North's
auto workers in Seven Against the Years demand union recognition, a grievance procedure, acceptance of the seniority principle in layoffs, minimum hourly rates and ten-minute rest periods. Mike Pell's seamen in S. S. Utah (1933) demand double pay
for overtime work on Sundays and one day off in port. Leane
Zugsmith's strikers in A Time to Remember demand a forty-
hour week, a ten percent raise, an hour for lunch, twenty-min-
ute relief periods and recognition of their union. Specific demands, specific conditions, specific tactics are always detailed
in the strike novels.

The mania for authenticity often leads to the inclusion of
easily recognizable incidents taken from actual strikes of the
period. One which had the greatest impact on the strike novelists was the textile strike in Gastonia, North Carolina in 1929.
The strike was a dramatic one, which utilized some completely
new strike tactics, resulted in ugly violence, and ended with the
indictment of sixteen strike leaders for murder. No less than
six strike novels published within a four-year period were based
on the Gastonia strike: Sherwood Anderson's Beyond Desire,
Olive Tilford Dargan's Call Home the Heart, Grace Lumpkin's
To Make My Bread, Dorothy Myra Page's Gathering Storm
(1932), William Rollins' The Shadow Before (1934) and Mary
Heaton Vorse's Strike!. (Willie Ethridge's Mingled Yarn, 1938,
which is not a "strike novel," is also based on the Gastonia
Strike).

During the strike mass picketing became one of the essential tactics, and the picket lines took on drama and color
when picketers began to sing the songs of a talented folk-bal-
ladeer, Ella May Wiggins, one of the strikers. Women and
children joined the picket lines and helped significantly in the

organization of a strikers' relief apparatus issuing food, clothing, blankets and fuel to the strikers and providing housing when strikers' families were evicted. For the first time in the South the strike united black and white workers and, also for the first time on such a mass scale, the Communist Party played an active and public organizing role.

One of the strike leaders indicted for murder wrote a book-length circumstantial account of the Gastonia events. Fred Beal's Proletarian Journey (1937) falls into two distinct, hardly related, parts: the Gastonia incidents and Beal's disillusioning sojourn in the Soviet Union after he jumped bail. Beal's account of the strike succeeds in evoking both the exhilaration during its early stages and the tense bitterness when violence and legal battles followed. The labor songs of Ella May Wiggins and her death at the hands of snipers, the singing mass picket lines, and the public role of the Communist Party during the strike are especially attractive literary devices for the strike novelists.

Sherwood Anderson's sympathetic use of the Gastonia strike as the central theme of Beyond Desire was greeted with hosannas by the Marxist critics of the time. In 1929 Joseph Freeman had accused Anderson of serving as "the voice of the harassed middle-class,"[15] of being preoccupied with his own feelings and of lacking the ability to distill much general human wisdom from his experiences. But Sergei Dinamov, reviewing Beyond Desire in 1933, can hardly restrain his enthusiasm. It is not Anderson's literary style that entrances Dinamov (he hardly mentions that aspect), but Anderson's new political attitude. Dinamov complains that Anderson still has not learned much about the life of the workers, but he is delighted that Anderson now realizes that the workers are exploited and suffocated by capitalism. "He describes the curse of toiling for others, the hardships and slavery of involuntary labor in a capitalist facto-

ry.... Sherwood Anderson is on the right road,"[16] Dinamov concludes.

In addition to the pivotal use of the strike and the earnest
effort to document the strike authentically, the strike novels usually have to deal in one way or another with the literary and philosophical problem of the individual against the collective. There
can be no doubt that in its full bloom the strike novel was less
concerned with probing the individual in depth than with examining the effect of society upon him. The good novelists in the
group persisted in exploring the problems of fiction in their own
way. John Steinbeck, for instance, never subordinated his interest in the human being to social theory. To Steinbeck, as a
matter of fact, the group-man, the mindless nonindividual created by the collective is a frightening phenomenon. Doc Burton
characterizes him in In Dubious Battle:

> 'A man in a group isn't himself at all, he's a cell
> in an organism that isn't like him any more than
> the cells in your body are like you.'[17]

Sherwood Anderson, Thomas Bell, Meyer Levin and Elliot Paul,
although less skilled than Steinbeck, still do not capitulate entirely. They write about individual men who respond as individuals
to events around them. To the orthodox strike novelist, however,
the response of any single man is entirely conditioned by movements of the mass. To McAlister Coleman and Stephen Rauschenbush in Red Neck, for example, the origin of a strike is not an
event in which individuals have come together from a complex
variety of reasons but an inexorable clash of two irreconcilable
groups, the arrogant capitalists and the tough-fibered exasper-
ated workers. Or Jack Conroy's narrator in The Disinherited is
liberated only when he learns to submerge his individuality in the
fortunes of his class. When he is no longer tempted by ambition
or troubled by shame, then he can "rise with his class. "

A sensitive critic like Ralph Fox tried valiantly to warn

against mechanical applications of Marxist philosophy to literature:

> For Marxism does not deny the individual. It does not
> see only masses in the grip of inexorable economic
> forces.... novelists ... have failed to rise to the great-
> ness of their theme of man changing himself through
> the process of changing nature and creating new eco-
> nomic forces. [18]

Nobody seemed to be listening to Fox's warnings. In 1962 Margot Heinemann somberly conceded that "in the older working-
class novel, the group was so strongly exalted that often the human being as a separate individual was little developed."[19] The
drastic swing of the pendulum from the rampant individualism of
the past to mindless collectivism is not completely without a redeeming benefit. When the American novelist rejected utter devotion to the group--as he very soon did--he never returned to
complete acceptance of a ruthless world in which each man
makes it on his own and only the fittest survive. Novelists
since the Thirties have had to fight, bit by bit, for some sort
of tenable position on man's responsibility to himself and to the
society he lives in.

There is one notable literary achievement in most of the
strike novels. All but the very poorest succeed in capturing the
rhythm of a strike. All strikes proceed with an emotional development that has little to do with the particularities of industry,
place, or strike demands. The first days of the strike are always a period of excitement, elation and joy. After the irrita-
tions and frustration of the pre-strike period and after the hesi-
tations and fear until the strike decision is made, the determination to strike comes as a relief. The first reaction of the strikers as a sense of joy is documented by Robert Cantwell in The
Land of Plenty, by Jack Conroy in The Disinherited and dramatically by John Steinbeck in In Dubious Battle:

The moment he stopped talking a turbulence broke out.

> Shouting and laughing, the men eddied. They seemed
> filled with a terrible joy, a bloody lustful joy. [20]

The gaiety soon gives way to apathy and boredom as the strike
continues. The idle workers start to bicker among themselves
as hunger and anxiety begin to take their toll. When sheriffs or
police or vigilantes move in, however, and attack the strikers
and their families, there is a new lift in spirits and a closing of
ranks. The strikers realize they have a collective strength and
that in the course of the strike they have acquired a new and important expertise. When the violent clash finally comes, it is an
ugly and brutal experience but a cleansing one, too. The strikers seem to need the physical contact with the enemy in order
to discover how profoundly committed they are to their own
cause. There are innumerable descriptions in almost all of the
strike novels of violent clashes between strikers and armed police. William Attaway's Blood on the Forge and Sterling North's
Seven Against the Years describe the mingled fear and sense of
power during police attacks on strikers, but the most gripping
description of all is in Steinbeck's In Dubious Battle. In two
sentences he gives us the effect of a brutal attack on the shaken
strikers.

> Now that the fury was past, the strikers were
> sick, poisoned by the flow from their own anger
> glands. They were weak; one man held his head
> between his hands as though it ached terribly. [21]

Inevitably, once the battle is over, the strikers become
aware of a new solidarity and a new hope--for the future, if not
for this particular strike. All the strike novels end with the conviction that workers will continue to organize, not only for the
improvement of their working conditions but for the ultimate reorganization of the whole society. The strike novelists almost
all capture the ebb and flow of the human spirit that is a part of
every strike.

To most of the novelists writing strike novels during the
Thirties and the early years of the Forties, and to most of the
Marxist critics of the period, the political implications of the
novels were of greater importance than the literary. The strike
is a symbol of the coming Socialist revolution. The novelist will
be praised for his success in making his novel such a symbol,
far more than for any subtlety of characterization or insight into
human motives which the novel may reveal. Some of the novelists ingeniously translate the strike into additional symbols, although still closely related to the idea of revolution. The strike
can stand for the death of the old and the birth of the new, or it
can become a metaphor for health, for strength, for renewal, for
rebirth--all rather unsubtle shorthand for the hope of an imminent cleansing revolution.

The strikes in these novels are always battles in the ever-
raging war between the classes. In Coleman and Rauschenbush's
Red Neck, Clifton Cuthbert's Another Such Victory, Meyer Levin's Citizens (1940) and Dorothy Page's Gathering Storm the
characters explicitly equate the strike with a war. In most of
the other novels the implications of a continuing class war are
strongly evident. Critics of the time insisted that the strike novel show the class war dramatically through the strike. They apparently had very little faith that readers could draw revolutionary conclusions for themselves. So, in the end, the novelists
are doing exactly what their predecessors did before them--
preaching a sermon to their readers, a sermon with a different
moral, but a sermon nevertheless. The critics and novelists
hoped that they were raising the level of consciousness of their
readers to the point of both revolutionary fervor and revolutionary action. Philip Rahv, for example, wrote in Partisan Review
in 1934:

> The primary merit of Parched Earth and The Shadow
> Before lies in the fact that their authors are acutely

> conscious of the material reality of act and character.
> And it is precisely this consciousness of the economic
> factor as the leading factor in the determinism of life
> under capitalism that makes it possible for them not
> merely to state the mounting contradiction between the
> classes but also to resolve it. [22]

Somehow the novel would not merely clarify for its readers the
class war but would impel them to do something about it. How
much any novel or piece of literature actually influences action
remains an open question, but the strike novels written to such
a narrow formula became less and less effective, not only as
propaganda but as novels.

The capitalists in these novels, almost always shadowy
characters seen only from a distance, are arrogant and authoritarian. Charles McMahon, the superintendent of Robert Cantwell's lumber mill in The Land of Plenty, for example, yearns
for the simple unquestioned authority that the military can command. "'They pay those fellows a dollar a day. Never a mur-
mur. If they kick, they lock them up. '"[23] He would like the
chance to run his mill like an army. The families of the bosses
consist of frivolous parasites, devoted to la dolce vita, and
leeches upon the productive members of society. Wastrel sons,
thrill-seeking daughters, bickering parents are the rule for the
capitalist families in the strike novels--Robert Cantwell's Mc-
Mahons in The Land of Plenty, Clifton Cuthbert's Lymans in
Another Such Victory, Walter Havighurst's Lannings in Pier 17,
John Klempner's Ellenbogens in Once Around the Block, Sterling
North's Bluchers in Seven Against the Years and Clara Weatherwax's Baylisses in Marching! Marching! Despite their responsible positions, the managers and supervisors of capitalist enterprises are incompetent and utterly unable to run the factories
without the workers, who do the real organizing of the complex
technical processes.

The middle class characters in the strike novel are sterile, unproductive, and without substance unless they fight on the side of the worker. Sherwood Anderson's Red Oliver, in Beyond Desire, doubts his manliness, his courage, his convictions, even his reality. He thinks longingly: "'I wish I could be something real. '"24 Larry Marvin, William Rollins' union organizer in The Shadow Before, exclaims: "'There ain't a damn thing about the bourgeoisie that's real. '"25 Harry Baumann, in the same novel, son of the mill owner but sympathetic to the strikers, becomes real when he helps their cause actively. Ned Bascom, related to the owner of the struck factory in Elliot Paul's The Stars and Stripes Forever (1939), is indecisive and useless and he envies the calm and confident sense of direction of Wojciechowski, the factory worker.

The working class characters in the strike novels are naturally in blatant contrast to the capitalists. They take pride in their skill and productivity. Mike Dobrecjak, the Polish steelworker in Thomas Bell's Out of This Furnace describes his attitude toward his work ecstatically: "'It's a terrible and beautiful thing to make iron.... I feel big and strong with pride. '"26 Communist Ed Hurley angrily chides Vera Damaszek in Cuthbert's Another Such Victory when she suggests sabotaging the machines in the textile mill. Workers take pride in the intricate machines, the product of human labor and ingenuity. It is also suggested that since the Socialist revolution is so imminent, the machines will soon become the workers' property and should therefore be cherished.

In contrast to the cutthroat competition inseparable from capitalist ideology, workers voluntarily cooperate with each other in the collective enterprise required by modern factories. They are the ones who really run the factories although their skill and intelligence are unrecognized and unrewarded. When the power fails in Cantwell's lumber mill, in The Land of Plenty; the super-

visors grope helplessly while the workers find their way about,
shut off the switches to save the machines from damage, and
combine forces to release a worker pinned underneath a beam.
The workers are so much the masters of the factory in all but
ownership that they communicate with each other wordlessly, almost instinctively. News of an impending layoff travels swiftly
through the factory, long before the official notices appear, and
an accident unites the workers in a way the managers cannot
even understand, let alone emulate.

   Women and Negroes, the natural allies of the working
class because they are themselves the victims of capitalism,
must also be shown as militant, confident and revolutionary.
Women, as a matter of fact, are often pictured in the strike novels as far more militant than the men. Ishma Hensley, the intrepid heroine of Olive Dargan's Call Home the Heart and A Stone
Came Rolling, bears with superhuman fortitude backbreaking labor, police violence, hunger and private emotional upheavals.
Grace Lumpkin's To Make My Bread portrays several indomitable women strikers: Emma McClure, Bonnie Calhoun, Ruth
Gordon. For the first time, the theme of cooperation between
Negro and white workers becomes an important one in the strike
novels. Negro-white unity is stressed in all the novels based on
the Gastonia strike, as it was during the actual strike. The attempt to organize black and white sharecroppers is the theme of
Charlie May Simon's The Share-Cropper. Both Scott Nearing's
Free Born (1932) and William Attaway's Blood on the Forge document the use of Negroes newly migrated from the South as strikebreakers and both novels emphasize the necessity for unity
among black and white workers.

   The working class, inherently progressive and courageous, since it has nothing to lose and everything to gain from a
Socialist revolution, nevertheless needs organization before it

can win power. A mob becomes the victim of its own disorgani-
zation and is easily dispersed and beaten by the disciplined enemy: the police during the microcosmic strike, the capitalist
class in the ultimate conflict to come. In Arnold Armstrong's
Parched Earth the cannery workers' strike, a disciplined organized fight led by Dave Washburn, succeeds, but the leaderless
mob of the unemployed which storms the cannery is beaten back
by deputies armed with tear-gas, blackjacks and guns. The Finnish, Filipino and Anglo workers in Clara Weatherwax's Marching! Marching! are brutally exploited as long as they remain
suspicious of each other. When they organize, they succeed in
preventing the eviction of Granny Whittle.

          To the orthodox strike novelist the most effective force
for the organization of the workers into revolutionary shock
troops is the Communist Party. Even those novelists who distrust or despise the Communists pay tribute to their discipline,
their selflessness and their effectiveness. Sherwood Anderson's
protagonist, Red Oliver, in Beyond Desire, fears the Communists, who are willing to sacrifice themselves and any number
of individual workers for the sake of Marxist theory and for the
chance of strengthening the Party. But he grants them the ability, which no one else seems to have, to weld an amorphous mass
into an effective unified force:

> They knew how. That was something. They had or-
> ganized the disorganized workers, had taught them to
> sing songs, had found out the leaders among them, the
> song-makers, the courageous ones. They had taught
> them to march shoulder to shoulder. [27]

John Steinbeck is also repelled by Communist dedication but in
In Dubious Battle he credits them with the ability to organize the fruit pickers effectively.

          The emphasis on organization in the strike novels is not
merely for the tactical value of discipline. The underlying theorem of the strike novel--that the workers will ultimately take

over state power--makes it necessary for the novelist to prove
that the working class would be able to run the state, and to run
it better than the servants of capitalism do. The ability to organize strike meetings, food kitchens, a defense apparatus, the
ability to formulate strike demands and to work together har-
moniously to achieve them are exemplified over and over again
in the strike novels. Such organizational ability could easily be
translated into the qualities necessary to run a government when
the time came.

Because the strike stood for ultimate revolution and the
takeover of the means of production by the workers, one form
of strike is especially important in the strike novels. The "sit-
down" strike, a tactic used extensively in some of the real
strikes of the Thirties, in which strikers actually occupied the
factories, is exactly what the strike novelist needed to complete
his analogy. Workers who sit in are really taking over what
should belong to them--the means of production. The sitdown
strikers protect the machines and tools and take better--be-
cause more knowledgeable--care of the factory than its owners
have ever done. The worker is concerned for the manufacture
of products which will ease or enrich human life. To the capitalist the sitdown strike is frightening because it is easy to proceed from sitting in to taking over. Upton Sinclair describes,
in Little Steel (1938), the petrifying effect of the sitdowns on
"the masters of American big business" as "the nightmare
which had been haunting their dreams for nearly twenty years,
ever since they had seen events in Russia. "[28] In Robert Cantwell's The Land of Plenty the workers invade the factory and in
the process lose their fear of the police. Cantwell's inclusion of the sitdown is purposeful. In a New Masses article
he talked about some of the literary problems he was trying
to solve with the use of the factory takeover.

> I tried to imagine what would actually happen in the
> sort of community I pictured, when the workers
> entered the factories, what new factors entered a
> strike situation, what advantages were gained, what
> new hazards were encountered. It seemed to me
> that the problem was important, one the working-
> class of this country must some day face. [29]

Cantwell meant the reader to see the strike as an omen of
the revolution about to begin and, more, meant the reader
to see the sitdown strike as a preparation for the workers
to own and run the socialized factories.

The strike novels emphasize that no lost strike is
ever a complete defeat, just as no strike is ever a complete
victory. As long as the workers have not won possession of
the mines and mills and the state power to retain them, the
gains in any strike are only temporary. The strike is the
school in which the working class learns the skills it will
need in the revolution. As a matter of fact, most of the
novels end with the strike either unresolved or lost, but the
strike novelists' reasons are very different from those of
earlier novelists whose strikes were also, more often than
not, defeated. The strike novelist is faced with a problem
which only history can solve. He cannot show the strike as
a total victory because the revolution is not yet a reality in
the United States. Since his strike mirrors a revolution in
miniature, he must leave its success undecided or must suggest that the next strike or the one after that will signal the
beginning of the workers' revolution. Strikers in Leane Zugsmith's A Time to Remember, Dorothy Myra Page's The
Gathering Storm and Elliot Paul's The Stars and Stripes
Forever all see their strikes as revolutionary preliminaries
and express their impatience with this transition period. The
novelist Jack Conroy recognized the problem of the still un-
fought revolution and tried to deal with it in his novels. In

an address to the first American Writers' Congress Conroy
spoke of this dilemma facing the strike novelist:

> American proletarian fiction must of necessity deal
> with prophecy, with hopes, with the decay of society
> and the manifestations of such decay in the lives of
> people, with temporary defeats, with temporary tri-
> umphs represented by successful strikes and demon-
> strations of working-class strength. [30]

By the beginning of the Forties the strike novel had
been locked into such an inflexible formula that it could no
longer develop.   Every strike novel had to include exactly the
same ingredients in precisely the form prescribed by the
Marxist critics.   Granville Hicks in The Great Tradition,
for example, appreciated some of Robert Cantwell's problems
and praised him generously, but still sternly demanded that
Cantwell learn more about strike strategy and incorporate
that knowledge into his novels.   A. B. Magil's criticism of
Grace Lumpkin's To Make My Bread was much harsher.
Grace Lumpkin was a far less skillful novelist than Cantwell,
but it was not for any literary ineptitude that Magil scolded
her.   He accused her of failing to make the class struggle
the central issue of her novel.   Even worse to Magil was
her omission of a tidy list of the strikers' exact demands.
The coup de grâce, however, came from Anna Elistratova,
an influential Soviet literary critic, who took the New Masses
bitterly to task for failing to deal with every strike according
to her rigid formula.   In an article in International Literature,
in 1932, she complained that New Masses failed to summarize
and generalize from each strike it reported.   In the literary
work it published there were too many abstractions and not
enough concrete lists of just what was attempted and learned
in each struggle.   Stories in New Masses neglected to show
"any militant solution of the contradictions of the capitalist

system. " Workers were too often depicted as downhearted
and subdued; their clashes with police and their strikes were
too often spontaneous or accidental. Workers must always
be shown as militant and organized.

Mme. Elistratova's insistence on the portrayal of the
working class as militant and organized is not quite as crotchety as it may appear to be. It results from the importance
Marxists assign to struggle. Mere passive acceptance of life,
even active participation without conscious ideology, will not
bring about revolutionary change. The highest level of experience comes only in the process of engaging actively and
consciously in a struggle which will change not only material
conditions but man himself. The ultimate goal of the Socialist revolution is not the establishment of the Socialist state
but the creation of a Socialist man who will be cooperative
rather than competitive, socially responsible rather than ma-
terialistic, dedicated to the collective good rather than personally ambitious. By her philosophical lights the Soviet
critic has reason for insisting on a greater emphasis on
conscious militancy. Very few of the strike novels indicate
even a dim awareness of the revolutionary concept which
foresees the creation of a new kind of human being, and the
critic's authoritarian dogma did little to help a young novelist
toward such awareness.

The critical straitjacket of the Marxists ultimately
guaranteed the production of strike novels which religiously
adhered to the formula but ceased to be interesting except
perhaps as museum pieces illustrative of the genre. The
one really fine novel, and far and away the best of the group,
is John Steinbeck's In Dubious Battle, and it is probably because Steinbeck ignored the rules of the critics that he could
create this memorable work. The novel deals with the or-

ganization of a fruit pickers' strike by two Communist organizers, the young recruit, Jim Nolan, and the veteran organizer, Mac. Steinbeck, like the Marxists, recognizes the need
for organization of the agricultural workers and admires
Mac's adroit education of some of the fruit tramps' natural
leaders as they prepare to strike. With the help of Doc Burton the pickers organize an efficient headquarters on Anderson's ranch (Steinbeck's account is based on a magnificent
achievement during a real strike near Corcoran, California
in 1934). Doc Burton is a complex and interesting character
committed to no political ideology and motivated by his desire
for a humane society. Mac insists on the formation of a
democratic community with self-imposed discipline, shared
tasks and an elected leadership. When negotiations with the
local Growers' Association begin and the orchard owners re-
taliate with vigilante action against the pickers, the typical
confrontation between two irreconcilable classes develops.
Mac's moves are all coldly calculated. A picker falls out
of a tree, and Mac uses the accident to whip up anger among
the pickers. A picker's daughter is giving birth, and Mac
volunteers to serve as midwife, carefully drawing the implied
lessons: the lack of medical care, the efficacy of collective
action, the unrecognized talents and abilities among the pickers themselves. Jim Nolan is killed during a clash, and
Mac deliberately uses his dead comrade's corpse to enrage
the pickers. Mac forces himself to remain emotionally un-
involved. He will not even allow himself to give way to his
feeling for a couple of fine pointer dogs on the Anderson
ranch, not to mention his growing fatherly feelings for young
Jim Nolan. Steinbeck is not quite sure what impels a man
like Mac. He suggests that Mac is able to submerge his
individuality in the collective because of his religious fervor

for the hypothetical revolution of the future. He is bewildered
and repelled by the motivations and the tactics of the Communists, but the novel gives an honest and factual account of
their role among California's agricultural workers. Steinbeck is passionately concerned with the outcome of this particular strike; novelistically, he has no interest in "the final
conflict. " He is deeply involved with the individual strikers
and organizers; he abhors the "group-man" and the fanatic
devotion of his Communist characters to impersonal theory
and coldblooded expediency.

A superb reporter, Steinbeck recognized the rapacious-
ness of uncontrolled capitalism in the California fruit orchards.
In Their Blood is Strong (1938) he wrote with indignation of
the peon class created and maintained by the industrialized
farming operations in California. A few corporations owning
thousands of acres of land used wandering fruit tramps for
the brief harvest period, then turned them loose to starve
for the rest of the year. To ensure continuation of the system the growers used terror and violence. Themselves tight-
ly organized into the Associated Farmers, they fought furious-
ly any attempt at united action by the migrant pickers. Especially vicious was the treatment of the Communist organizers who tried to organize the pickers into unions. In Dubious Battle, however, is not a sociological tract. Steinbeck
transforms his raw materials into a powerful novel which explores, not ideologies but human beings.

Louis Filler, in his vitriolic introduction to The Anxious Years (1952), condemns In Dubious Battle as a "communist novel. " Filler is dead wrong. The novel is a taut,
superbly written strike novel. It is concerned with the way
men act under the stress and tensions of a bitter strike. It

is not an apology for Communism nor for the Communist
Party but a work of art from which we learn a great deal
about men who are Communists, like Mac or Jim, or strikers, like London or Sam, or men who are committed only to
doing something that needs doing, like Anderson or Doc Burton.   Steinbeck's insight enabled him to perceive that essentially the Communist drew his confidence and courage from
a kind of enlightened self-interest.   Because he wished to in-
tensify the meaning of his own life he sought his individual
salvation in the ennobling of the group.

By 1945 the strike novel was almost extinct.   Sapped
internally by the deadening demands of the Left and externally
by the new materials and preoccupations of the war, the
strike novel offered less and less as a fictional vehicle.

In the course of about seventy years the strike has
entered American fiction, come to dominate one type of novel, evolved into a distinctive genre, and then practically disappeared, at least for a time, from the American novel.
The uses of the strike have left some indelible effects on
the American novelist.   He can make unhesitating use of
working class life and working class characters.   He no longer accepts middle class ideas as unquestioned truths.   He
can draw upon a corpus of literary examples attempting to
come to philosophical terms with the complexities of violence,
of freedom, of individualism.   Even those novelists who will
never use a strike have been freed, in part, from the con-
fining limits of the nineteenth century American novel by the
pioneering work of novelists who explored the ways in which
to deal with the strike.

Notes

1. V. F. Calverton, The Newer Spirit; a Sociological Criti-
    cism of Literature (New York: Boni and Liveright,
    1925), p. 144.

2. James T. Farrell listed all the possible variations in
    his rather waspish but serious analysis in A Note
    on Literary Criticism: "It seems to me that there
    are the following possible definitions of proletarian
    literature: it can be defined as creative literature
    written by a member of the industrial proletariat
    regardless of the political orientation of the author;
    as creative literature that reveals some phase of
    the experience of the industrial proletariat, regard-
    less of the political orientation of the author; as
    creative literature written by a member of the in-
    dustrial proletariat who is class-conscious in the
    Marxian sense, and a member of the proletarian
    vanguard; as creative literature written by a class-
    conscious member of the proletariat and treating
    solely (or principally) of some phase of the life of
    that group; as creative literature written about that
    group within the proletariat regardless of the author's
    class status or his group status within his class; as
    creative literature written in order to enforce,
    through its conclusions and implications, the views
    of the proletarian vanguard; as creative literature
    read by the proletariat; as creative literature read
    by the proletarian vanguard; or as creative literature
    combining these features in differing combinations. "
    --James T. Farrell, A Note on Literary Criticism
    (New York: Vanguard Press, 1936), pp. 86-87.

3. Henry Hart, ed. , American Writers' Congress (New
    York: International Publishers, 1935), p. 165.

4. Melvin P. Levy, "Stories of Workers, " New Masses,
    VI:12 (May, 1931), p. 19.

5. Edwin Seaver, "What Is a Proletarian Novel?" Partisan
    Review, II:7 (April/May, 1935), p. 8.

6. Leon Trotsky, Literature and Revolution (New York:
    International Publishers, 1925), p. 14.

7. Howard Fast, Literature and Reality (New York: International Publishers, 1950), p. 28.

8. Walter B. Rideout, The Radical Novel in the United States, 1900-1954 (Cambridge, Mass.: Harvard University Press, 1956), p. 171.

9. Robert Cantwell, The Land of Plenty (New York: Farrar and Rinehart, 1934), p. 304.

10. Fielding Burke (Olive Tilford Dargan), A Stone Came Rolling (New York: Longmans, Green and Co., 1935), p. 179.

11. Anna Elistratova, "Jack Conroy: American Worker-Writer," International Literature, no. 1 (7), (1934), p. 116.

12. Granville Hicks, "Revolution and the Novel, part 5: Selection and Emphasis," New Masses, XI:6 (May 8, 1934), p. 24.

13. Sherwood Anderson, Beyond Desire (New York: Liveright Publishing Corp., 1961), p. 287.

14. Philip Rahv, "The Cult of Experience in American Writing," Partisan Review, VII:6 (November/December, 1940), p. 420.

15. Joseph Freeman, "Sherwood Anderson's Confusion," New Masses, IV:9 (February, 1929), p. 6.

16. Sergei Dinamov, "Sherwood Anderson: American Writer," International Literature, no. 4 (1933), p. 91.

17. John Steinbeck, In Dubious Battle (New York: Modern Library, 1936), p. 144.

18. Ralph Fox, The Novel and the People (New York: International Publishers, 1937), p. 23.

19. Margot Heinemann, "Workers and Writers," Mainstream, XV:6 (June, 1962), p. 17.

20. Steinbeck, op. cit., p. 132.

21. Ibid., p. 180-181.

22. Philip Rahv, "The Novelist as a Partisan," Partisan
     Review, I:2 (April/May, 1934), p. 50.

23. Cantwell, op. cit., p. 155.

24. Anderson, op. cit., p. 314

25. William Rollins, Jr., The Shadow Before (New York:
     Robert M. McBride and Co., 1934), p. 204.

26. Thomas Bell, Out of This Furnace (Boston: Little,
     Brown and Co., 1941), p. 195.

27. Anderson, op. cit., p. 270.

28. Upton Sinclair, Little Steel (New York: Farrar and
     Rinehart, Inc., 1938), p. 83.

29. "Authors' Field Day: a Symposium on Marxist Criti-
     cism," New Masses, XXII:1 (July 3, 1934), p. 27.

30. Hart, op. cit., p. 84.

BIBLIOGRAPHY

Primary Sources

NOVELS:

Adamic, Louis, Grandsons: a Story of American Lives, New
    York, Harper and Bros. , 1935.
Adams, William T. (Oliver Optic), Plane and Plank; or, The
    Mishaps of a Mechanic, Boston, Lee and Shepard, 1890.
Aldrich, Thomas Bailey, The Stillwater Tragedy, Boston,
    Houghton-Mifflin & Co. , 1908 (c. 1880).
Anderson, Sherwood, Beyond Desire, New York, Liveright
    Publishing Corp. , 1961 (c. 1932)
_____ , Kit Brandon: a Portrait, New York, Charles
    Scribner's Sons, 1936.
_____ , Marching Men, New York, B. W. Huebsch, Inc. ,
    1921.
_____ , Poor White, New York, B. W. Huebsch, Inc. ,
    1920.
_____ , Windy McPherson's Son, New York, John Lane
    Co. , 1916.
Appel, Benjamin, The Power-House, New York, E. P. Dut-
    ton and Co. , 1939.
"Argus, " Lights and Shades of a Factory Village: a Tale of
    Lowell, Lowell, Mass. , Vox Populi Office, 1849.
Armstrong, Arnold B. , Parched Earth, New York, Macmillan
    Co. , 1934.
Arthur, Timothy Shay, The Strike at Tivoli Mills; and What
    Came of It, Philadelphia, Garrigues Bros. , 1879.
Atherton, Sarah, Mark's Own, Indianapolis, Bobbs-Merrill
    Co. , 1941.
Attaway, William, Blood on the Forge, New York, Doubleday,
    Doran and Co. , 1941.
Barber, Harriet Boomer (Faith Templeton), Drafted In; a
    Sequel to The Breadwinners, a Social Study, New York,
    Bliss Publishing Co. , 1888.
Basso, Hamilton, In Their Own Image, New York, Charles
    Scribner's Sons, 1935.
Beals, Carleton, The Stones Awake, Philadelphia, J. B.

185

Lippincott Co. , 1936.

Beard, Dan, Moonblight and Six Feet of Romance, New York, Charles L. Webster and Co. , 1892.

Bech-Meyer, Nico, A Story from Pullmantown, Chicago, Charles H. Kerr and Co. , 1894.

Bell, Thomas, All Brides Are Beautiful, Boston, Little, Brown and Co. , 1936.

_____, Out of This Furnace, Boston, Little, Brown and Co. , 1941.

_____, The Second Prince, New York, G. P. Putnam's Sons, 1935.

Bellamy, Charles Joseph, The Breton Mills, New York, G. P. Putnam's Sons, 1879.

Bellamy, Edward, Looking Backward, 2000-1887, New York, Modern Library, 1951 (c. 1887).

Benedict, Frank L. , Miss Van Kortland, New York, Harper and Bros. , 1870.

Benjamin, Charles, The Strike in the B-- Mill; a Study, Boston, Ticknor and Co. , 1887.

Bishop, R. F. , Camerton Slope; a Story of Mining Life, Cincinnati, Cranston and Curts; New York, Hunt and Eaton, 1893.

Bishop, William Henry, The Golden Justice, Boston, Houghton Mifflin Co. , 1887.

Bisno, Beatrice, Tomorrow's Bread, Philadelphia, Jewish Publication Society of America, 1938.

Blake, William J. , The Painter and the Lady, New York, Simon and Schuster, 1939.

Brenholtz, Edwin Arnold, The Recording Angel, Chicago, Charles H. Kerr and Co. , 1905.

Breuer, Bessie, The Daughter, New York, Simon and Schuster, 1938.

Brody, Catharine, Nobody Starves, New York, Longmans, Green and Co. , 1932.

Bromfield, Louis, A Good Woman, New York, Frederick A. Stokes Co. , 1916.

_____, The Green Bay Tree, New York, Frederick A. Stokes Co. , 1926.

Brower, James H. , The Mills of Mammon, Joliet, Ill. , P. H. Murray and Co. , 1909.

Brown, Rollo Walter, The Firemakers; a Novel of Environment, New York, Coward-McCann, 1931.

Burnett, Frances Hodgson, Haworth's, New York, Charles Scribner's Sons, 1879.

Byrne, Donn, The Stranger's Banquet, New York, Harper and Bros. , 1919.

Cahan, Abraham, The Rise of David Levinsky, New York,

Harper and Bros., 1917.

_____, Yekl: A Tale of the New York Ghetto, New York, D. Appleton and Co., 1896.

Caldwell, Erskine, God's Little Acre, New York, Modern Library, c. 1933.

Campbell, Helen, Roger Berkeley's Probation, Boston, Roberts Bros., 1888.

Cantwell, Robert, The Land of Plenty, New York, Farrar and Rinehart, 1934.

Carryl, Guy Wetmore, The Lieutenant-Governor, Boston, Houghton Mifflin Co., 1903.

Cassady, Constance, This Magic Dust, Indianapolis, Bobbs-Merrill, 1937.

Cherouny, Henry W., The Burial of the Apprentice, New York, Cherouny Printing and Publishing Co., 1900.

Churchill, Winston, The Dwelling-Place of Light, New York, Macmillan Co., 1917.

Cline, Leonard, God Head, New York, Viking Press, 1927.

Cohen, Hyman and Lester, Aaron Traum, New York, Horace Liveright, 1930.

Coleman, McAlister and Rauschenbush, Stephen, Red Neck, New York, Harrison Smith and Robert Haas, 1936.

Colman, Louis, Lumber, Boston, Little, Brown and Co., 1931.

Conroy, Jack, The Disinherited, New York, Hill and Wang, 1963 (c. 1933).

_____, A World to Win, New York, Covici, Friede Publishers, 1935.

Converse, Florence, The Burden of Christopher, Boston, Houghton Mifflin Co., 1900.

_____, The Children of Light, London, J. M. Dent Sons, Ltd., n. d. (c. 1912).

Cook, George Cram, The Chasm, New York, Frederick A. Stokes Co., 1911.

Corbett, Elizabeth, Charley Manning, New York, D. Appleton-Century Co., 1939.

Cullum, Ridgewell, The Trail of the Axe, New York, A. L. Burt Co., 1910.

Cummings, Ariel Ivers, The Factory Girl: or Gardez la Coeur, Lowell, Mass., J. E. Short and Co., 1847.

Cuthbert, Clifton, Another Such Victory, New York, Hillman-Curl, Inc., 1936.

Daniels, Gertrude Potter, The Warners; an American Story of Today, Chicago, Jamieson-Higgins Co., 1901.

Dargan, Olive Tilford (Fielding Burke), Call Home the Heart, New York, Longmans, Green and Co., 1932.

_____, A Stone Came Rolling, New York, Longmans,

Green and Co., 1935.

Davenport, Marcia, The Valley of Decision, New York,
Charles Scribner's Sons, 1943.

Davis, Clyde Brion, "The Great American Novel--," New
York, Farrar and Rinehart, 1938.

(Davis, Rebecca Harding), Margret Howth. A Story of Today, Boston, Ticknor and Fields, 1862.

Deland, Margaret, The Rising Tide, New York, Harper and
Bros., 1916.

Delany, J. (Joel Y. Dane), The Christmas Tree Murders,
New York, Doubleday, Doran and Co., Inc., 1938.

Dell, Floyd, Diana Stair, New York, Farrar and Rinehart,
Inc., 1932.

Denison, Thomas Stewart, An Iron Crown; a Tale of the
Great Republic, Chicago, T. S. Denison, 1879.

Dixon, Thomas, Jr., Comrades, New York, Grosset and
Dunlap, 1909.

Dos Passos, John, Adventures of a Young Man, New York,
Harcourt, Brace and Co., 1938.

Douglas, Amanda M., Hope Mills; or, Between Friend and
Sweetheart, Boston, Lee and Shepard, 1879.

Dowling, George Thomas, The Wreckers; a Social Study,
Philadelphia, J. B. Lippincott Co., 1886.

Doyle, Arthur Conan, "Valley of Fear" in The Complete
Sherlock Holmes, New York, Garden City Publishing Co.,
1938.

Dreiser, Theodore, Sister Carrie, New York, B. W. Dodge
and Co., 1907 (c. 1900).

Duffus, R. L., Night Between the Rivers, New York, Macmillan Co., 1937.

(Duzanne, Augustine Joseph Hickey), The Tenant-House: or,
Embers from Poverty's Hearthstone, New York, International Book Co., 1860?

Eastman, Max, Venture, New York, Albert and Charles Boni,
1927.

Eddy, Arthur Jerome, Ganton and Co., Chicago, A. A. Mc-
Clurg and Co., 1908.

Edwards, Albert, Comrade Yetta, New York, Macmillan Co.,
1913.

Elliott, Sarah Barnwell, Jerry, New York, Henry Holt and
Co., 1891.

Engstrand, Stuart David, The Invaders, New York, Alfred A.
Knopf, 1937.

Ethridge, Willie Snow, Mingled Yarn, New York, Macmillan
Co., 1938.

Everett, Henry L., The People's Program; the Twentieth
Century is Theirs, New York, Workmen's Publishing Co.,
1892.

Farnum, Mabel A., The Cry of the Street, Boston, Angel Guardian Press, 1913.

Field, Rachel, And Now Tomorrow, New York, Macmillan Co., 1942.

Fitch, Thomas and Anna M., Better Days: or, A Millionaire of To-Morrow, San Francisco, Better Days Publishing Co., 1891.

Foote, Mary Hallock, Coeur D'Alène, Boston, Houghton Mifflin Co., 1894.

Foran, Martin A., The Other Side, Washington, D.C., W. A. Ingham, 1886.

Ford, Paul Leicester, The Honorable Peter Stirling and What People Thought of Him, New York, Henry Holt and Co., 1900 (c. 1894).

France, Royal Wilbur, Compromise, Philadelphia, Dorrance and Co., 1936.

Frank, Waldo, The Death and Birth of David Markand, New York, Charles Scribner's Sons, 1934.

Frederic, Harold, The Lawton Girl, New York, Charles Scribner's Sons, 1897 (c. 1890).

Freeman, Joseph, Never Call Retreat, New York, Farrar and Rinehart, Inc., 1943.

Freeman, Mary E. Wilkins, The Portion of Labor, New York, Harper and Bros., 1901.

French, Alice (Octave Thanet), The Man of the Hour, New York, Grosset and Dunlap, 1905.

Friedman, Isaac Kahn, By Bread Alone, New York, McClure, Phillips and Co., 1901.

_____, The Radical, New York, D. Appleton and Co., 1907.

Fuller, Edward, Complaining Millions of Men, New York, Harper and Bros., 1886.

Garland, Hamlin, Hesper, New York, Harper and Bros., 1903.

Garrett, Garet, The Cinder Buggy: a Fable in Iron and Steel, New York, E. P. Dutton and Co., 1923.

Gibbs, George, The Joyous Conspirator, New York, J. H. Sears and Co., 1927.

Gilfillan, Lauren, I Went to Pit College, New York, Viking Press, 1934.

Gilligan, Edmund, Boundary Against Night, New York, Farrar and Rinehart, Inc. 1938.

Givens, Charles G., The Devil Takes a Hill Town, Indianapolis, Bobbs-Merrill Co., 1939.

Gollomb, Joseph, Unquiet, New York, Dodd, Mead and Co., 1935.

Grant, Robert, Face to Face, New York, Charles Scribner's

Sons, 1886.

Grey, Zane, The Desert of Wheat, New York, Harper and Bros., 1919.

Hale, Edward Everett, How They Lived in Hampton. A Study of Practical Christianity Applied in the Manufacture of Woollens, Boston, J. Stilman Smith and Co., 1888.

Hamblen, Herbert Elliott, The General Manager's Story: Old-Time Reminiscences of Railroading in the United States, New York, Macmillan Co., 1898.

Hammett, Dashiell, "Red Harvest" in The Novels of Dashiell Hammett, New York, Alfred A. Knopf, 1965 (c. 1929).

Harris, Frank, The Bomb, London, John Long, 1908.

Harrison, Charles Yale, A Child Is Born, New York, Jonathan Cape and Harrison Smith, 1931.

Havighurst, Walter, Pier 17, New York, Macmillan Co., 1935.

(Hay, John), The Bread-Winners; a Social Study, New York, Harper and Bros., 1884.

Helm, Flora, Between Two Forces, Boston, Arena Publishing Co., 1894.

Herbst, Josephine, The Executioner Waits, New York, Harcourt, Brace and Co., 1934.

_____, Pity Is Not Enough, New York, Harcourt, Brace and Co., 1933.

_____, Rope of Gold, New York, Harcourt, Brace and Co., 1939.

Herrick, Robert, The Memoirs of an American Citizen, Cambridge, Mass., Harvard University Press, 1963 (c. 1905).

_____, The Web of Life, New York, Macmillan Co., 1914 (c. 1900).

Howells, William Dean, A Hazard of New Fortunes, New York, E. P. Dutton and Co., 1952 (c. 1890).

Huie, William Bradford, Mud on the Stars, New York, L. B. Fischer, 1942.

Hurt, Walter, The Scarlet Shadow, a Story of the Great Colorado Conspiracy, Gerard, Kansas, The Appeal to Reason, 1907.

Jackson, Charles Tenney, My Brother's Keeper, Indianapolis, Bobbs-Merrill Co., 1910.

Jay, Junius, Open-Air Politics and the Conversion of Governor Soothem, Boston, Houghton Mifflin Co., 1914.

Jenkins, Burris, Fresh Furrow, Chicago, Willett, Clark and Co., 1936.

Jeter, Goetze, The Strikers, New York, Frederick A. Stokes Co., 1937.

Johnson, Josephine, Jordanstown, New York, Simon and Schuster, 1937.

Jones, Idwal, Steel Chips, New York, Alfred A. Knopf, 1929.
(Judd, Sylvester), Richard Edney and the Governor's Family,
  Boston, Phillips, Sampson and Co. , 1850.
Kagey, Rudolf (Kurt Steel), Judas, Incorporated, Boston, Lit-
  tle, Brown and Co. , 1939.
Kauffman, Reginald Wright, The House of Bondage, New York,
  Moffat, Yard and Co. , 1911.
_____ , The Spider's Web, New York, Macaulay Co. , 1914.
Keenan, Henry Francis, The Money-Makers: a Social Para-
  ble, New York, D. Appleton and Co. , 1885.
Kelland, Clarence Budington, Dynasty, New York, Harper
  and Bros. , 1929.
Kester, Vaughan, The Manager of the B and A, New York,
  Harper and Bros. , 1901.
Kimbrough, Edward, From Hell to Breakfast, Philadelphia,
  J. B. Lippincott Co. , 1941.
King, Charles, An Army Wife, New York, F. Tennyson Neely,
  1896.
_____ , Foes in Ambush, Philadelphia, J. B. Lippincott Co. ,
  1893.
_____ , A Tame Surrender; a Story of the Chicago Strike,
  Philadelphia, J. B. Lippincott Co. , 1896.
King, Edward, Joseph Zalmonah, Boston, Lee and Shepard,
  1893.
Klempner, John, Once Around the Block, Charles Scribner's
  Sons, 1939.
Lanham, Edwin, The Stricklands, Boston, Little, Brown and
  Co. , 1939.
Larsson, Gösta, Our Daily Bread, New York, Vanguard Press,
  1934.
Leavitt, John McDowell, Kings of Capital and Knights of
  Labor, Cincinnati, Skelton and Bulkley Book Co. , 1886.
Lee, Day Kellogg, The Master Builder: or, Life at a Trade,
  New York, Redfield, 1853.
_____ , Merrimack: or, Life at the Loom, New York, Red-
  field, 1854.
Levin, Meyer, Citizens, New York, Viking Press, 1940.
_____ , The Old Bunch, New York, Macfadden-Bartell Corp. ,
  1962 (c. 1937).
Lewis, Sinclair, "Babbitt" in Lewis at Zenith, New York,
  Harcourt, Brace and World, Inc. , 1961 (c. 1922).
Linn, Bettina, Flea Circus, New York, Harrison Smith and
  Robert Haas, 1936.
Lippard, George, New York: Its Upper Ten and Lower Mil-
  lion, Cincinnati, E. Mendenhall, 1854.
London, Jack, The Iron Heel, New York, International Publish-
  ers, n. d. (c. 1907).

191

_____, Valley of the Moon, New York, International Publishers, n. d. (c. 1913).

Loring, Emilie, Today Is Yours, New York, Farrar and Rinehart, Inc., 1937.

Lumpkin, Grace, To Make My Bread, New York, Macaulay Co., 1932.

Lush, Charles, The Federal Judge, Boston, Houghton Mifflin Co., 1898.

Mainwaring, Daniel (Geoffrey Homes), The Doctor Died at Dusk, New York, William Morrow and Co., 1936.

Malkiel, Theresa Serber, Diary of a Shirtwaist Striker, New York, Cooperative Press, 1910.

Mathews, Cornelius, Big Abel, and the Little Manhattan, New York, Wiley and Putnam, 1845.

McCardell, Roy L., The Wage Slaves of New York, New York, G. W. Dillingham Co., 1899.

McCowan, Archibald (Luke A. Hedd), Philip Meyer's Scheme; a Story of Trades Unionism, New York, J. S. Ogilvie, 1892.

McGibeny, Donald, Slag, a Story of Steel and Stocks, Indianapolis, Bobbs-Merrill Co., 1922.

McIntyre, John T., Ferment, New York, Farrar and Rinehart, Inc., 1937.

McKenney, Ruth, Jake Home, New York, Harcourt, Brace and Co., 1943.

McLeod, Norman, The Bitter Roots, New York, Smith and Durrell, 1941.

McMahon, John R., Toilers and Idlers, New York, Wilshire Book Co., 1907.

McMahon, Patrick Justin, Philip; or, the Mollie's Secret. A Tale of the Coal Regions, Philadelphia, H. L. Kilner and Co., 1891.

Merwin, Samuel and Webster, Henry Kitchell, Calumet "K", New York, Macmillan Co., 1901.

Meyersburg, Dorothy, Seventh Avenue, New York, E. P. Dutton and Co., Inc., 1941.

Mitchell, Ruth Comfort, Of Human Kindness, New York, D. Appleton-Century Co., 1940.

Moore, Ward, Breathe the Air Again, New York, Harper and Bros., 1942.

Morris, Henry O., Waiting for the Signal, Chicago, Schulte Publishing Co., 1904.

Myers, Cortland, Would Christ Belong to a Labor Union? or Henry Fielding's Dream, New York, Street and Smith, 1900.

Nason, Frank Lewis, The Blue Goose, New York, McClure, Phillips and Co., 1903.

Nearing, Scott, Free Born: An Unpublishable Novel, New
    York, Urquhart Press, 1932.
Newhouse, Edward, This Is Your Day, New York, Lee Fur-
    man, Inc. , 1937.
_____, You Can't Sleep Here, New York, Macaulay Co. ,
    1934.
Nitsch, Helen Alice Matthews (Catherine Owen), Gentle Bread-
    winners, The Story of One of Them, Boston, Houghton
    Mifflin Co. , 1888.
Norris, Charles G. , Flint, Garden City, N. Y. , Doubleday,
    Doran and Co. , 1941.
Norris, Frank, The Octopus, a Story of California, Garden
    City, N. Y. Doubleday and Co. , n. d. (c. 1901).
North, Sterling, Seven Against the Years, New York, Mac-
    millan Co. , 1939.
Oppenheim, James, The Nine-Tenths, New York, Harper
    and Bros. , 1911.
(Ornitz, Samuel), Haunch, Paunch and Jowl, an Anonymous
    Autobiography, New York, Boni and Liveright, 1923.
Overton, Gwendolen, Captains of the World, New York, Mac-
    millan Co. , 1904.
Page, Dorothy Myra, Gathering Storm; a Story of the Black
    Belt, New York, International Publishers, 1932.
Page, Thomas Nelson, John Marvel, Assistant, New York,
    Charles Scribner's Sons, 1909.
Paul, Elliot, The Stars and Stripes Forever, New York,
    Random House, 1939.
Pell, Mike, S. S. Utah, New York, International Publishers,
    1933.
Phillips, David Graham, The Conflict, New York, D. Apple-
    ton and Co. , 1911.
Pidgin, Charles Felton, Labor; or, The Money-God! Which?
    a Story of the Times, Boston, Mayhew Publishing Co. ,
    1908.
Pier, Arthur Stanwood, Jerry, Boston, Houghton Mifflin Co. ,
    1927.
Poling, Dan, The Furnace, New York, Geo. H. Doran Co.
    1925
Poole, Ernest, The Habor, New York, Macmillan Co. , 1916.
Preston, John Hyde, The Liberals, New York, John Day Co. ,
    1938.
Prince, Helen Choate, The Story of Christine Rochefort,
    Boston, Houghton Mifflin Co. , 1895.
Rice, Elmer, Imperial City, New York, Coward-McCann,
    Inc. , 1937.
Rinehart, Mary Roberts, A Poor Wise Man, New York, Re-
    view of Reviews Co. , 1920.

Rodney, George Brydges, Jim Lofton, American, New York, James A. McCann Co. , 1920.

Roe, Abigail (C. M. Cornwall), Free, Yet Forging Their Own Chains, New York, Dodd, Mead and Co. , 1876.

Rollins, William, Jr. , The Shadow Before, New York, Robert M. McBride and Co. , 1934.

Rood, Henry Edward, The Company Doctor, an American Story, New York, Merrian Co. , 1895.

Ross, Clinton, The Silent Workman, a Story, New York, G. P. Putnam's Sons, 1886.

Rothermell, Fred, The Ghostland, Philadelphia, J. B. Lippincott Co. , 1940.

Rowan, Thomas, Black Earth, New York, Hillman-Curl, Inc. , 1935.

Rush, Caroline, The Dew-Drop of the Sunny South: a Story Written from Every Day Life, Philadelphia, Cressy and Markley, 1851.

Russell, Ruth, Lake Front, Chicago, Thomas S. Rockwell Co. , 1931.

Rutzeback, Hjalmar, My Alaskan Idyll, New York, Boni and Liveright, 1922.

Sandoz, Mari, Capital City, Boston, Little, Brown and Co. , 1939.

Scott, Leroy, The Walking Delegate, New York, Doubleday, Page and Co. , 1905.

Scott, Milton R. , Ernest Marble, the Labor Agitator, Newark, Ohio, Tribune Book Print, 1895.

Scudder, Viola D. , A Listener in Babel, Boston, Houghton Mifflin Co. , 1903.

Sheldon, Charles M. , The Crucifixion of Phillip Strong, Chicago, A. C. McClurg and Co. , 1894.

Sherman, Ray W. , The Other Mahoney, New York, Ives, Washburn, Inc. , 1944.

Simon, Charlie May, The Share-Cropper, New York, E. P. Dutton and Co. , Inc. , 1937.

Sinclair, Upton, Boston, New York, Albert and Charles Boni, 1927.

_____ , The Jungle, New York, Doubleday, Page and Co. , 1906.

_____ , King Coal, n. p. , Upton Sinclair, 1929.

_____ , Little Steel, New York, Farrar and Rinehart, Inc. , 1938.

_____ , Oil!, Pasadena, Upton Sinclair, 1926.

Smedley, Agnes, Daughter of Earth, New York, Coward-McCann, Inc. , 1935 (c. 1929).

Smith, Edgar Maurice, A Daughter of Humanity, Boston, Arena Publishing Co. , 1895.

(Smith, Elizabeth), The Newsboy, New York, J. C. Derby, 1854.

Smith, Francis Hopkinson, Tom Grogan, Boston, Houghton Mifflin Co., 1896.

Spadoni, Adriana, Not All Rivers, New York, Book League of America, 1937.

Steinbeck, John, In Dubious Battle, New York, Modern Library, n. d. (c. 1936).

Stockton, Frank R., The Hundredth Man, New York, Charles Scribner's Sons, 1899 (c. 1886).

Storm, Hans Otto, Pity the Tyrant, New York, Longmans, Green and Co., 1937.

Swafford, Charles Carroll, The Silent Conflict; a Story of Industrial Warfare, Boston, Roxburgh Publishing Co., 1916.

Swift, Morrison I., The Monarch Billionaire, New York, J. S. Ogilvie Co., 1903.

(Talcott, Hannah Elizabeth Bradbury Godwin), H. G. H., Madge: or, Night and Morning, New York, D. Appleton and Co., 1863.

Teilhet, Darwin L., Journey to the West, New York, Doubleday, Doran and Co., 1938.

Teller, Charlotte, The Cage, New York, D. Appleton and Co., 1907.

Tippett, Tom, Horse Shoe Bottoms, New York, Harper and Bros., 1935.

Tobenkin, Elias, The Road, New York, Harcourt, Brace and Co., 1922.

Tourgée, Albion W., Murvale Eastman, Christian Socialist, Montreal, William Foster Brown and Co., 1889.

Townsend, Virginia F., The Mills of Tuxbury, Boston, Lee and Shepard, 1896 (c. 1871).

Train, Arthur, The Needle's Eye, New York, Charles Scribner's Sons, 1924.

Trammell, William Douglas, Ça Ira, New York, United States Publishing Co., 1874.

Tyler, Martha W., A Book without a Title: or, Thrilling Events in the Life of Mira Dana, Boston, Printed for the Author, 1855.

Van Vorst, Marie, Amanda of the Mill, New York, Dodd, Mead and Co., 1905.

Van Vechten, Carl, Peter Whiffle, New York, Modern Library, n. d. (c. 1929).

Vorse, Mary Heaton, Strike!, New York, Horace Liveright, 1930.

Walker, Charles Rumford, Bread and Fire, Boston, Houghton Mifflin Co., 1927.

Walter, Eugene, Paid in Full, New York, G. W. Dillingham
Co., 1908.
Ward, Elizabeth Stuart Phelps, The Silent Partner, Boston,
Houghton Mifflin Co., 1871.
Warner, Charles Dudley, A Little Journey in the World, New
York, Harper and Bros., 1896 (c. 1889).
Weatherwax, Clara, Marching! Marching!, New York, John
Day Co., 1935.
Webster, Henry Kitchell, An American Family, Indianapolis,
Bobbs-Merrill Co., 1918.
White, William Allen, In the Heart of a Fool, New York,
Macmillan Co., 1919.
Wiener, Philip (Thomas Burton), And So Dedicated, New
York, Harrison-Hilton Books, 1940.
Williams, William Carlos, White Mule, Norfolk, Conn., New
Directions, 1937.
Williamson, Thames, Hunky, New York, Coward-McCann,
Inc., 1929.
Wilson, Anne Florence, The Wars of Peace, Boston, Little,
Brown and Co., 1903.
Winslow, Helen M., Salome Shepard, Reformer, Boston,
Arena Publishing Co., 1893.
Wood, Clement, Mountain, New York, E. P. Dutton and Co.,
1920.
Wood, Henry, Edward Burton, Boston, Lee and Shepard,
1890.
Woods, Katherine Pearson, Metzerott, Shoemaker, New York,
Thomas Y. Crowell and Co., 1889.
Wright, Harold Bell, Helen of the Old House, New York, D.
Appleton and Co., 1921.
Wright, James North, Where Copper Was King, Boston,
Small, Maynard and Co., 1905.
Zara, Louis, Give Us This Day, Indianapolis, Bobbs-Merrill
Co., 1936.
Zugsmith, Leane, The Summer Soldier, New York, Random
House, 1938.
_____, A Time to Remember, New York, Random House,
1936.

SHORT STORIES:

Bunner, H. C., Zadoc Pine and Other Stories, New York,
Charles Scribner's Sons, 1891.
(Davis, Rebecca Harding), "Life in the Iron Mills," The At-
lantic Monthly, vol, VII, no. 42, April, 1861, p. 430-451.
Deland, Margaret, The Wisdom of Fools, Boston, Houghton
Mifflin Co., 1897.

French, Alice (Octave Thanet), The Heart of Toil, New York, International Association of Newspapers and Authors, 1901.
_____, Otto the Knight and Other Trans-Mississippi Stories, Boston, Houghton Mifflin Co., 1891.
Mind amongst the Spindles: a Selection from "The Lowell Offering," London, Charles Knight and Co., 1845.

Secondary Sources

BOOKS:

Aaron, Daniel, Writers on the Left, Episodes in American Literary Criticism, New York, Harcourt, Brace and World, Inc., 1961.
Adams, Jr., Frederick B., Radical Literature in America, Stamford, Conn., Overbrook Press, 1939.
Addams, Jane, Forty Years at Hull House, New York, Macmillan Co., 1935.
Allen, James B., The Company Town in the American West, Norman Okla., University of Oklahoma Press, 1966.
Beale, Fred, Proletarian Journey, New York, Hillman-Curl, Inc., 1937.
Beard, Charles A. and Mary R., America in Midpassage, New York, Macmillan Co., 1939.
Beer, Thomas, The Mauve Decade; American Life at the End of the Nineteenth Century, New York, Random House, 1960.
Bennett, Robert, The Wrath of John Steinbeck, or St. John Goes to Church, Los Angeles, Albertson Press, 1939.
Bimba, Anthony, The History of the American Working Class, New York, International Publishers, 1927.
_____, The Molly Maguires, New York, International Publishers, 1932.
Blotner, Joseph, The Modern American Political Novel, 1900-1960, Austin, Texas, University of Texas Press, 1966.
Bowman, John Scott, The Proletarian Novel in America, Pennsylvania State College, 1939 (Dissertation).
Bremner, Robert H., From the Depths, New York, New York University Press, 1956.
Brooks, Thomas R., To Build a New World, New York, League for Industrial Democracy, 1965.
Brown, Deming, Soviet Attitudes toward American Writing, Princeton, Princeton University Press, 1962.
Browne, Ray B., Winkelman, Donald M., and Hayman, Allen (eds.), New Voices in American Studies, West Lafayette, Ind., Purdue University Studies, 1966.
Buchanan, Joseph R., The Story of a Labor Agitator, New

197

York, Outlook Co., 1903.

Calverton, V. F., The Newer Spirit; a Sociological Criticism
of Literature, New York, Boni and Liveright, 1925.

Commons, John R. and others, History of Labor in the
United States, New York, Macmillan Co., 1921.

Cowley, Malcolm (ed.), After the Genteel Tradition, New
York, W. W. Norton and Co., Inc., 1937.

_____, Think Back on Us ...; a Contemporary Chronicle
of the 1930's, Carbondale, Southern Illinois University
Press, 1967.

Craven, Avery, Johnson, Walter and Dunn, F. Roger, A
Documentary History of the American People, Boston,
Ginn and Co., 1951.

Davidson, Lallah S., South of Joplin, New York, W. W.
Norton and Co., 1939.

Dickens, Charles, American Notes, New York, Charles
Scribner's Sons, 1907.

Drinnon, Richard, Rebel in Paradise, Chicago, University
of Chicago Press, 1961.

Du Breuil, Alice Jouveau, The Novel of Democracy in
America, Baltimore, J. H. Furst Co., 1923.

Dulles, Foster Rhea, Labor in America, New York, Thomas
Y. Crowell Co., 3rd ed., 1966.

Dunlap, George Arthur, The City in the American Novel,
1789-1900, University of Pennsylvania, 1934 (Dissertation).

Egbert, Donald Drew and Persons, Stow (eds.), Socialism
and American Life, Princeton, N. J., Princeton University
Press, 1952.

Farrell, James T., A Note on Literary Criticism, New
York, Vanguard Press, 1936.

Fast, Howard, Literature and Reality, New York, International Publishers, 1950.

Filler, Louis (ed.), The Anxious Years: America in the
Nineteen Thirties, New York, G. P. Putnam's Sons, 1952.

Flory, Claude Reherd, Economic Criticism in American
Fiction, 1792-1900, University of Pennsylvania, 1936
(Dissertation).

Fox, Ralph, The Novel and the People, New York, International Publishers, 1937.

Freeman, Joseph, An American Testament; a Narrative of
Rebels and Romantics, London, Victor Gollancz, Ltd.,
1938.

Garraty, John A., (ed.), Labor and Capital in the Gilded
Age: Testimony Taken by the Senate Committee upon the
Relations between Capital and Labor, 1883, Boston, Little, Brown and Co., 1968.

Geismar, Maxwell, Rebels and Ancestors, Boston, Houghton,

Mifflin Co. , 1953.

Gilbert, James Burkhart, Writers and Partisans: A History of Literary Radicalism in America, New York, John Wiley and Sons, Inc. , 1968.

Ginzberg, Eli and Berman, Hyman, The American Worker in the Twentieth Century, Glencoe, Ill. , Free Press, 1963.

Goldman, Emma, Living My Life, New York, Alfred A. Knopf, 1931.

Hart, Henry (ed.), The American Writers' Congress, New York, International Publishers, 1935.

_____, The Writer in a Changing World, n. p. , Equinox Cooperative Press, 1937.

Hicks, Granville, The Great Tradition, New York, Macmillan Co. , rev. ed. , 1935.

_____, Part of the Truth, New York, Harcourt, Brace and World, Inc. , 1965.

Hofstadter, Richard, Miller, William and Aaron, Daniel, The United States, Englewood Cliffs, N. J. , Prentice-Hall, Inc. , 2nd ed. , 1967.

Howe, Irving, Sherwood Anderson, n. p. , William Sloane Associates, 1951.

_____, Steady Work, New York, Harcourt, Brace and World, Inc. , 1966.

_____, A World More Attractive, New York, Horizon Press, 1963.

Irvine, Leigh H. , Historic Strikes and their Settlement, San Francisco, Calkins Newspaper Syndicate, 1907.

Jane Addams; a Centennial Reader, New York, Macmillan Co. , 1960.

Johnson, Robert E. , The American Political Novel, 1792-1950; a Survey, University of California at Los Angeles, 1956 (Dissertation).

Kazin, Alfred, Contemporaries, Boston, Little, Brown and Co. , 1962.

_____, On Native Grounds, New York, Harcourt, Brace and Co. , 1942.

_____, Starting Out in the Thirties, Boston, Little, Brown and Co. , 1965.

_____ and Shapiro, Charles (eds.), The Stature of Theodore Dreiser, Bloomington, Ind. , Indiana University Press, 1955.

Kempton, Murray, Part of Our Time, New York, Simon and Schuster, 1955.

Lovell, John, Jr. , Champions of the Workers in American Literature of the Forties, University of California at Berkeley, 1938 (Dissertation).

Lukacs, George, Essays über Realismus, Berlin, Aufbau-
    Verlag, 1948.
_____, The Meaning of Contemporary Realism, London,
    Merlin Press, 1962.
Lynn, Kenneth S. , The Dream of Success, Boston, Little,
    Brown and Co. , 1955.
Madden, David (ed.), Proletarian Writers of the Thirties,
    Carbondale, Ill. , Southern Illinois University Press, 1968.
Martineau, Harriet, Society in America, New York, Saunders
    and Otley, 1836.
Matthiesen, F. O. , Theodore Dreiser, n. p. , William Sloan
    Associates, 1951.
Mayberry, George, Industrialism and the Industrial Worker
    in the American Novel, 1814-1890, Harvard University,
    1942 (Dissertation).
McKenney, Ruth, Industrial Valley, New York, Harcourt,
    Brace and Co. , 1939.
Millett, Fred B. , Contemporary American Authors, New
    York, Harcourt, Brace and Co. , 1940.
Neidle, Cecyle S. , The New Americans, New York, Twayne
    Publishers, 1967.
Nevins, Allan, The Emergence of Modern America, 1865-
    1878, New York, Macmillan Co. , 1927 (A History of
    American Life, v. VII).
Nevius, Blake, Robert Herrick: The Development of a Nov-
    elist, Berkeley, University of California Press, 1962.
Parrington, Vernon Louis, Main Currents in American
    Thought, New York, Harcourt, Brace and Co. , 1930.
Pinkerton, Allan, The Molly Maguires and the Detectives,
    New York, G. W. Carleton and Co. , 1877.
_____, Strikers, Communists, Tramps and Detectives,
    New York, G. W. Dillingham Co. , 1878.
Proletarian Literature in the United States; an Anthology,
    New York, International Publishers, 1935.
Rideout, Walter B. , The Radical Novel in the United States,
    1900-1954, Cambridge, Mass. , Harvard University Press,
    1956.
Romanciers américains contemporains, Paris, Librairie
    Didier, 1946.
Rowan, Richard Wilmer, The Pinkertons: a Detective Dy-
    nasty, Boston, Little, Brown and Co. , 1931.
Salzman, Jack (ed.), Years of Protest, New York, Pegasus,
    1967.
Schneider, Robert W. , Five Novelists of the Progressive
    Era, New York, Columbia University Press, 1965.
Shannon, David A. , Twentieth Century America, Chicago,
    Rand McNally and Co. , 1963.

Sprigg, Christopher St. John (Christopher Caudwell), Studies in a Dying Culture, London, John Lane, 1938.

Steinbeck, John, Their Blood Is Strong, San Francisco, Simon J. Lubin Society, 1938.

Symes, Lillian and Travers, Clement, Rebel America, New York, Harper and Bros., 1934.

Taft, Philip, Organized Labor in American History, New York, Harper and Row, 1964.

Taylor, Walter Fuller, The Economic Novel in America, Chapel Hill, N.C., University of North Carolina Press, 1942.

Thompson, Fred, The I.W.W.: Its First Fifty Years, 1905-1955, Chicago, Industrial Workers of the World, 1955.

Trotsky, Leon, Literature and Revolution, New York, International Publishers, 1925.

U.S. Bureau of Labor, Bulletin, No. 59, Washington, D.C., Government Printing Office, 1905.

_____, Bulletin, No. 61, Washington, D.C., Government Printing Office, 1905.

_____, Bulletin, No. 105, Washington, D.C., Government Printing Office, 1912.

U.S. Bureau of Labor Statistics, Bulletin, No. 651, Washington, D.C., Government Printing Office, 1938.

U.S. Commissioner of Labor, First Annual Report, Washington, D.C., Government Printing Office, 1886.

_____, Third Annual Report, Washington, D.C., Government Printing Office, 1888.

_____, Seventh Annual Report, Washington, D.C., Government Printing Office, 1892.

Van Doren, Carl, The American Novel, New York, Macmillan Co., 1940.

_____, Contemporary American Novelists, 1900-1920, New York, Macmillan Co., 1928.

Van Vorst, Mrs. John and Marie, The Women Who Toil, being the Experiences of Two Ladies as Factory Girls, New York, Doubleday, Page and Co., 1903.

Werstein, Irving, The Great Struggle, New York, Charles Scribner's Sons, 1965.

Wilson, Edmund, The Shores of Light, New York, Farrar, Straus and Young, Inc., 1952.

Wister, Fanny Kemble (ed.), Owen Wister Out West, Chicago, University of Chicago Press, 1958.

Wright, Lyle H., A Few Observations on American Fiction, 1851-1875, Worcester, Mass., American Antiquarian Society, 1955.

Yellen, Samuel, American Labor Struggles, New York, Harcourt, Brace and Co., 1936.

Young, Art, Art Young: His Life and Times, New York,
Sheridan House, 1939.

ARTICLES:

Aaron, Daniel, "A Decade of Convictions: the Appeal of
    Communism in the 1930's, " Massachusetts Review, vol.
    II, no. 4, Summer, 1961, p. 736-747.
_____, "The Thirties - Now and Then, " American Scholar,
    vol. XXXV, no. 3, Summer, 1966, p. 490-494.
Anderson, Sherwood, "Let's Have More Criminal Syndicalism, "
    New Masses, vol. VII, no. 9, February, 1932, p. 3-6.
Armfield, Eugene, "The Second Writers' Congress, " Satur-
    day Review of Literature, vol. XVI, no. 7, June 12, 1937,
    p. 7, 17.
Aubery, Pierre, "Les Industrial Workers of the World dans
    l'Oeuvre d'Upton Sinclair, " La Revue Socialiste, nouvelle
    série, no. 99, July, 1956, p. 178-197.
"Author's Field Day: a Symposium on Marxist Criticism, "
    New Masses, vol. XII, no. 1, July 3, 1934, p. 27-32.
Barnes, L. (pseud. Russell Ames?), "The Proletarian Nov-
    el, " Mainstream, vol. XVI, no. 7, July, 1963, p. 51-57.
Bittner, William, "Waldo Frank as Novelist, " Literary Re-
    view, vol. I, no. 4, Summer, 1958, p. 478-484.
Bonosky, Philip, "Thomas Bell's In the Midst of Life, "
    Mainstream, vol. XIV, no. 12, December, 1961, p. 56-
    58.
Brewster, Dorothy, "The Interpretation of Social Change in
    Literature, " Science and Society, vol. V, no. 3, Summer,
    1941, p. 234-242.
Briffault, Robert, "The Left Turn in Literature, " Scribner's
    Magazine, vol. XVII, no. 2, August, 1932, p. 88-90.
Bryant, Jerry H. , "The Last of the Social Protest Writers, "
    Arizona Quarterly, vol. XIX, no. 4, Winter, 1963, p.
    315-325.
Burgum, Edwin Berry, "The Function of the Critic in Our
    Day, " Science and Society, vol. V, no. 3, Summer, 1941,
    p. 243-254.
Calmer, Alan, "Portrait of the Artist as a Proletarian, "
    Saturday Review of Literature, vol. XVI, no. 14, July
    31, 1937, p. 3-4, 14.
Calverton, V. F. , "The Liberation of American Literature, "
    Scribner's Magazine, vol. XCI, no. 3, March, 1932, p.
    143-146.
_____, "Sherwood Anderson: A Study in Sociological
    Criticism, " Modern Quarterly, vol. II, no. 2, Fall,

1924, p. 4-21.

_____, "Sociological Criticism of Literature," Modern Quarterly, vol. II, no. 1, Summer, 1924, p. 4-21.

Chamberlain, John, "The Businessman in Fiction," Fortune, vol. XXXVIII, no. 5, November, 1948, p. 134-148.

"Communism and the American Writer, a Report on the Tenth Newberry Library Conference on American Studies," Newberry Library Bulletin, vol. V, no. 3, August, 1959, p. 84-116.

Cowley, Malcolm, "A Remembrance of the Red Romance," Esquire, vol. LXI, no. 3 and 4, March and April, 1964, p. 124-130 and p. 78-81.

_____, "While They Waited for Lefty," Saturday Review, vol. XLVIII, no. 23, June 6, 1964, p. 16-19, 61.

Dell, Floyd, "On Being Sherwood Anderson's Literary Father," Newberry Library Bulletin, vol. V, no. 9, December, 1961, p. 314-321.

Dinamov, Sergei, "Sherwood Anderson: American Writer," International Literature, vol. 1933, no. 4, p. 84-91.

Dunne, Bill, "Gastonia: A Beginning," New Masses, vol. V, no. 2, July, 1929, p. 3-5.

Elistratova, Anna, "New Masses," International Literature, vol. 1932, no. 1, p. 107-114.

_____, "Jack Conroy: American Worker-Writer," International Literature, vol., 1934, no. 1 (7), p. 112-118.

Fadiman, Clifton, "The American Novel of the Truce," Saturday Review of Literature, vol. XXVII, no. 32, August 5, 1944, p. 19-21.

Farrell, James T., "The Last Writers' Congress," Saturday Review of Literature, vol. XVI, no. 6, June 5, 1937, p. 10, 14.

Fast, Howard, "My Decision," Mainstream, vol. X, no. 3, March, 1957, p. 29-38.

Filler, Louis, "Political Literature: a Post-Mortem," Southwest Review, vol. XXXIX, no. 3, Summer, 1954, p. 185-193.

_____, "The Reputation of David Graham Phillips," Antioch Review, vol. XI, no. 4, December, 1951, p. 475-488.

Freeman, Joseph, "Sherwood Anderson's Confusion," New Masses, vol. IV, no. 9, February, 1929, p. 6.

Getzels, Jacob Warren, "William Dean Howells and Socialism," Science and Society, vol. II, no. 3, Summer, 1938, p. 376-386.

Glicksberg, Charles L., "The Decline of Literary Marxism," Antioch Review, vol. I, no. 4, Winter, 1941, p. 452-462.

Goldman, Emma, "Between Jails," Mother Earth, vol. XII, no. 6, August, 1917, p. 207-212.

_____, "The Tragedy of Woman's Emancipation," Mother Earth, vol. I, no. 1, March, 1906, p. 9-18.

Harris, Mrs. L. H., "The Walking Delegate Novelist," Independent, vol. LX, no. 2999, May 24, 1906, p. 1213-1216.

Heinemann, Margot, "Workers and Writers," Mainstream, vol. XV, no. 6, June, 1962, p. 10-22.

Herbst, Josephine, "Ubiquitous Critics and the Author," Newberry Library Bulletin, vol. V, no. 1, December, 1958, p. 1-13.

Hicks, Granville, "The Crisis in American Criticism," New Masses, vol. VIII, no. 7, February, 1933, p. 3-5.

_____, "Revolution and the Novel," New Masses, vol. XI, nos. 1, 2, 3, 4, 6, 7 and 8, April 3, 10, 17, 24 and May 8, 15 and 22, 1934, p. 20.

_____, "The Thirties: a Reappraisal," Saturday Review, vol. XLVI, no. 18, May 4, 1963, p. 27-28.

Hoffman, Frederick J., "The Voices of Sherwood Anderson," Shenandoah, vol. XIII, no. 3, Spring, 1962, p. 5-19.

Humboldt, Charles, "Fiction on the Left," Mainstream, vol. X, no. 3, March, 1957, p. 48-50.

_____, "The Novel of Action," Mainstream, vol. I, no. 4, Fall, 1947, p. 389-407.

Jackson, Kenny A., "Robert Herrick's Use of Chicago," Midcontinent American Studies Journal, vol., V, no. 1, September, 1964, p. 24-32.

Jerome, V. J., "Remembering Dashiell Hammett," Mainstream, vol. XVI, no. 5, May, 1963, p. 60-61.

_____, "Toward a Proletarian Novel," New Masses, vol. VIII, no. 2, August, 1932, p. 14-15.

Kazin, Alfred, "Howells: A Late Portrait," Antioch Review, vol. I, no. 2, Summer, 1941, p. 216-233.

Kirk, Rudolf and Clara M., "Abraham Cahan and William Dean Howells: The Story of a Friendship," American Jewish Historical Quarterly, vol. LII, no. 1, September, 1962, p. 27-57.

Levy, Melvin P., "Stories of Workers," New Masses, vol. VI, no. 12, May, 1931, p. 19-20.

Magil, A. B., "To Make My Bread," New Masses, vol. VIII, no. 7, February, 1933, p. 19-20.

McCarthy, Mary, "Two in our Time," Partisan Review, vol. VI, no. 4, Summer, 1939, p. 111-114.

Montgomery, David, "The Working Classes of the Pre-Industrial American City, 1780-1830," Labor History, vol. IX, no. 1, Winter, 1968, p. 3-22.

Nichols, William W. , "A Changing Attitude toward Poverty
in The Ladies' Home Journal: 1895-1919, " Midcontinent
American Studies Journal, vol. V, no. 1, Spring, 1964,
p. 3-16.
"The 1930's, a Symposium, " Carleton Miscellany, vol. VI,
no. 1, Winter, 1965, p. 6-113.
Phelps, Wallace and Rahv, Philip, "Criticism, " Partisan
Review, vol. II, no. 7, April/May, 1935, p. 16-31.
_____, "Problems and Perspectives in Revolutionary
Literature, " Partisan Review, vol. I, no. 3, June/July,
1934, p. 3-10.
Phillips, William and Rahv, Philip, "Some Aspects of Liter-
ary Criticism, " Science and Society, vol. I, no. 2, Win-
ter, 1937, p. 212-220.
_____, "What Happened in the 30's, " Commentary, vol.
XXXIV, no. 3, September, 1962, p. 204-212.
Rahv, Philip, "The Cult of Experience in American Writing,"
Partisan Review, vol. VII, no. 6, November/December,
1940, p. 412-424.
_____, "The Novelist as a Partisan, " Partisan Review,
vol. I, no. 2, April/May, 1934, p. 50-52.
_____, "Proletarian Literature: a Political Autopsy,"
Southern Review, vol. IV, no. 3, Winter, 1939, p. 616-
628.
_____, "Trials of the Mind, " Partisan Review, vol. IV,
no. 5, April, 1938, p. 3-11.
Reed, John, "War in Paterson, " The Masses, June, 1913
in Echoes of Revolt: The Masses, 1911-1917, Chicago,
Quadrangle Books, 1966, p. 143.
Reynolds, Robert L. , "The Coal Kings Come to Judgment, "
American Heritage, vol. XI, no. 3, April, 1960, p. 55-
61, 94-100.
Rollins, William, Jr. , and Lloyd, Jessie, "The Gastonia
Trial, " New Masses, vol. V, no. 5, October, 1929,
p. 3-4.
Rose, Lisle Abbott, "A Bibliographical Survey of Economic
and Political Writings, 1865-1900, " American Literature,
vol. XV, no. 4, January, 1944, p. 381-410.
Russell, Francis, "The Strike that Made a President, "
American Heritage, vol. XIV, no. 6, October, 1963, p.
44-47, 90-94.
Schlauch, Margaret, "Criticism and Scholarship, " Main-
stream, vol. X, no. 5, May, 1957, p. 1-10.
Seaver, Edwin, "What Is a Proletarian Novel?" Partisan
Review, vol. II, no. 7, April/May, 1935, p. 5-15.
"The Situation in American Writing, " Partisan Review, vol.
VI, no. 4 and 5, Summer and Fall, 1939, p. 25-51 and

103-123.

Sühnel, Rudolf, "The Marxist Trend in Literary Criticism in the U. S. A. in the Thirties," Jahrbuch für Amerika-studien, vol. VII, 1962, p. 53-66.

"Symposium, Thirty Years Later: Memories of the First American Writers' Congress," American Scholar, vol. XXXV, no. 3, Summer, 1966, p. 495-516.

Tresca, Carlo, "On Strike with Bill Haywood," New Masses, vol. IV, no. 9, February, 1929, p. 18-20.

Trilling, Lionel, "Young in the Thirties," Commentary, vol. XLI, no. 5, May, 1966, p. 43-51.

Watkins, T. H., "Requiem for the Federation," The American West, vol. III, no. 1, Winter, 1966, p. 4-12, 91-95.

Weisberger, Bernard A., "The Working Ladies of Lowell," American Heritage, vol. XII, no. 2, February, 1961, p. 42-45, 83-90.

Williams, Cratis D., "Kit Brandon, A Reappraisal," Shenandoah, vol. XII, no. 3, Spring, 1962, p. 55-61.

Williams, Raymond, "Realism and the Contemporary Novel," Promethean Review, vol. I, no. 2, March/April, 1959, p. 6-12.

Wright, Conrad, "The Sources of Mr. Howells's Socialism," Science and Society, vol. II, no. 4, Fall, 1938, p. 514-517.

Wüstenhagen, Heinz, "Harold Frederic's The Lawton Girl," Zeitschrift für Anglistik und Amerikanistik, vol. XII, no. 1, 1964, p. 32-53.

ANNOTATED BIBLIOGRAPHY

1845

Mathews, Cornelius, Big Abel, and the Little Manhattan,
New York, Wiley and Putnam.
A brief, occasionally moving hymn to New York City. Big
Abel, a descendant of Henry Hudson, and Little Manhattan,
last survivor of an Indian tribe, have convinced themselves
they are the rightful heirs to New York. They wander
through the city observing the lives of its multitude of in-
habitants and invite some of them--hucksters, seamstresses,
writers, sea captains--to a feast. As they wander they observe with an eye for colorful authentic detail but with much
sugary sentimentality the busy lives of shipyard workers,
milliners, iron workers and the wretched lives of beggars,
drunkards, prostitutes. The Indian, dying at the end of the
book, resigns himself to the disappearance of Indians and of
Nature from the busy, thriving city.

1847

Cummings, Ariel Ivers, The Factory Girl: or Gardez la
Coeur, Lowell, Mass., J. E. Short and Co.
A poorly written, syrupy novel about a young girl who leaves
her Vermont farm to work in a Lowell factory. She helps
pay for her brother's education, works hard, prays often
and contributes articles to the Lowell Offering, the millworkers' magazine. All ends well when her brother becomes a minister and she marries a young doctor.

1849

"Argus, " Norton: Lights and Shades of a Factory Village;
a Tale of Lowell, Lowell, Mass., Vox Populi Office.
Although it deals with girls working in the Lowell textile
mills, this novel is really a moral tale meant to warn
against the dangers lying in wait for factory girls and not
an attempt to picture actual factory life. Julia, who begins
by complaining about the fourteen-hour working day, attends

a card party with the villain, Alfred Caldwell, drinks a mint
julep, is seduced by Caldwell, and dies when he deserts her.

1850

(Judd, Sylvester), Richard Edney and the Governor's Family,
  Boston, Phillips, Sampson and Co.
A long rambling account of the career of Richard Edney,
country boy turned sawmill worker. Richard wins the hand
of Melicent, the Governor's daughter, after he disentangles
himself from the clutches of Plumy Alicia Eyre, a textile
mill operative. The author treats his readers to long dis-
cursive essays on the city, nature, religion and other philosophical topics but manages to describe in some detail the
workings of a sawmill.

1853

Lee, Day Kellogg, The Master Builder; or, Life at a Trade,
  New York, Redfield.
The rise of Arthur Sumner, a foundling who becomes a carpenter, architect and master builder. The novel includes
some rather detailed descriptions of the tools and techniques
of working carpenters. There is a happy ending when Arthur discovers he is the kidnaped son of a well-to-do couple
and he marries his childhood sweetheart.

Lippard, George, New York: Its Upper Ten and Lower Million, Cincinnati, H. M. Rulison.
An extravagantly melodramatic tale of seven contenders for
a multi-million dollar bequest. Identical twins, infants
spirited away from their homes, murder, suicide, a mysterious Papal legate cram the closely printed double-col-
umned pages of this novel. The author is fascinated by the
more sensational aspects of the lives of the poor, and has
chosen as one of the possible heirs a noble minded carpenter
with Socialist convictions.

1854

Lee, Day Kellogg, Merrimack; or, Life at the Loom, New
  York, Redfield.
Mercy Winthrop, orphaned young, leaves domestic service
for work in a textile mill. She is industrious and pious
and strives earnestly to improve herself. While avoiding
the temptations of fine clothes and other vanities, she works
for a reprieve for her younger brother, an innocent victim

of circumstantial evidence. She receives her eventual reward in Walter's vindication and in her marriage to the
young attorney who defends him.

(Smith, Elizabeth), The Newsboy, New York, J. S. Derby.
Bob, an orphan newsboy, supports himself and two foundling
children whom he adopts. He falls deeply in love with the
young daughter of a prosperous merchant. When she is
kidnaped and spirited away to Cuba, Bob becomes her father's
foster-son, is given an education and eventually becomes a
partner in the firm. He is the prime agent in the restora-
tion of the kidnaped Imogen Dinsmoor to her family, then
nobly gives her up to the man she loves. The novel is ap-
pallingly bad, but includes some scenes of the life of newsboys and other street denizens--apple sellers, hot corn vendors, crossing sweepers, etc.

1855

Tyler, Martha W. , A Book without a Title: or, Thrilling
     Events in the Life of Mira Dana, Boston, Printed for
     the Author.
A disjointed account of Mira Dana's life from her childhood
on a New England farm, work in a Lowell textile mill, marriage to a sea captain, early widowhood, and a second marriage to a Southerner who neglects and mistreats Mira.
This novel has only one distinction--it is the first to depict
a "turn-out" and to portray the heroine as the strike leader.

1860

(Duzanne, Augustine Joseph Hickey), The Tenant-House; or,
     Embers from Poverty's Hearthstone, New York, Inter-
     national Book Co.
A sentimental and melodramatic portrayal of the poverty-
stricken interwoven lives of the tenants of two sprawling
tenements, Foley's Barracks and Kolephat College. Noble
newsboys, overworked seamstresses, gouging rent collectors
abound.

1862

(Davis, Rebecca Harding), Margret Howth. A Story of To-
     Day, Boston, Ticknor and Fields.
A dour picture of life in an Indiana woolen mill. Margret
marries the mill owner but only after it is destroyed in a
fire and he comes to a realization of his inhumane ruthless-

ness. The mill itself becomes a sinister destructive force
and those who work in it, epitomized by Lois Yare, crippled
in a mill accident as a child, become brutalized subhumans.

1863

H. G. H. (Hannah Elizabeth Bradbury Godwin Talcott),
  Madge; or, Night and Morning, New York, D. Appleton
  and Co., 1863.
The story of a young orphan girl who escapes from a harsh
mistress to whom she has been bound into a job as a factory
girl in Preston. She lives frugally, avoids temptation and
holds fast to two abiding ambitions: her desire for an education and her love for the son of her former mistress.
By unstinting industry and with the help of a generous doctor
(who turns out to be her dead mother's cousin) Madge manages to acquire an education and a teacher's job. Her fi-
delity to Maurice is finally rewarded when he realizes he
loves her.

1870

(Benedict, Frank L.), Miss Van Kortland, New York, Harper
  and Bros.
The novel contrasts the hardworking life in Upsden, a Pennsylvania mining town, and the idle dissipated life of New
York's high society. When the coal miners strike, Alan
Prescott, the manager of the mine, exhibits coolheaded re-
sourcefulness. He rescues Margaret Dane and Gay Van
Kortland when the strikers besiege them in their isolated
cottage and Margaret realizes Alan's superiority to the idle
neurotic New Yorker, Noel Seaton. It takes a mine cave-
in to bring Seaton to his senses and when he reforms, Gay
Van Kortland consents to marry him.

1871

Ward, Elizabeth Stuart Phelps, The Silent Partner, Boston,
  J. R. Osgood and Co.
Mrs. Ward writes with feeling and some authenticity but the
strike scenes ring false. They are used to further the author's thesis that the concern and Christian love of the factory owners can prevent strikes. There are some harrowing scenes of working class life in a New England mill town
and rather touching glimpses of young-old children, female
drudges and desperate blacklisted men. Perley Kelso, the
heroine, changes from a thoughtless young society girl to a

deeply concerned woman, no longer content to be "a silent partner." Mrs. Ward, unfortunately, is unable to resist climaxing her story with a cataclysmic flood.

1876

Roe, Abigail (C. M. Cornwall), Free, Yet Forging Their
    Own Chains, New York, Dodd, Mead and Co.
Pennsylvania coal miners strike against a ten percent wage cut. The owners of the mine are either callous or weak, but Maurice Graham, the mine superintendent, combines resoluteness with humaneness. He pleads for trust between employers and employees and succeeds in persuading Julia Earle, sister-in-law of one of the mine owners, that her social position imposes a responsibility for "stewardship" upon her. Graham wins her hand, becomes a partner in the mine. The strike is disposed of in half a sentence at the end of the novel.

1879

Arthur, Timothy Shay, The Strike at Tivoli Mills; and What
    Came of It, Philadelphia, Garrigues Bros.
A blatant temperance tract. Strikes are the result of over-indulgence in strong drink. With the money saved by temperate workers they can buy their own homes, open their own businesses and become contented, comfortably established citizens. When the Commonwealth Mills in the town of Tivoli exact a temperance pledge from all their workers, strikes cease.

Bellamy, Charles Joseph, The Breton Mills, New York, G.
    P. Putnam's Sons.
Curran, the strike leader, comes off as the most fascinating character in the novel. His power and conviction win aristocratic and snobbish Bertha Ellingsworth's love. Although she leaves him and marries Philip Breton (bigamously), it is only after Curran's death that she can at last give her wholehearted love to Breton, the ostensible hero of the novel. The strike, called in response to Ezekiel Breton's unfeeling defiance of the workers' needs, ends when Ezekiel dies and his enlightened son, Philip, takes over the mill. But another strike is in the making at the end of the novel when Philip washes his hands of the whole enterprise and goes off to Europe with Bertha.

Burnett, Frances Hodgson, Haworth's, New York, Charles

Scribner's Sons.
The authenticity of the Lancashire locale adds interest to
this novel about the rise of Jem Haworth from poorhouse
runaway to owner of a thriving foundry. The strike is fomented by the most incompetent, drunken workers in the
foundry. Haworth defies them, but loses his works anyway
because of his infatuation for aristocratic Rachel Ffrench,
who throws Haworth over for a rich French nobleman.

Denison, Thomas Stewart, An Iron Crown; a Tale of the
    Great Republic, Chicago, T. S. Denison.
The contrasted story of Tom Norwell, a rich wastrel, and
Arthur Wilson, a young man fresh from the farm. Tom
loses his fortune gambling in the stock market and ends up
a lonely man when his fiancée dies of tuberculosis. Arthur
makes a fortune in a rich gold strike, then loses it in a
panic engineered by a stock manipulator. He settles down
to a quiet country life with the young schoolteacher he marries. There are two strikes, one by miners, the other by
railroad workers, both violent and neither having much relevance to the already confused plot. The author is writing a con-
demnation of Wall Street manipulators and a warning to young
men to avoid get-rich-quick schemes. The strikes are only another example of the economic chaos Wall Street is creating.

Douglas, Amanda M., Hope Mills; or, Between Friend and
    Sweetheart, Boston, Lee and Shepard.
A plea for cooperatives, the novel contrasts a bitter strike
against unfeeling mill-owners with a strike in Jack Darcy's
cooperatively run mill. Darcy's men rally round loyally,
refuse to be misled by strike agitators. Overloaded with
propaganda for cooperatives and Christian Socialism, the
book is dull and tendentious.

1880

Aldrich, Thomas Bailey, The Stillwater Tragedy, Boston,
    Houghton, Mifflin Co.
When the workers at Slocum's Marble Yard strike for a
twenty-five cent weekly raise, the hero, Richard Shackford,
wages a clever, resourceful and determined fight against
Torrini and Durgin, the malicious strike leaders. Durgin
is revealed as the murderer of Richard's cousin and Richard
marries his boss's daughter and becomes a partner in the firm.

1884

(Hay, John), The Bread-Winners, a Social Study, New York,

Harper and Bros.
A melodramatic recreation of the 1877 railroad strike. The
hero, Arthur Farnham, defends himself and the girl he loves
against rioting strikers by organizing and equipping a private
army. Farnham succeeds in exposing Offitt, the union official, as a thief, murderer and lecher.

1885

(Keenan, Henry Francis), The Money-Makers, a Social Para-
    ble, New York, D. Appleton and Co.
Two young journalists, Archibald Hilliard and Fred Carew,
begin their careers as friends but quickly take vastly different directions. Hilliard becomes rich and famous but sacrifices his independence and integrity. Carew remains sturdily
honest as the editor of a Valedo (read Chicago) newspaper.
Carew reports a strike of anthracite coal miners truthfully
although he is fired for his efforts, but when his own printers strike against him, he hires scabs and sets type himself.
Fred is also involved in the railroad strike, editorializing
equally strongly against the capitalists and the violent unionists. At the end Hilliard is making shady deals with playboy stock manipulator Herbert Grimstone while Carew is offered a Congressional nomination which he refuses.

Leavitt, John McDowell, Kings of Capital and Knights of
    Labor for the People, New York, J. S. Willey Publishing
    Co.
An absurd novel replete with lost children, Russian princes-
ses, fires, explosions, seductions, et al. Despite the title
the book is not about the Knights of Labor. The strike at
the Alma locomotive works is fomented by Diable, a Russian
Nihilist, who turns out to be Ruric, a Russian nobleman.
John Standfast, a loyal workman, thwarts Diable's plots as
RECTITUDE and BENEVOLENCE (in blazing capitals) triumph.

1886

Dowling, George Thomas, The Wreckers, a Social Study,
    Philadelphia, J. B. Lippincott Co.
The novel recounts the long involved search of Mike Barney
for his daughter Kate, who is abducted, abandoned, adopted
by a rich woman and finally reunited years later with her
father. The strike in DeCamp's woolen mills occurs because
the owner is indifferent to the needs of his workers. His
competitor, Russell, on the other hand, is never threatened

with strikes because he establishes a reading room for his
workers where he plays checkers with them one night a week.

Foran, Martin A., The Other Side, Washington, D.C., W.
    A. Ingham.
Richard Arbyght becomes a cooper in Chicago and rescues
his long-lost sister from a fate worse than death. Richard
and his fellow workers in a pork-packing plant are incensed
by irregular paydays and outrageous prices in the company
store. Richard organizes them and leads them in a successful strike, then establishes his own manufacturing company
organized on a profit-sharing system.

Fuller, Edward, Complaining Millions of Men, New York,
    Harper and Bros.
Edward Baretta, the son of a Hungarian barber and a New
England millhand, desperately tries to make his way into
Boston society. Thwarted in his ambition, he joins forces
with some dastardly union organizers who foment a violent
strike at the South Boston Iron Works. At the end, Baretta,
now completely mad, shoots himself. The author pokes fun
at Hamlin Garland, whom he introduces into the novel as
Hamilton Wreath, an untidy, bearded, arrogant radical reformer from "the wild and woolly West."

Grant, Robert, Face to Face, New York, Charles Scribner's
    Sons.
The story of Evelyn Pimlico, a young English girl, who
comes to America determined to earn her own living. She
fortuitously inherits a great fortune and hires Andrew De
Vito to manage the Wisabel Mill. De Vito stirs up a disastrous strike but redeems himself when he dies saving the
life of Ernest Clay, an industrious inventor who believes
that the leisure class has a responsibility to improve society.
Evelyn marries Clay at the end of the novel.

Ross, Clinton, The Silent Workman, a Story, New York, G.
    P. Putnam's Sons.
Ebenezer Randall, a steel mill worker, stirs up a strike in
the mill because he blames the owner, Philip Twickenham,
for the death of his fiancée. Randall shoots Twickenham,
then runs away to live out his life as a taciturn farm worker
called "The Silent Workman." Twickenham recovers and the
strike is settled. The strike is used purely as a device
upon which to hang a sensational tale of passion and violence
with a final happy ending.

214

Stockton, Frank R. , The Hundredth Man, New York, Century
   Co.
An unusual novel for its time because it handles the strike
of restaurant waiters humorously.   The writing is vigorous
and professional with some rather brightly conceived charac-
ters--the garrulous Mrs. People, the shrewd farmer Enoch
Bullripple and the determined Martha Stull.   The strike is
not very relevant to the plot and the novel is not an important one, but it is a refreshing cut above most of the novels
employing strikes in this period.

1887

Bellamy, Edward, Looking Backward, 2000-1887, Boston,
   Ticknor and Co.
An imaginative version of a Socialist Utopia into which Julian
West awakens in 2000 A. D.   This influential novel set the
pattern for a number of succeeding Utopian novels and still
reads well.   The strikes in the Boston of 1887 are contrasted to the serene, ingeniously comfortable life in the Boston
of the year 2000.

Benjamin, Charles, The Strike in the B-- Mill; a Study,
   Boston, Ticknor and Co.
An execrably written novel which shows strikers as deluded
fools who follow false leaders and destroy not only their employers' property but their own hopes for bettering their lot.
One striker, shaken by the violence he has helped loose,
finally turns his back on unionism and recognizes that workingmen can depend only on their own hard work and the generosity of their employers.

Bishop, William Henry, The Golden Justice, Boston, Houghton, Mifflin Co.
The Golden Justice is a gilded statue above Keewaydin's City
Hall in which David Lane has hidden the evidence of his
criminal negligence in a bridge accident resulting in several
deaths.   This transparent symbolism, glittering Justice with
a criminal secret at its heart, characterizes the exposé of
political corruption with which the novel is concerned.   The
strike of longshoremen turns into a riot when Polish scabs
are sent in and serves the author as a vehicle for exhibiting
the heroism of Paul Barclay.   Barclay, the hero of the novel, who confronts and exposes Lane, fearlessly addresses
the rioting strikers and helps restore order.

215

1888

Barber, Harriet Boomer (Faith Templeton), <u>Drafted In; a</u>
  <u>Sequel to The Bread-Winners, a Social Study</u>, New York,
  Bliss Publishing Co.
A sequel to John Hay's <u>The Bread-Winners</u>, the novel carries on the story with several of the same characters.
Arthur Farnham, the anti-labor hero of Hay's book, comes
upon bad times and learns from illness, a murder indictment, and a strike against an unjustified wage cut that workers are badly treated by arrogant irresponsible employers.
Farnham becomes a convert to the cooperative movement.
Some incredibly bad writing.

1889

Tourgée, Albion W., <u>Murvale Eastman, Christian Socialist</u>,
  New York, Fords, Howard and Hulbert.
A long tedious novel in which the sincere, humanitarian
preacher hero works incognito as a horse-car driver, pleads
for the rights of the workmen and wins a strike settlement
for them from the Belt and Cross-Cut Co. He becomes in-
nocently involved in a scandal, almost loses his ministry on
a charge of heresy but is vindicated and marries a good
woman. There are interminable sermons lauding Christian
Socialism and the usual assortment of abductions, long-lost
children and bomb plots.

Warner, Charles Dudley, <u>A Little Journey in the World</u>,
  New York, Harper and Bros.
The story of a sensitive, highly moral girl, Margaret Henderson, whose marriage to a rising financier gradually dead-
ens her sensibilities as she accedes to his ruthless driving
money-making methods. The strikes, only obliquely mentioned, are attributed to the unequal distribution of wealth
and to the stock manipulations of men like tycoon Rodney
Henderson. Warner writes competently and wisely restricts
himself to characters he thoroughly understands, but as a
result the strikes and the strikers remain shadowy.

(Woods, Katherine Pearson), <u>Metzerott, Shoemaker</u>, New
  York, Thomas Y. Crowell and Co.
Weepy and sentimental, the novel describes a successful co-
operative venture which falls apart because its leader, Karl
Metzerott, has not learned to temper his Socialism with
Christianity. A member of a commune, Metzerott goes
berserk when the local mill cuts wages and strikers' families

go hungry. He whips a sullen group of strikers into fury, leads them in an attack on the mill owner and becomes an eye-witness to the death of his own son in the subsequent riot. Chastened by his son's sacrifice Metzerott becomes a pious Christian and forswears all violent action.

1890

Frederic, Harold, The Lawton Girl, New York, Charles
    Scribner's Sons.
A thoughtful attempt to show the real life in a factory town in upper New York State, the novel fails because it capitulates to contemporary literary conventions. The working class heroine is courageous, dignified and self-reliant but dies melodramatically because she has been seduced. Her seducer is portrayed as weak rather than evil. His lack of principle helps to suck him into a financial conspiracy with two scoundrels who deliberately engineer a strike in order to enable them to take over the Minster iron-works. The conspiracy is thwarted by Reuben Tracy, an upright lawyer, whom Jessica Lawton loves and for whom she sacrifices her life. There are some very well-written scenes describing Jessica's homelife with her drunken ne'er-do-well father and slatternly stepmother but the strike is neither realistic nor credible.

Howells, William Dean, A Hazard of New Fortunes, New
    York, Harper and Bros.
One of the most successful efforts of this period to use a strike creatively in a novel. The New York City street-car strike erupts into a violent attack on strikebreakers and police in which Conrad Dryfoos loses his life. The roles played by several of the characters during and after the strike reveal their real personalities: Basil March stands by helpless and indecisive; Conrad goes almost willingly to his death in order to redeem the sins of his father; Lindau, the Socialist, springs to the defense of the strikers and ultimately dies of his injuries; Jacob Dryfoos learns a bitter lesson from his son's death. No one in the novel is left untouched or unchanged by the strike.

1891

Fitch, Thomas and Anna M., Better Days: or, a Millionaire
    of To-Morrow, San Francisco, Better Days Publishing Co.
A terrible Utopian novel in which a general strike results in the death of industrialist Lorin French. Just before he

dies he realizes the necessity for cooperative factories.
His ideas are carried into effect by his heir, David Morning, who makes such a rich gold-strike that he becomes the
richest man in the world. He uses his fortune to revolu-
tionize the international economy and strikes become a thing
of the past.

McMahon, Patrick Justin, Philip; or, The Mollie's Secret,
    A Tale of the Coal Regions, Philadelphia, H. L. Kilner
    and Co.
A confused story of the evil doings of the Mollie Maguires.
Philip, of unknown parentage, turns out to be the son of
Sweeney, the mine boss. Amid fires, explosions, gun-bat-
tles and abductions James McKenna investigates the Mollies,
reveals he is McParlan, a Pinkerton detective, and brings
twenty miners to trial for murder. The strike with which
the book begins has been called in protest against severe
wage cuts but it quickly peters out. McMahon's thesis is
that the Mollie Maguires have been subverted from their
original fraternal purpose by reckless, irreligious men acting out of pure malice.

1892

Beard, Daniel Carter, Moonblight and Six Feet of Romance,
    New York, Charles L. Webster and Co.
The novel turns out to be the dream--or nightmare--of a
Pennsylvania mine owner. He learns that the mines are
owned by rapacious brutes who use murderous Pinkertons
to intimidate and incite desperate workers. The blunt honest mine superintendent Clint Butts tries to defend the strikers against the Pinkertons but when a woman is killed a
riot begins and the mine owner awakens.

Everett, Henry L., The People's Program: the Twentieth
    Century Is Theirs, New York, Workmen's Publishing Co.
An utterly disorganized, thoroughly dull Utopian novel in
which a general strike is supposed to establish George
Streeter as an international leader of men. The author becomes so involved, however, in plots for the Spanish throne,
the organization of a Peace Congress, a revivalist movement among college students and other assorted high jinks
that he loses sight of the strike completely and it quietly
expires.

McCowan, Archibald (Luke A. Hedd), Philip Meyer's Scheme,
    a Story of Trades Unionism, New York, J. S. Ogilvie.

This novel of the future, dedicated to the author of Looking Backward, hardly matches the vigor and ingenuity of Bellamy's novel. Philip Meyer's scheme, the establishment of one universal union to which all workers belong, puts an effective end to all strikes since it eliminates all strikebreakers. In 1905 a coal strike breaks down after five weeks and marks the last strike in the United States.

1893

Bishop, R. F., Camerton Slope, a Story of Mining Life, Cincinnati, Cranston and Curts; New York, Hunt and Eaton.
A novel which exposes the evil machinations of the Mollie Maguires among the Pennsylvania miners. The Mollies conspire to foment an unjustified strike and to murder the mine superintendent and those miners who oppose the Mollies. The author, a minister, advocates "extra-judicial" methods of dealing with criminal conspiracies (a kangaroo trial in the book sentences the Mollie leaders to banishment from the area). James Shryock, the town's Sunday School teacher, preaches long sermons to the miners which induce some of them to defy Pat McCoy, the union leader.

King, Charles, Foes in Ambush, Philadelphia, J. B. Lippincott Co.
From Tucson where they have been fighting off Apache raids, an army troop led by Lieutenant Drummond is assigned to Chicago to control rioting railroad strikers. Drummond and Sergeant Feeny attack the strikers with rifle butts, then shoot the strike leader who turns out to be an army deserter. A typical Western "shoot-em-up" with a completely synthetic strike background.

King, Edward, Joseph Zalmonah, Boston, Lee and Shepard.
A badly written but interesting portrayal of early struggles to organize Jewish garment workers in New York City's lower East Side. The lively Yiddish theater plays an important role in dramatizing the demands of the strikers among the immigrants. The story of Joseph Zalmonah's attraction to Bathsheba, wife of a theater violinist, is sympathetically handled. There are many descriptions (not always accurate) of Jewish religious and cultural customs. Zalmonah is an unusual character in the novels of this period--a completely sincere and dedicated union organizer.

Winslow, Helen M., Salome Shepard, Reformer, Boston,

Arena Publishing Co.
Salome Shepard, owner of the Shawsheen Mills, resents the strike in her mill but learns that the strikers' demands are justified. Salome's callous superintendent and hoodlum elements among the workers are equally responsible for stirring up trouble and the strike is settled through the efforts of Villard, the assistant superintendent of the mill, who has risen from the ranks and understands the workers. The style is treacly, the characterizations shallow and the solutions pat.

1894

Bech-Meyer, Nico, A Story from Pullmantown, Chicago, Charles H. Kerr and Co.
A puerile story of the desperate lives of the workers in Pullmantown owned by Mr. HOARD (always printed in caps in the book). A dedicated group led by Mr. Wright, a store-keeper, and including Mrs. Wright, Mark Wallace, a painter, and Miss Kean, a secretary, begins to organize the Pullmantown workers. The novel ends as the first strike in Pullmantown's history begins.

Foote, Mary Hallock, Coeur d'Alène, Boston, Houghton, Mifflin Co.
An early Western with much gunplay and horsemanship. The strike is a vicious conspiracy by the union, headquartered in Butte, which stirs up the more skilled copper miners to demand a raise. The union meets its match in Jack Darcie, who eventually reveals that he is really John Darcie Hamilton, the son of one of the mine owners. Jack wins the hand of pure, lovely, courageous Faith Bingham and the strike ends when troops arrive to rescue the beleaguered mine owner.

Ford, Paul Leicester, The Honorable Peter Stirling and What People Thought of Him, New York, Henry Holt and Co.
A political novel which shows Peter Stirling's development from a taciturn, socially inept young lawyer to a powerful political figure. When a railroad strike breaks out, Peter, a colonel in the militia, protects the strikebreakers and brings them safely through an attack by a mob of ten thousand (!) enraged strikers. Ponderously overwritten, the novel ends with Peter happily married and newly elected Governor of New York, a living example of the positive value of political bossism when the boss is a man of integrity.

Sheldon, Charles M., The Crucifixion of Phillip Strong,
Chicago, A. C. McClurg and Co.
An extended sermon. Phillip Strong, a dedicated clergyman,
tries to live as Christ might have in a large manufacturing
town. Phillip is against the strike but deeply moved by the
desperate conditions of the factory workers. He wins the
loyal support of the mill workers by his defense of their
demands and succeeds in moving the hard hearts of a few
of his rich parishioners. The strike on its way to settlement, Phillip dies at the foot of the cross in his church.

1895

Prince, Helen Choate, The Story of Christine Rochefort,
Boston, Houghton, Mifflin Co.
Christine Rochefort is the bored wife of Gaston, the owner
of a chocolate factory in Blois. She is attracted to the anarchist, Paul de Martel, and sides with him when he stirs
the workers up to strike. Christine comes to her senses
when a mob of hungry strikers attacks her house. Paul is
killed by a maddened striker and Christine and Gaston realize they are still deeply in love with each other. The locale is unusual in this period, but the buckets of sentimental
tears and the melodramatic plot are quite typical.

Rood, Henry Edward, The Company Doctor, an American
Story, New York, Merriam Co.
The strike in a Pennsylvania anthracite mine is described
from the point of view of Malcolm Curtis, the company doctor. The dreaded secret Mollie Maguires are believed to
be at the bottom of the violent riots, during which an armed
priest on horseback singlehandedly stops an infuriated mob
and armed guards, called Hawkeyes, protect the strikebreakers. Curtis marries the daughter of the mine owner and
they leave the minefields. Curtis blames unrest and violence
among miners on unchecked immigration.

Scott, Milton R., Ernest Marble, the Labor Agitator, Newark, Ohio, Tribune Book Print.
Ernest Marble is the minister of a rich church in the company town of Penrose. He sympathizes with the railroad
car workers' strike even though Andrew Penrose, the owner
of the company, is an important contributor to his church.
Marble resigns from the church when the strike fails, goes
to work among the poor and is ultimately rewarded for his
idealism when Penrose realizes his worth and Ernest marries his daughter Lucy. Another Christian Socialist tract,

221

the novel is really one long boring sermon.

1896

King, Charles, <u>An Army Wife,</u> New York, F. Tennyson
    Neely.
Randy Merriam, a U.S. army officer at Fort Sedgwick, is
detailed to strike duty, protecting struck railroad trains to
ensure the movement of the U.S. mails.   He engages in
combat with strike rioters, foils some Mexican bandits,
rescues fair ladies from predatory Apaches.   All ends
well, and who really cares?

King, Charles, <u>A Tame Surrender; a Story of the Chicago</u>
    <u>Strike</u>, Philadelphia, J. B. Lippincott Co.
Charles King, himself an army officer, made a career of
producing novels about the gallant role of the U.S. Army in
Western outposts.   In this one Captain Floyd Forrest tangles
with Socialists during the Chicago Pullman strike of 1894.
King makes no secret of his contempt for strikers, foreigners, socialists and all who "preach sedition and rebellion. "
His hero is the U.S. Army and Forrest its living embodi-
ment.   Forrest courageously "holds misguided, drink-crazed,
demogogue-excited mobs at bay, " rescues distressed damsels,
and receives a promotion in rank and the love of a good
woman as reward.   Admiration for the discipline and order
of the Army prompts one of King's characters to recommend
that all workers be regularly enlisted--and charged with desertion when they quit or mutiny when they strike.

Smith, Francis Hopkinson, <u>Tom Grogan</u>, Boston, Houghton,
    Mifflin Co.
Tom Grogan is a most unconventional heroine in this syrupy
novel.   She is a Staten Island stevedore, running her own
company and supporting an invalid husband, a teen-age
daughter and a crippled son.   Tom defies the union and the
corrupt walking delegate but finally agrees to settle the
strike in order to spare the strikers' families suffering.

1897

Lush, Charles K. , <u>The Federal Judge</u>, Boston, Houghton,
    Mifflin Co.
Tracy Dunn is a firm, incorruptible and stubborn man but
he gradually falls under the influence of Elliot Gardwell,
head of the Trans-American Railroad, to whom he owes his
appointment as a Federal judge.   When the railroad workers

strike, Gardwell exacts a Federal injunction order from
Dunn. At the end of the novel Dunn recognizes that he has
been duped and denounces the corrupting influence of the
corporations before resigning from the bench. The novel
is too obvious, but there are interesting glimpses of the relationships between the world of high finance and the judici-
ary.

Morris, Henry O. , Waiting for the Signal, Chicago, Schulte
    Publishing Co.
John Stearns, an active member of the Seamen's Union, is
killed during a strike. His son becomes a reporter on a
Chicago muckraking newspaper and the novel zooms into
prophecy. After President McKinley's election a series of
strikes leads to an almost bloodless revolution and the establishment of the Universal Brotherhood of Man. This is
hardly a novel, more a string of speeches, lectures, sermons and predictions, all dull.

1898

Hamblen, Herbert Elliott, The General Manager's Story:
    Old-Time Reminiscences of Railroading in the United
    States, New York, Macmillan Co.
The author's descriptions of railroaders' work, lives and
jargon are authentic and interesting; the story much less
so. The narrator tries desperately to keep the men from
striking but is defeated by the railroad company's stubborn
refusal to negotiate. The strike is broken and M--, the
narrator, starts at the bottom again as a pick-and-shovel
man. He works his way up the ladder until he is appointed
general manager of the railroad line. When a strike breaks
out, he puts his knowledge to good use. He breaks the
strike by utilizing blacklists, strikebreakers, intimidation
and force. The novel is naively honest and preaches no
morals.

1899

McCardell, Roy L. , The Wage Slaves of New York, New
    York, G. W. Dillingham Co.
A ridiculous novel with no redeeming feature except for the
social historian. The strikers ask for a share of the profits in a New York silk mill and help the real but defrauded
owner of the mill, Arthur Barrison, to regain his inheritance. He reorganizes the factory as a "Socialistic experiment" and all is sweetness and light.

Cherouny, Henry W., The Burial of the Apprentice, New
    York, Cherouny Printing and Publishing Co.
An utterly inept religious tract, only faintly disguised as a
novel. The apprentice printer, Charlie, attends Sunday
School and works hard but is led astray by his German anarchist father and his father's trade union cronies. Charlie
joins the printers when they strike, quickly contracts a gal-
loping case of consumption, and dies. His father, realizing
his guilt, goes mad.

Converse, Florence, The Burden of Christopher, Boston,
    Houghton, Mifflin Co.
Christopher Kenyon runs his shoe-factory on a profit-sharing
plan and supports the striking workers of the competitive
Watson Company where the workers are underpaid and without the protection of a union. When it is discovered that
Christopher has misused a trust fund he administers, he
commits suicide. The novel is talky and very slow-moving.
Christopher, an advocate of Socialism, is portrayed as a
victim of the competitiveness and ruthlessness of capitalism.
Although there are a few scenes in the shoe factory itself,
the novel focuses on the Kenyons rather than on the strikers.

Dreiser, Theodore, Sister Carrie, New York, Doubleday,
    Page and Co.
An important American novel. Carrie's rise from factory
girl to successful actress, her matter-of-fact liaisons with
several men and the authentic pictures of Chicago and New
York make use of material completely new to American fiction in 1900. Dreiser also uses a strike as a powerful literary device. Hurstwood, already demoralized by his theft of
money from his employers in order to carry on his affair
with Carrie, becomes a strikebreaker during a violent streetcar strike in New York. His decision marks the final turn-
ing-point in his moral disintegration. Hurstwood recognizes
that he is a defeated man, contemptible even to the police-
man assigned to guard him. Dreiser has created memorable
characters in the novel, dealt with important philosophical
themes and used a strike to dramatize his ideas without
preaching at his readers.

Herrick, Robert, The Web of Life, New York, Macmillan
    Co.
Herrick is a thoughtful and close observer of the Chicago scene.
He uses the Pullman strike as the objective counterpart for

the disintegrating hope and pride of Dr. Harold Sommers.
The hopeless love affair between Sommers and tarnished,
neurotic Alves Preston is movingly unfolded against the
background of the defeated strike but Herrick's style is
clumsy and the novel peters out irresolutely.

Myers, Cortland, Would Christ Belong to a Labor Union?
    or, Henry Fielding's Dream, New York, Street and Smith.
"Yes, " says the novel, "Christ would join a union but he
would not force anyone else to join. " An extended sermon
on the responsibilities of the Church toward oppressed workers. When Reverend David Dowling proves (by very long
sermons) that he supports labor's legitimate demands, he
is elected an honorary union member by the striking streetcar workers and Henry Fielding, who has been doubting the
church, becomes one of Dowling's parishioners, marries a
rich wife, and establishes a factory which he runs on true
Christian principles without strikes.

1901

Daniels, Gertrude Potter, The Warners; an American Story
    of Today, Chicago, Jamieson and Higgins Co.
Cyrus Warner is a quiet hard-working dependable factory
worker with a loving wife until he is misled by the malicious
agitator Kirby and his termagant of a mistress, Ida Fisher.
They deliberately foment a bloody strike as part of their plot
to make the United States a Socialist state. Kirby and Ida,
carrying their young son, lead the strikers in a head-on
clash with the police. The bomb they explode kills the boy
and Kirby goes to prison for a long term. Cyrus has
learned his lesson. Even when he confronts the seducer of
his daughter, Cyrus is unable to bring himself to use violence. Atrociously written, The Warners shows some knowledge of working class life but absolutely none of strikes or
trade unions.

Freeman, Mary E. Wilkins, The Portion of Labor, New
    York, Harper and Bros.
Ellen Brewster, daughter of a shoe-factory worker, grows
up among poverty and ignorance but manages to graduate
from high-school. Despite an offer of help from rich Cyn-
thia Lennox, Ellen goes to work in the shoe factory and becomes active in the strike which breaks out when wages are
cut ten percent. As the strike drags on, Ellen realizes she
was wrong and returns to work, defying the desperate strikers. The strike is lost and Ellen eventually marries Robert
Lloyd, the nephew of the factory owner. The moral of the

story is that "labor is not for silver and gold but for the growth in character of the laborer. " The novel founders badly. It is ineptly written with precious little character in it and less growth.

Friedman, Isaac Kahn, By Bread Alone, New York, McClure, Phillips and Co.
Blair Carrhart becomes a minister in a rich Chicago church but leaves to go to work at the North-Western Rolling Mills, owned by his fiancée's father. Carrhart leads the workers when they go out on strike. He is beset, on the one hand, by the employers who use strikebreakers and martial law against the strikers and, on the other, by the violent anarchist movement exemplified by the chemist La Vette and the passionate Sophia Goldstein. The workers win a few concessions but the strike is lost. Blair is reunited with his fiancée, Evangeline Marvin, and leaves the factory determined to run for the Senate and fight for Socialist legislation. The plot is full of creaky anachronisms and incredible melodrama, and the author veers between pity and contempt for factory workers.

Kester, Vaughan, The Manager of the B and A, New York, Harper and Bros.
Dan Oakley, a tough two-fisted railroad man, is appointed general manager of the Buckhorn and Antioch Railroad. During a strike against a ten percent pay cut he stands firm against the strikers' demands but refuses to bring in scabs and is fired by the owner. He proves himself, however, by singlehandedly running a relief train into a town isolated by a forest fire and becomes general manager of Consolidated Railroad in New York. Hurrah!

Merwin, Samuel and Henry Kitchell Webster, Calumet "K", New York, Macmillan Co.
The strike in the two million bushel grain elevator under construction in this novel is organized by the unscrupulous walking delegate, Grady, and opposed by the vigorous young foreman, Charlie Bannon. It ends when the A. F. L. district leadership replaces Grady and workers and management combine to finish the elevator in time to meet contract obligations. The novel is strictly for popular consumption but some of the construction techniques are described quite vividly.

Carryl, Guy Wetmore, <u>The Lieutenant-Governor</u>, Boston,
 Houghton, Mifflin and Co.
The mill strike in this novel is fomented by the labor boss,
McGrath, with the active connivance of the Democratic Governor, Elijah Abbot, of "Alleghania," elected by a labor-re-
form coalition. Peter Rathbawne, owner of the struck mill,
stubbornly resists any attempts by labor to dictate how he
runs his mill. John Barclay, the Lieutenant Governor, opposes Abbot's policies. When Abbot is shot, Barclay calls
out the troops, declares martial law and breaks the strike.
There are no subtleties in this novel. Characters are all
good or all bad. The only way to oppose malicious labor
agitators is by strict adherence to law and order, rugged
individualism, duty and responsibility.

Garland, Hamlin, <u>Hesper</u>, New York, Harper and Bros.
A formula-ridden story of a Western gold-miners' strike led
by Jack Munro, a cashiered West Pointer. The hero, Rob
Raymond, is an independent miner who overpowers Munro
and delivers him up to the U.S. Cavalry who restore order.
Rob marries his rich New York lady-love, Ann Rupert, when
she realizes the rugged West is superior to effete New York.

Nason, Frank Lewis, <u>The Blue Goose</u>, New York, McClure,
 Phillips and Co.
The novel begins with an auctorial lecture against labor unions. It depicts a gold miners' strike in Colorado connived
at by the labor agitator, Patrick Morison, and Pierre La
Martine, owner of the Blue Goose saloon and gambling hall.
A shipment of gold bullion is hijacked, armed strikebreakers
clash with strikers, La Martine and Morison are killed.
Firmstone, superintendent of the mine who remains firm as
a stone against the strikers, succeeds in routing them and
chasing them out of the area.

Scudder, Vida D., <u>A Listener in Babel</u>, Boston, Houghton,
 Mifflin Co.
Hilda Lathrop is contrasted with her lifelong friend, Dorothy
Ferguson. Hilda, a spinster, has dedicated herself to work
in Langley House, a slum settlement. She becomes intimately involved in the planning of a local strike. Eventually she
decides to devote herself even more closely to the workers
by becoming a factory worker herself. Dorothy has married
the man Hilda loves, is raising two fine children yet feels
lonely and lost. She envies Hilda's sense of mission and

her busy, happy life. The novel is stuffed with interminable intellectual discussions and simplistic analyses of current economics. The workers' lives and the strikers' struggles are only talked about, never shown. The reader comes away with the feeling that Hilda will be more trouble than help to her fellow factory workers.

Swift, Morrison I., The Monarch Billionaire, New York, J. S. Ogilvie Co.
An atrocious novel in which Giles Wyndon, owner of the Amalgamated Fish, Ship, Iron, Transportation, Coal and Steel Company (honest!) discharges several employees because they don't greet him one morning and precipitates a strike. "Giles, to minimize the instructiveness of the revolt, hastily received the discharged men back and for that time ended the industrial rebellion and lowering cataclysm." So much for the strike. More than half of the book consists of long discourses on capital, labor, economics and politics --dull, dull, dull.

Wilson, Anne Florence, The Wars of Peace, Boston, Little, Brown and Co.
Theodore Harding uses reason and moderation to win over the strikers in his father's mill. He breaks decisively with his father when Harding, Sr. becomes one of the organizers of a developing trust. Theodore sets up his own small mill, determined to oppose concentration of power in the American Combine. When his father's workers strike over a twenty percent wage cut, Theodore and his fiancée help the strikers. The Combine hires an agitator to blow up Theodore's mill. He is badly hurt in the explosion but rescued by the millworkers. His father learns his lesson and dies a broken man. Mostly drivel.

1904

Overton, Gwendolen, Captains of the World, New York, Macmillan Co.
Neil Manning, a steel worker at the Bessemer mill owned by Alan Tennant, wrecks his chances for advancement out of the ranks and for marrying Tennant's daughter, Beatrice, by becoming an active union member. Throughout the strike which soon breaks out, Manning insists on the necessity for unions but opposes all forms of violence. The strike defeated, Manning leaves the state but rises rapidly in the union until he is elected president. His adamant position against chicanery and violence and for the establishment

of an arbitration board finally wins the support of a majority
of the workers and Manning marries the by now orphaned,
impoverished and chastened Beatrice Tennant.   The novel
is trite, syrupy, unbelievable.

<u>1905</u>

Brenholtz, Edwin Arnold, <u>The Recording Angel</u>, Chicago,
    Charles H. Kerr and Co.
The steel mill strike in this novel begins when the workers
refuse to be addressed by numbers instead of names.   Led
by Charles Arndt the thirty thousand strikers follow a course
of nonviolence despite desperate provocations by the management of the mill.   The novel is full of ridiculous coinciden-
ces and unbelievable plot devices.   Arndt is a dedicated
Socialist and regards the union and the strike as temporary
steps toward an imminent worldwide Socialist victory.

French, Alice (Octave Thanet), <u>The Man of the Hour</u>
    Indianapolis, Bobbs-Merrill Co.
This one is a real dilly with a schizophrenic hero, John/
Ivan Winslow, who has trouble deciding whether he is the
son of his Russian Nihilist princess mother or his self-
made New England capitalist father.   He begins by leading
some mischievous strikes and flirting with Socialism.   Finally, he finds himself during a steel strike when he organizes Negro strikebreakers, intimidates the strikers by
threats and violence and succeeds in breaking the strike.
"The Anglo-Saxon in me has conquered, " he exults and
shouting the Harvard battle-cry (so help me!) he leads the
way for the National Guard, inherits his father's factory
and marries his childhood sweetheart.

Herrick, Robert, <u>The Memoirs of an American Citizen,</u>
    New York, Macmillan Co.
An interesting novel portraying the rise of meat-packing tycoon, Van Harrington, from obscurity to riches.   Harrington
is involved in two strikes.   He serves on the jury of the
Haymarket Anarchists' trial which grows out of the McCormick Reaper strike and he later breaks a strike in one of his
own plants.   Harrington is unhampered by ethical scruples
and convinces himself that the country needs strong, forceful men if it is to expand and develop.

Scott, Leroy, <u>The Walking Delegate,</u> New York, Doubleday,
    Page and Co.
The rather touching story of Tom Keating, a skilled construc-

tion worker (in the days when they earned three dollars a day), who learns trade unionism through painful experience. Tom opposes the corrupt walking delegate, Buck Foley, who has used his position in the union to line his own pockets. Tom's pathetic love affair with a sympathetic secretary and his tremendous struggle to retain integrity in the midst of graft and corruption are honestly, if somewhat sentimentally, portrayed. Although overdrawn, the novel is an early example of realism in the labor novel. Union meetings, the life of the walking delegate, struggles to make unions democratic, and behind-the-scenes strike negotiations are well reported although Scott's style is undistinguished and his plot overcomplicated.

Van Vorst, Marie, Amanda of the Mill, New York, Dodd, Mead and Co.
An early picture of the devasting effects on Blue Ridge mountain people when they move to Southern cotton mill towns. The author knows her people--their dialect, their folkways, their poverty and their pathetic efforts to organize unions in secret. Her hero, walking delegate Henry Euston, is a barely reformed drunkard married to a slattern. Unfortunately her heroine Amanda is too good to be true and Mrs. Vorst has been unable to resist stock melodramatic devices. Amanda becomes the protégé of a rich lady who finances her education, Euston is revealed as the long-lost son of the millowner, the lovers are reunited when the dam breaks. But the descriptions of the organization of the mill strikes, smashed again and again, and of the lives of the cotton mill workers ring true.

Wright, James North, Where Copper Was King, Boston, Small, Maynard and Co.
Young Clarence Hayden becomes manager of a Wisconsin copper mine in 1865 and meets his first challenge when the miners strike for higher wages. He refuses to deal with them and defies Dick Jeffrey, the Cornish spokesman of the union delegation. The strike ends when it is revealed that Jeffrey had planned to dynamite the mine. The author knows mining and the Northern woods well and includes some detailed descriptions of mine workings, forest fires and a rescue from a mine fire.

1906

Sinclair, Upton, The Jungle, New York, Doubleday, Page and Co.

An authentic classic still as fresh and vigorous as it was in 1906 when it led to reforms in the Pure Food and Drug Laws. Sinclair's descriptions of the lives of Chicago stockyard workers at home and on the job are shocking and compelling. The strike is used masterfully to educate Jurgis Rudkis, the sturdy hero. When he agrees to become a scab, the company uses his natural talents to lead and organize the strikebreakers. As a worker, he is given only the most disgusting and backbreaking jobs in the stockyard. For Jurgis the strike is his introduction to Socialism as a solution to the labor problem.

1907

Friedman, Isaac Kahn, The Radical, New York, D. Appleton and Co.
The radical of the novel is Bruce McAllister, who is elected to Congress by the Chicago Democratic machine, then turns on his bosses by fighting for enlightened labor legislation. During a series of crippling and violent strikes McAllister deplores the violence but insists that "the altar fires of Law and Order must not be fed with the substance and the life blood of his people" (a pretty fair example of Friedman's turgid prose). Eventually McAllister resigns from the Senate intending to devote himself to organizing labor into a political force.

Hurt, Walter, The Scarlet Shadow; a Story of the Great Colorado Conspiracy, Gerard, Kansas, The Appeal to Reason.
Based on the violent Cripple Creek, Colorado miners' strike and the subsequent trial of Bill Haywood and other leaders of the Western Federation of Miners, this novel weaves actual and fictional events together into a wild mélange of murders, kidnappings, conspiracies and suicides. The author is sympathetic to the striking miners, but with such a friend, they don't need enemies.

London, Jack, The Iron Heel, New York, Macmillan Co.
A disturbingly prescient description of the rise of a Fascist-like dictatorship in the United States. Ernest Everhard and his wife, Avis, fight against the rise of the Iron Heel and, as guerillas, when the dictatorship takes over the country. The new order begins after a series of disastrous strikes in the course of which the labor movement is decisively smashed. Although the novel is unrestrained, the writing is forceful. The story moves swiftly and delivers a still shocking impact.

McMahon, John R. , Toilers and Idlers, New York, Wilshire
    Book Co.
Otis Rensen, bored young owner of a foundry, takes a job
as a laborer in the mill unknown to the other workers. He
becomes interested in their lives and welfare and supports
them when they decide to strike. Two anarchists, Zienski
and Sonia Sofronsky, precipitate a riot. When it is over,
Rensen reveals his identity and reorganizes the works as
the Brotherhood Foundry. He has become a fervent Socialist dedicated to reforming the whole society. Another naive,
badly written tract.

Teller, Charlotte, The Cage, New York, D. Appleton and
    Co.
Anne Forester leaves her well-to-do home to do social work
on Chicago's West Side, She falls in love with a Socialist
minister and both of them become deeply involved in a lumber workers' strike. The strike has estranged lumber mill
owner, Alexander Sloane, from his son who supports the
strikers. Sloane and his son are reunited during the trial
of the Haymarket anarchists when Sloane, Sr. contributes
money for their defense. The plot is fantastically complicated, the characters uniformly wooden and the final outcome predictably unreal.

                            1908

Eddy, Arthur Jerome, Ganton & Co. , Chicago, A. A. Mc-
    Clurg and Co.
Ganton & Co. is a Chicago meat-packing plant troubled by
union agitators who are trying to stir up a strike. Corrupt
union leaders have been terrorizing the meat-packers with
strike threats in order to collect bribes from the owners.
Young Allan Borlan, one of the meat-packers, decides to
fight back and defy the union. Despite vacillating factory-
owners, venal unionists and busybody settlement workers
Borlan stands firm. His absolute refusal to submit to arbitration finally puts some spine into the other meat-packers and the strike is broken. The author does not hide his
admiration for tough old John Ganton, not above dishonesty
when he can get away with it, shrewd and a complete individualist. By the end of the novel, however, Ganton is
dying of cancer, and the old robber barons are giving way
to a new breed of factory-owners. Allan Borlan, who might
have carried on the Ganton tradition, sells out his plant (for
a tidy sixteen million dollars), and it is evident that the
capitalists will be doing business with the unions.

Pidgin, Charles Felton, Labor; or, the Money-God! Which?
    A Story of the Times, Boston, Mayhew Publishing Co.
Myrtle Melton, granddaughter of a textile millowner, works
with Captain Dudley, superintendent of the mill and a captain in the militia, to keep an explosive labor situation from
breaking out into the open. They are helped by Tom Potter,
one of the millworkers, but the strike erupts and the mill is
set on fire. With the arrival of Dudley's militiamen, however, the strike is settled and Myrtle and Dudley run the
mill peaceably. The book is incredibly bad with some of
the worst writing imaginable. It pleads for "a more equitable distribution of the results of capital and labor" presumably through the generosity of enlightened capitalists.

Walter, Eugene, Paid in Full, New York, G. W. Dillingham
    Co.
The author is really not interested in the strike or in the
strikers. He uses it merely as a device to contrast Jim
Smith, the intrepid superintendent of the Latin-American
Steamship Line, with bluff, ruthless Captain Amos Williams,
President of the Line, and weak, dishonest Joe Brooks, ac-
countant for the firm. Williams absolutely refuses to negotiate with his employees, Brooks embezzles sixteen thousand dollars from the firm while Smith faces down the striking longshoremen. When he announces that he has enlisted
an army of three thousand strikebreakers and is prepared
to use them, the longshoremen capitulate and Smith's honesty
and decisiveness are vindicated.

1909

Dixon, Thomas, Jr. , Comrades, New York, Doubleday,
    Page and Co.
The novel portrays an attempt to set up a Socialist communal
experiment on the island of Ventura, California. Trouble
breaks out among the Socialists over unequal pay rates, and
the farmers of the settlement strike against the skilled
craftsmen. The strike is settled amicably by vote but the
community falls apart anyway because of the lechery of its
leader, Herman Wolf.

Page, Thomas Nelson, John Marvel, Assistant, New York,
    Charles Scribner's Sons.
The intermingled lives of three college classmates: Henry
Glave, the narrator, who becomes a lawyer; Leo Wolffert,
who becomes a social worker; and John Marvel, who becomes a minister. Glave is a dilettante stock speculator

who gradually becomes committed to social reform under
the influence of Marvel and Wolffert. A violent streetcar
strike convinces Glave that unions are necessary but that
they have to be held in check. Wolffert is killed during the
strike and Marvel devotes his life to a ministry among the
poor. The novel is extremely long and tiresome. There is
little real understanding of the lives of workers, and John
Marvel is too saintly to be believed. Social issues are
touched upon but resolved sentimentally and unrealistically.

1910

Cullum, Ridgwell, The Trail of the Axe, New York, A. L.
    Burt Co.
The strike of lumberjacks in Red Sand Valley, Canada gives
the hero of this badly-written outdoor novel a chance to show
off his great physical courage and strength of character.
His readiness with his fists and his knowledge of the men
who work for him win for Dave not only the heart of Betty
Somers but also the loyalty of his men who abandon the
strike when Dave promises them a bonus at the end of the
logging season.

Jackson, Charles Tenney, My Brother's Keeper, Indianapolis,
    Bobbs, Merrill Co.
Based vaguely on the Cripple Creek, Colorado strike this
rambling novel uses many of the outworn clichés of the
period--bomb-throwing foreign agitators, a long-lost brother,
dynamite plots and assassination. The novel spins intricate
connections among Demetra, married to Corbett Ennisley,
and Herford Rand, son of the struck plant's owner. Rand
is killed during the strike and the estranged Corbett and
Demetra are reunited.

Malkiel, Theresa Serber, Diary of a Shirtwaist Striker, New
    York, Co-operative Press.
So naive that it becomes charming, this supposed diary
shows Mary's development from a thoughtless flibbertygibbet
into an earnest union member who suffers hunger, fatigue
and even jailing for the cause. Mary's steadfastness eventually wins the strike and persuades Jim, Mary's stubborn
fiancé, that she is right.

1911

Kauffman, Reginald Wright, The House of Bondage, New
    York, Moffat, Yard and Co.

An expose of the white slave traffic, melodramatic and sentimental. The strike of shirtwaist workers drives Carrie Berkowicz into prostitution.

Oppenheim, James, The Nine-Tenths, New York, Harper and Bros.
Joe Blaine runs a weekly labor paper, The Nine-Tenths, which prints labor news excluded from the commercial press. His partner, Sally Heffer, becomes involved in a garment strike and Joe agrees to let the strikers use his home as their headquarters. Myra Craig, the schoolteacher whom Joe loves, learns from the strike to discard her snobbishness toward the working class. When the strike ends, Myra and Joe marry, resolved to continue their dedication to the labor movement.

Phillips, David Graham, The Conflict, New York, D. Appleton and Co.
Victor Dorn, Socialist crusader and editor of The New Day, a Socialist paper, leads the fight for election of a reform mayor. A bitter streetcar strike breaks out during the campaign and Dorn exposes the intricate web of bibery and corruption among union leaders, party bosses and weak-kneed reform candidates. Phillips knows the political arena but his writing is undistinguished and his characters unrealized.

1912

Converse, Florence, The Children of Light, Boston, Houghton, Mifflin Co.
A naive plea for Socialism centering about a mayoralty campaign. A strike of women garment-workers serves to differentiate Lucian Emery and Llewellyn Evans, the Socialists, from Tristram Lawrence, the reform candidate. Emery and Evans put up an active and determined fight for their beliefs but the cynical Lawrence caves in when the election fight becomes intense and is willing to compromise his ideals. The strike escalates into a general strike. When it is broken, Emery goes to prison but Lawrence has been exposed as a double-dealer, a liar and a tool of reaction.

1913

Bullard, Arthur (Albert Edwards), Comrade Yetta, New York, Macmillan Co.
The rise of Yetta Rayefsky from garment-worker to Socialist

leader. Some of the strike scenes in the garment industry
are taken from actual events and Yetta's sympathetic portrayal is somewhat unusual for the period, but the author's
earnest advocacy of the oppressed does not overcome his
lack of skill as a novelist.

Farnum, Mabel A., The Cry of the Street, Boston, Angel
  Guardian Press.
A nonsensical story about Austin Bellingham, a lawyer involved in the Lawrence textile strike of 1912, who finds his
true love in Jacqueline Recamier, a beautiful mill worker.
The leader of the strike turns out to be Bellingham's long-
lost brother. At the end, the strike leader is converted
from Socialism and all ends happily in the peal of merry
wedding bells.

Kauffman, Reginald Wright, The Spider's Web, New York,
  Moffat, Yard and Co.
A completely unsuccessful attempt to picture capitalism as a
vast threatening spider's web which entangles and destroys
mankind. Luke Huber, a crusading lawyer, tries to smash
the web but is caught in it and is killed at the end. The
author is obsessed with violence, almost visibly licks his
chops during a vivid rape scene. He uses the strike primarily as a convenient way to show strikers and strikebreakers locked in violent conflict.

London, Jack, Valley of the Moon, New York, Macmillan
  Co.
A long novel full of London's personal crotchets but interesting for the first half because it presents an authentic picture of working class life. The Oakland teamster's strike
in which the hero, Billy Roberts, takes an active part is
realistically described. London is less successful with his
descriptions of a Carmel artists' colony and the Sonoma
Valley wanderings of Billy and his wife Saxon.

1914

Jay, Junius, Open-Air Politics and the Conversion of Governor Soothem, Boston, Houghton Mifflin Co.
While Governor Soothem is on a hunting trip in the remote
wooded back country a group of fantastic unions (the Brotherhood of Expert Woodsmen and the Confederate Company of
Complete Cooks, for example) call a general strike and plot
assassinations, sabotage and anarchy. The Governor changes
his conciliatory tactics, calls out the troops and restores
order.

1915

Poole, Ernest, The Harbor, New York, Macmillan Co.
A thoughtful, occasionally moving novel recounting the spiritual education of the narrator.   From a sheltered sensitive boy Bill grows into a competent reporter married to a charming rich girl.   He is pushed inexorably into close contact with the lives of the workers in New York harbor and eventually into active participation in a bitterly contested general strike.   Out of the hunger, brutality and sheer incompetence Bill encounters among the striking workers he nevertheless extracts a deeper meaning: the strike is only an early portent of a brighter future for all men, a future they will build for themselves through their collective action.

1916

Anderson, Sherwood, Windy McPherson's Son, New York,
John Lane Co.
Sam McPherson overcomes the disadvantages of a shiftless, incompetent father and an overworked, uneducated mother to become rich and powerful but he fails to find any real meaning in life.   Anderson leaves the problem unsolved although he suggests through Sam's participation in a garment worker's strike that accepting responsibility gives depth and meaning to an individual's life.

Deland, Margaret, The Rising Tide, New York, Harper and
Bros.
The energetic society heroine of this infantile love story realizes during her participation in a rubber strike that in true love lies a woman's real happiness.   Brave, stubborn and headstrong Freddy Payton is tamed by her strike experience into a good and contented wife.

Swafford, Charles Carroll, The Silent Conflict; a Story of
Industrial Warfare, Boston, Roxburgh Publishing Co.
Luke Darrell, hero of this melodramatic and preachy novel, pleads for rational behavior by the oppressed coal miners. When the strike breaks out, Luke serves as the workers' spokesman and is badly hurt when the mine is blown up. He becomes superintendent of the mine and is later elected to the Pennsylvania state legislature, where he fights for enlightened labor legislation.   The novel is full of auctorial lectures on tariffs, the irresponsible press, the educational system and "man's inhumanity to man. "

237

Anderson, Sherwood, Marching Men, New York, John Lane
Co.
Beaut McGregor's tormented search for order and beauty
after his early years in an ugly, strike-torn mining town.
In the rhythmic disciplined ranks of the Marching Men whom
Beaut (what a nickname!) organizes he finds a harmonious
collective which he contrasts to the irrational and ineffective
violence of a tumultuous teamsters' strike. A thoughtful
novel but Anderson leaves unresolved the questions it raises.
The vague goals of the Marching Men make it a disturbing,
rather than a harmonious organization.

Cahan, Abraham, The Rise of David Levinsky, New York,
Harper and Bros.
A thoroughly believable portrait of a young Jewish immigrant
who starts in the clothing industry, saves and borrows
enough money to begin his own business. By ruthless exploitation of his employees and by driving himself mercilessly Levinsky becomes a rich but lonely, disillusioned man.
Strike follows strike in the garment industry and David uses
all his native shrewdness to defeat them.

Churchill, Winston, The Dwelling-Place of Light, New York,
Macmillan Co.
Janet Bumpus joins the infuriated strikers at Chippering Mill
in New England solely because she is wildly vindictive
against the mill owner who has seduced and betrayed her.
Ditmar, the mill owner, is killed by the strikers and the
strike ends. Janet is helped back to serenity by her friendship with the philosophical writer, Insall. She dies relatively resigned and contented. A superficial and badly written
novel.

Pier, Arthur Stanwood, Jerry, Boston, Houghton, Mifflin Co.
Jerry Donohue, a young steel worker, joins the militia and
patrols the mill when a strike is called against the twelve-
hour day. In the fight that develops between strikers and
strikebreakers Jerry's sympathies veer between the contending groups. The rest of the novel is concerned with Jerry's
rapid rise, first on the police force and then as an Assistant
District Attorney when Jerry fights political corruption. The
novel is a poor one, notable only for its sympathetic picture
of working class life.

Sinclair, Upton, King Coal, New York, Macmillan Co.

The adventures of Hal Warner, a young college student, in
a series of coal-mining jobs.   Hal develops a warm sympathy for the miners and becomes a close friend of the union organizer who is secretly signing the men up into the
union.   Although Hal is the son of a coal magnate he supports
the miners when they strike.   The strike is lost but union
organization among the miners continues.   There are a few
vigorously written scenes but this is not one of Sinclair's
best efforts.

1918

Webster, Henry Kitchell, An American Family, Indianapolis,
    Bobbs-Merrill Co.
Written in a competent forthright style this novel has some
interesting sections but bogs down in an overlong, overcomplicated plot.   Hugh Corbett tries to influence his grandfather, his father and his brother to run their wagon factory
with some intelligent concern for the welfare of their workers.   Anarchists in the plant stir up a strike and when
Hugh's grandfather dies, both sides freeze into intransigent
positions.   So far, so good.   But then Hugh is attracted to
Helena Golicz, one of the strike leaders.   He marries her
and she leads him a merry chase until he discovers that
she is sexually shameless (she enjoys intercourse with Hugh)
and a German agent to boot.   A lover kills her and Hugh is
free to turn his factory to full-scale war production.

1919

Byrne, Donn, The Stranger's Banquet, New York, Harper
    and Bros.
A trashy work liberally sprinkled with Gothic elements, anti-
Semitism, xenophobia and utterly incredible characters.
During the shipyard strike, Angus Campbell manages then
works for Dereth Keogh, who has inherited the shipyard
from her father.   He protects the rather witless Dereth
from lustful terrorists and she finally realizes that he is
her true love.

Grey, Zane, The Desert of Wheat, New York, Harper and
    Bros.
A violent sermon against foreigners, the I. W. W. and the
brutal Hun.   German agents combine with the I. W. W. to
foment strikes among wheat harvesters but courageous Kurt
Dorn outfights and outwits them.   Dorn joins vigilantes who
lynch Glidden, the I. W. W. leader, then fights valiantly with

the A. E. F. in France and returns to the arms of Lenore
Anderson, a banker's daughter.

White, William Allen, In the Heart of a Fool, New York,
    Macmillan Co.
A very long novel beginning with the founding of Harvey,
Kansas in 1870 and ending with Grant Adams' martyrdom
during a disastrous general strike.   A passionate plea for
Socialism, the novel is an extended allegory.   Grant Adams
is a contemporary Christ who sacrifices himself for the redemption of mankind.   The strike points up the intolerable
oppression of the poor.   Although it is lost, the real victory
of the workers lies in their ability to keep the strike nonviolent.   Adams' example lives on among the workers after
his brutal lynching by vigilantes.

1920

Anderson, Sherwood, Poor White, New York, B. W. Huebsch,
    Inc.
A sensitive account of the rise of Hugh McVey.   Born into
a poor shiftless Tennessee family Hugh becomes a rich man
through an agricultural machinery invention.   The strike in
the novel is the last doomed effort of a group of factory
workers to resist the Juggernaut of materialism.   Hugh
recognizes when the strike fails that individuality, creativity
and dignity have all been swept away by the victory of the
Machine Age.

Rinehart, Mary Roberts, A Poor Wise Man, New York,
    George H. Doran Co.
A subliterary account of society girl Lily Cardew's infatuation with a scoundrel who uses her as a pawn in an anarchist conspiracy.   In the general strike which the anarchists
precipitate Lily learns that her real love is Willy Cameron,
a chemist who leads a Vigilance Committee in illegal raids
on the strikers' printing presses, organizes two thousand
vigilantes as strikebreakers, "fights like a demon" and
when the strike is finally quelled marries Lily.   Pulp for
the woman's magazine market.

Rodney, George Brydges, Jim Lofton, American, New York,
    James A. McCann Co.
A blatant screed in defense of American nationalism full of
tirades against all foreigners.   Jim Lofton, an unemployed
engineer, goes to work as a miner in Denver, Colorado.
He foils an attempt by strikers under the influence of the

240

I. W. W. to sabotage a mine tipple. Jim is tried on a
trumped-up murder charge which grows out of the strike,
but he confounds the perjured witnesses who testify against
him and is acquitted. The author is familiar with mining
and is trying to show the transformation of his hero from
footloose wanderer to responsible adult, but his unrestrained
prejudices and awkward style make for a silly novel.

Wood, Clement, Mountain, New York, E. P. Dutton and Co.
Wood's description of the education of Pelham Judson is an
interesting one. Unloved son of a rich and ruthless father,
Judson marries a social worker with a dilettante's interest
in Socialism. He becomes deeply involved in the lives of
the miners. When they go out on strike, Judson supports
them, breaks with his family and finds himself alienated
from his wife. The strike is the catalyst which separates
Judson irrevocably from his own capitalist class without
giving him entry into the working class. His personal life
and his career are shattered as a result of the strike and
at the end of the novel Judson is a disillusioned failure.

1921

Wright, Harold Bell, Helen of the Old House, New York,
   D. Appleton and Co.
A sentimentalized tale of industrial strife. The mill strike
is organized by Jake Vodell, the malicious union leader. It
is exacerbated by the crazed mill owner. When Vodell is
expelled from the town and the owner, Adam Ward, commits
suicide, the contending parties are reconciled and the mill
becomes a cooperative enterprise. The writing, plot and
characterizations are all incredibly bad.

1922

Lewis, Sinclair, Babbitt, New York, Harcourt, Brace and
   Co.
Lewis's acidulous, ironic portrait of the American business
man is very well done. Zenith telephone workers, dairy
workers and truck drivers strike against a wage cut. Babbitt recognizes the justice of their demands but hasn't the
guts to come out publicly in support of the strikers. He is
intimidated into joining the anti-labor Good Citizens' League
and loses his last chance to become a man of independence
and integrity.

McGibeny, Donald, Slag, a Story of Steel and Stocks,

Indianapolis, Bobbs-Merrill Co.
Steel worker David MacNamara and Alec Jeffries, nephew of
the steel mill owner, become good friends and work together
to circumvent murderous anarchistic L.W.W. leader, Glen-
denning, who is trying to stir up a steel strike. David's
brother, Jerry, at first attracted to the conspirators, sees
the light, joins forces with David and Alec and helps them
avert the strike. Poorly written and outrageously melodramatic, the novel has one slight redeeming quality: the
author obviously knows steel mills and their routines very
well.

Rutzeback, Hjalmar, My Alaskan Idyll, New York, Boni and
    Liveright.
An earnest attempt, partially autobiographical, to portray the
life of a young couple struggling against the elements in
Alaska. Although full of authentic detail, the novel fails to
convince because it lacks depth of characterization. We
follow Svend and Marion Norman through their adventures
but never really learn to know their minds. The strike for
an eight-hour day for gold-miners is organized and led to a
successful conclusion by Svend.

Tobenkin, Elias, The Road, New York, Harcourt, Brace and
    Co.
Hilda Thorsen bears her illegitimate child alone and works
in New York's garment industry to support herself and her
son. She is gradually drawn into union activity and a close
friendship with Socialist union organizer, Frank Hellstrom.
Hilda's sincerity, dedication and personal knowledge of the
working class make her a top-flight union organizer whose
life becomes absorbed in a series of strikes. Raymond
Evert, the father of her son, turns up again years later,
but by then Hilda realizes he is a weak and vacillating man.
In 1921 Hilda joins Frank in the Soviet Union where he has
become the superintendent of a Russian locomotive repair
plant. Tobenkin's sympathetic portrayal of Hilda is heightened by a style which owes much to Hemingway.

1923

Garrett, Garet, The Cinder Buggy: a Fable in Iron and
    Steel, New York, E. P. Dutton and Co.
Beginning with a prose poem to the American steel industry,
the author traces the rise of Alex Thane from lowly puddler
to head of a giant steel trust. At the end a strike forced
on the industry by sullen foreign workers results in Thane's
death.

242

(Ornitz, Samuel), Haunch, Paunch and Jowl, an Anonymous
  Autobiography, New York, Boni and Liveright.
A well-written account of the turbulent garment industry in
New York during the early years of the twentieth century.
Corruption, racketeering and waves of desperate strikes
mark the steady degeneration of Meyer Hirsch, an immigrant
garment worker who becomes the attorney for the garment
industry employers. As Hirsch becomes richer and fatter,
his life becomes emptier. His betrayal of family, friends
and workers leaves him a rich but lonely failure.

1924

Bromfield, Louis, The Green Bay Tree, New York, Frederick A. Stokes Co.
A novel which begins with a powerful description of the
blighting effects of industrialism and contrasts the two sisters, Lily Shane, who reaches out for love, and Irene, who
shrinks from human contact. The strike in the local mill
is used to dramatize the end of the era of rural peace and
beauty. The vigorous beginning soon gives way to absurd
melodrama. As plot complications in the novel multiply,
ideas soon peter out.

Train, Arthur, The Needle's Eye, New York, Charles
  Scribner's Sons.
John Graham, heir to a great fortune, proves his solid
worth when he pitches in to run one of his father's mines.
John defies the union organizing the miners. When they
strike, John is shot, the mine is blown up and John loses
control of the mine. The strike convinces him that unions
are a necessary protection for the workers but that the real
solution to labor troubles lies in conscientious employers
who live close to their plants, understand the problems of
the workers and run the operation personally.

1925

Cline, Leonard, God Head, New York, Viking Press.
A peculiar fantastic tale in which Paulus Kempf loses all
faith in humanity when a miners' strike in which he is involved fails disastrously. He is sheltered and protected by
a simple Finnish couple while sheriff's deputies hunt for him
because of his strike activities. Kempf is so bitter, however, that he becomes a Lemminkainen, a malicious spirit,
and wrecks the lives of his benefactors.

Poling, Daniel Alfred, The Furnace, New York, George H. Doran Co.
The post-war adventures of three veterans of World War I. Malcolm Frank, the son of a Finnish steel worker, becomes the superintendent of Oldsburg Steel Mill, while his friends, Haig Brant and Bruce Jane, become active in the United World Movement. Frank defends the workers in his mill when they strike and exposes the existence of a labor spy network in the industry. The United World Movement helps to publicize Frank's findings but Frank is forced to resign from his position. The author is clearly a passionate defender of justice and decency but fails sadly as a novelist. He relies far too much on preaching and unjustified coincidence, far too little on developing believable characters.

1926

Sinclair, Upton, Oil!, Pasadena, Upton, Sinclair.
The novel races along at a good pace, fine vigorous descriptions side by side with incredibly careless passages. Jim Ross, son of an oil millionaire, clings to a lifetime friendship with Socialist Paul Watkins. Under Paul's influence Jim gives substantial help in two different oilworkers' strikes but still finds plenty of time and money for sprees with his movie starlet mistress, editing a labor weekly and involvement in the Teapot Dome scandal. The strikes show capital and labor locked in a conflict which foreshadows the eventual Socialist revolution. For all his sympathy toward the workers, Jim's class is doomed.

1927

Bromfield, Louis, A Good Woman, New York, Frederick A. Stokes Co.
The overwritten saga of Philip Downes' unhappy marriage to Naomi Potts and his frustrated love affair with Mary Conyngham. After a miserable experience as a missionary in East Africa, Philip goes to work in a mill and joins the other workers when they strike, but the strike is lost and Philip dies of fever. The strike briefly symbolizes Philip's rebirth as an active fulfilled man, but the image soon bogs down in elopements, suicides and other stilted plot contrivances.

Eastman, Max, Venture, New York, Albert and Charles Boni.
Jo Hancock, son of a New England Episcopalian minister,

is caught between his middle class ideas and his admiration
for Big Bill Haywood, leader of the Paterson textile strikers.
Jo's sensitivity as a poet and his attraction to striker Vera
Smirnov pull him toward the Socialist cause but his envy for
the power of Forbes, the capitalist, makes it impossible for
Joe to choose either side decisively. There are some well-
realized scenes, but none of the characters ever really
come to life.

Gibbs, George, The Joyous Conspirator, New York, J. H.
    Sears and Co.
Joyce Bayly risks her life to warn Lord Pembury, the English mill owner, that strikers have planted dynamite. De-
feating their dastardly attempt to kidnap Joyce, Pembury reveals his love and the happy couple are united. Tripe
warmed over.

Sinclair, Upton, Boston, New York, Albert and Charles Boni.
Cornelia Thornwell, member of a prominent Boston family,
gets a job in a cordage factory. She is drawn into active
participation when a strike begins and she becomes a close
friend of Bartolomeo Vanzetti, one of the strike leaders.
When Vanzetti and his partner, Niccolo Sacco, are tried
for murder, Cornelia takes an active part in their defense.
Sinclair weaves a great deal of factual material into his
novel and saves it from tedium by rapid action and a zest-
ful swinging style.

Walker, Charles Rumford, Bread and Fire, Boston,
    Houghton, Mifflin Co.
The narrator, Harris Burnham, of a good New England
family, returns from World War I restless and unsure what
he wants to do with his life. He works briefly in a Bethle-
hem, Pennsylvania steel mill and participates in the 1919
industry-wide steel strike. Then he drifts into a group of
Socialist intellectuals who irritate him with their insincere
talk. A coterie of spoiled young society leaders are no
less irritating to the rootless Burnham. He seems to find
himself momentarily when he begins working in a copper
mill but mounting resentment among the workers, strike
threats and a mass layoff send Burnham into hopelessness
once more. At the end of the novel Burnham is once again
jobless and uncertain of the future. The strike, as well as
the other incidents of factory life, is knowledgeably and
credibly portrayed.

Hammett, Dashiell, Red Harvest, New York, Alfred A.
  Knopf.
A hard-hitting, crisply written novel of violence--granddaddy
of the "tough" detective story. The style is suited admirably
to the theme. Although Hammett never moralizes, his concern for justice is evident. The strike in Personville, a
corrupt mining town, has taken place before the novel begins.
Gangsters, brought in to defeat the strikers, now terrorize
the town. The narrator, Hammett's Continental Op, adroitly
eggs on rival gangs and they decimate each other.

Jones, Idwal, Steel Chips, New York, Alfred A. Knopf.
A well-written unpretentious novel about real steel workers.
Their work, their emotional lives and their relationships to
each other are simply and credibly portrayed. The strike
is seen through the eyes of machinist, Bram Dartnell, an
intelligent and very believable skilled worker and striker.

Kelland, Clarence Budington, Dynasty, New York, Harper
  and Bros.
Touted as "an answer to Babbitt" this novel relates the story
of Hyram Bond who creates and directs a vast financial empire. The steel strike is Bond's opportunity to pit his
strength of will and intelligence against the frightened in-
decisiveness of the strikers. His ruthlessness is a modern
adaptation of the American pioneer spirit, and his ambitious
drive is what has made America the great power she is.

Smedley, Agnes, Daughter of Earth, New York, Coward-
  McCann, Inc.
The life story of Marie Rogers who grows up in Colorado
mining camps where violent strikes are frequent and ugly.
From domestic jobs Marie proceeds to teaching, an unsuccessful marriage and finally work as a book reviewer
and writer in New York. Marie's early experiences in
strike-ridden mining towns convince her that America consists of two nations, the rich and the poor and that the only
solution for the poor lies in the solidarity of the workers.

Williamson, Thames, Hunky, New York, Coward-McCann,
  Inc.
Jencic is a powerful slow-witted Czech immigrant whose life
is focused around the master baker Krusach, whom he wor-
ships. Jencic, for all his strength, is a gentle pacific man.
When Krusach leads the bakery workers out on strike, Jencic

joins the strikers but is horrified when they destroy the
freshly baked loaves of bread. Jencic's nonviolent example
wins over Krusach and the strike is amicably settled. Altogether too naive to be credible.

1930

Cohen, Hyman and Lester, Aaron Traum, New York, Horace
    Liveright.
Another saga of Jewish immigrants swept into the tempestuous garment industry strikes at the turn of the century.
Aaron, a timid weak man, becomes an indefatigable organizer and courageous street fighter. He tries desperately to
work his way through medical school but family responsibilities force him back into the factory. Naive and sentimental.

Vorse, Mary Heaton, Strike!, New York, Horace Liveright.
An early fictional version of the Gastonia strike, this novel
describes in excruciating detail the efforts to organize a
Southern textile mill. Under the leadership of Ferdinand
Deane the workers strike, learn to cooperate, establish a
form of self-government and develop working class consciousness. They are defeated by the vicious combined attacks of
millowners and government agencies but determine to continue organizing until America has become a land of justice.
The author uses her experiences as a journalist, but the
book is more a step-by-step manual for strike organizers
than a realized novel.

1931

Brown, Rollo Walter, The Firemakers; a Novel of Environ-
    ment, New York, Coward-McCann, Inc.
Luke Dabney, a coal-miner at fourteen, becomes active in
a strike for safer working conditions. He is arrested for
arson but acquitted. Luke and his wife try to break away
from the hopelessness of the miners' lives by starting a
small pottery but are forced back when Luke's father-in-law
is blinded in a mine accident. The novel is old-fashioned.
The lustful striker of the 1880's has become an equally lustful captain in the militia. The strike is violent but incon-
clusive, and the hopeless circle goes on and on.

Colman, Louis, Lumber, Boston, Little, Brown and Co.
Jim Logan, a lumber worker, joins the I.W.W., participates in several violent lumber strikes and struggles with
debts, marital problems, illness and periods of unemploy-

ment. Jim can find nothing to believe in or fight for and
sinks into embittered disappointment before he is killed in
a sawmill accident. The book is an honest and authentic
portrayal of working class life but rather plodding and pedestrian.

Harrison, Charles Yale, A Child Is Born, New York, Jonathan Cape and Harrison Smith.
The violence-ridden story of a Brooklyn longshoreman, Edward Roberts, and his family. Roberts takes part in a
strike during World War I in which the longshoremen battle
not only oppressive shipyard bosses but their own corrupt
union. Roberts is killed, his daughter is raped and his son
is hurried off to a reformatory where the boys are brutally
handled. The novel uses an effective recurrent metaphor:
the kinesitherapist, Bernard Powers, who offers his physical culture lectures and health foods as a solution to all of
mankind's problems, but the unrelieved gloom of the novel
is not convincing.

Russell, Ruth, Lake Front, Chicago, Thomas S. Rockwell
Co.
James O'Mara is a young Chicago reporter in 1886 when the
Haymarket bomb explodes. He is sympathetic to the Mc-
Cormick Reaper strikers but revolted by the cynicism of the
Haymarket anarchists to whom workers are only a means to
a revolutionary end. By 1894 when the Pullman strike begins, O'Mara is rich, hard and ruthless. He personally
takes out a train and drives it through a mob of strikers,
killing one of them. The two strikes are cleverly used to
dramatize O'Mara's development, and there are several well-
done descriptions of nineteenth century Chicago.

1932

Anderson, Sherwood, Beyond Desire, New York, Liveright,
Inc.
Red Oliver, the son of a drunken doctor, undergoes his
strike baptism in a Georgia textile mill. He is hesitant
and indecisive, conscious of the growing discrepancy between
the ideals of both the strikers and their employers and their
practices. In a second strike near Birchfield, North Carolina (based on the actual Gastonia strike) Red is killed during a confrontation between strikers and militiamen. Anderson experiments with the use of short, staccato sentences,
the elimination of cant phrases and emotional passages, and
the use of realistic Southern dialect. He succeeds in evok-

ing sympathy for his very human millworkers. He sees the strike not so much as an economic conflict as a clash between man as he would like to be--simple, dignified and creative--and industrial man as he is--unscrupulous, dehumanized and lonely.

Brody, Catherine, Nobody Starves, New York, Longmans,
    Green and Co.
The story of the doomed marriage of Molly and Bill Redding during the Depression. Deeply in love, they both work in Michigan auto plants. After taking part in a lost strike, they lose their jobs. As the struggle to find work becomes more desperate, they begin to quarrel. Finally, Bill shoots Molly and plans his own suicide but is arrested before he can act. The novel is realistic and avoids becoming maudlin but it fails to give real insight into the characters.

Dargan, Olive Tilford (Fielding Burke), Call Home the Heart,
    New York, Longmans, Green and Co.
From an illiterate hill-farm girl in the Great Smokies of North Carolina Ishma Waycaster develops into an effective union organizer in Southern textile mills. She marries one man and runs away with another but really finds herself as an individual when she is drawn into the National Textile Union's organizing drives and as she begins to grapple with Communist philosophy and politics. The book is preachy and stuffed with endless theoretical discussions on dialectical materialism and the nature of the Socialist revolution. Many of the incidents are modelled on the Gastonia textile strike.

Dell, Floyd, Diana Stair, New York, Farrar and Rinehart,
    Inc.
Diana Stair is a liberated woman who tries her hand at stump-speaking for Abolition, teaching, labor organizing, smoking, love affairs, writing and communal living in a Socialist community in pre-Civil War New England. She is not a conspicuous success at any of her unorthodox experiments. Her involvement with a strike occurs in 1845 in the town of Pickering when she leads a walkout of women millworkers. Not only is the strike itself unsuccessful but Diana's impulsiveness causes dissension among the strikers. Accused of irresponsibility, she leaves town in the midst of a strike meeting. Dell's attempt to picture a free spirit is talky and tendentious.

Lumpkin, Grace, To Make My Bread, New York, Macaulay
    Co.

Another fictional account of the Gastonia textile strike and
one of the worst. The McClure family leaves its hill farm
for work in a Southern textile mill and endures misery and
exploitation. Under the leadership of Marxist John Stevens,
the millworkers organize secretly, then strike. Bonnie Mc-
Clure is killed during a confrontation of strikers and deputies and fifteen strikers are tried for murder, but Stevens
assures the strikers: "This is just the beginning."

Nearing, Scott, Free Born: An Unpublishable Novel, New
    York, Urquhart Press.
Jim Rogers begins life on a tenant farm in Georgia. After
a lynching he flees to a South Carolina mill town where he
works for a time. In 1917 Jim arrives in Chicago. As a
black man he endures hunger, discrimination and dreadful
poverty. Again and again Jim and those he loves can find
work only as menials or as strikebreakers. When Jim, under the guidance of Jane Wilson, a Communist, organizes a
strike of strikebreakers, he is indicted for assault and sentenced to five years in the penitentiary. His experiences
have taught him that the race question can be solved only
through the development of a class-conscious labor movement. The novel is too didactic but it deals with an important social issue.

Page, Dorothy Myra, Gathering Storm; a Story of the Black
    Belt, New York, International Publishers.
Still another novel based on the Gastonia strike, this one
emphasizes the need for unity between black and white workers not only in organizing Southern textile mills but in their
common struggle to overthrow capitalism. Tom Crenshaw,
the white organizer of the book, works closely with Fred
Morgan, a Negro strike leader. Both become Communists,
and the book ends with their reunion at a Communist Party
convention where William Z. Foster leads the singing of the
Internationale. Atrociously written, full of exhortatory
speeches, thoroughly dull.

1933

Caldwell, Erskine, God's Little Acre, Viking Press.
A memorable novel in which Will Thompson's obsessive
struggle to turn on the power of a struck Southern cotton
mill represents both his zest for life and his need to prove
he is a whole man. Although Will is killed in his successful attempt to pull the power switch, his act is recognized
by the strikers as symbolic of their collective power. The

novel was attacked because of its explicit sexual scenes, on
the one hand, and its unusual approach to labor conflict, on
the other. It remains a strong, well-written and integrated
novel making some important statements on the human condition.

Conroy, Jack, The Disinherited, New York, Covici Friede
  and Co.
A better than average proletarian novel portraying the education of Larry Donovan, son of a Missouri miner. Larry
learns slowly in the course of many jobs and many industrial strikes in mines, steel mills, railroads and migrant farm
labor that his individual salvation lies only in the awakened
militancy of the working class.

Pell, Mike, S. S. Utah, New York, International Publishers.
When the seamen on the S. S. Utah contrast their dismal
conditions with those of Russian seamen in Leningrad, they
go on strike. Led by Slim Rogers, a Communist member
of the Marine Workers Industrial Union, the crew learns to
fight the corrupt International Seaman's Union as well as the
exploiting shipowners. The book is so ineptly conceived and
written that it can hardly be called a novel at all.

1934

Armstrong, Arnold B., Parched Earth, New York, Macmillan Co.
Dave Washburn, a dedicated Communist, attempts to organize exploited California cannery workers thrown out of work
by mechanization. The whole town of Caldwell is destroyed
when the local dam is dynamited, but Dave escapes presumably to organize other workers more successfully. The
capitalists in the novel are morally despicable, the workers
confused and powerless because they have not yet learned
to take power by organized collective action. Obvious symbolism, undeveloped characters.

Cantwell, Robert, The Land of Plenty, New York, Farrar
  and Rinehart.
A competent and readable novel although it follows the orthodox formula for the strike novel of the Thirties. The workers in Cantwell's lumber mill have learned how to work together cooperatively while their incompetent foremen and
supervisors bicker and compete with each other. The exuberance of the early days of the lumber workers' strike
gives way to despair but the strikers soon learn how

251

to regroup skillfully and a new solidarity develops. Cantwell knows the inside workings of a lumber mill well and uses the strike as a model for the class conflict he believes is developing throughout the society. His account of the education of the young worker, Johnny Hagen, is touching and real. The conclusion of the strike is left unresolved at the end of the novel but even if it fails, the workers now know the extent of their collective power and will probably go on to take over the factories which are rightfully theirs.

Frank, Waldo, The Death and Birth of David Markand, New York, Charles Scribner's Sons.
In 1913 David Markand, an executive in his family's tobacco company, leaves his wife and two children to search for some kind of order and morality in a chaotic society. He works at a series of jobs and comes into intimate contact with a variety of strikers and organizers among coal miners, farmers, steel workers, railroad workers and textile mill workers. He discards in turn the methods and philosophies of traditional craft trade unionists, and the I.W.W. During a disastrous coal strike Markand is arrested but escapes after seeing his two closest colleagues killed. He returns to his family determined to help destroy capitalism. Frank introduces a great many diverse characters into his novel, none of them especially memorable. Markand himself is only superficially realized and his final commitment to an undefined "socialism" is more a matter of faith than of conviction.

Gilfillan, Lauren, I Went to Pit College, New York, Viking Press.
Lauren, just out of college, goes to Avelonia, Pennsylvania to observe a coal miners' strike. She lives with a striker's family, attends union meetings and takes part in the miners' social events. She notes with growing impatience the bickering between the United Mine Workers and the National Miners Union, rival organizing groups, and opposes the role of the Communist Party which is using the strike for its own devious purposes. In spite of her attraction to Johnny Cercil, a young miner, Lauren decides to leave Avelonia and return to her own world. A lightweight novel, obviously autobiographical, with a few good descriptions of life in a struck town but without much depth. Lauren comes off as a flighty dilettante who becomes a disturbing element among the strikers.

Herbst, Josephine, The Executioner Waits, New York, Har-

court, Brace and Co.
One volume of a trilogy, this novel describes the effect of
several strikes on the Wendel family.   The sisters, Rosamund and Vicky, are only briefly touched by the Seattle
general strike of 1918 and by another strike in Iowa in
which I. W. W. organizers are lynched.   Rosamund's husband,
Jerry Stauffer, a World War I veteran, is assigned to strikebreaking duties in a meat-packing plant.   He joins the strikers in their fight, is arrested, and becomes completely committed to the cause of the working class.   The development
of the plot and the characters is fairly interesting.

Larsson, Gösta, Our Daily Bread, New York, Vanguard
    Press.
As the world-wide depression deepens a dock strike in
Malmö, Sweden becomes a general strike.   The effects of
hunger and despair on the Hammar family are described in
purple prose.   The novel ends with the strike still continuing while a Socialist solidarity is developing among the
Swedish workers.

Newhouse, Edward, You Can't Sleep Here, New York,
    Macaulay Co.
Gene Marsay, an unemployed newspaperman, receives a
rapid political education when he helps Chuck Andor, a Communist, organize a hotel laundry workers' strike.   Chuck's
dedication and skill inspire Gene to lead the organization of
an Unemployed Council in the Shantytown where Gene is living.   In spite of a tear gas attack by police and his arrest
during the demonstration Gene continues in his determination
to ally himself with working class causes.   The description
of life in a Shantytown during the Depression is accurate.

Rollins, Jr. , William, The Shadow Before, New York,
    Robert M. McBride and Co.
Rollins has used a number of experimental techniques in this
strike novel which lift it above many of its contemporaries.
Set in a New England thread mill, the novel uses incidents
from the Gastonia textile strike.   Typographical innovations,
interior monologues, quickly changing and contrasted vignettes
and the use of newspaper clippings recall John Dos Passos'
U. S. A.   Although the strike is lost, it serves as a means
of redemption for several of the characters: Micky Bonner,
whom it rescues from a neurotic love affair with a wastrel;
Larry Marvin, the organizer, who will use his experiences
in this strike to win future strike victories; Harry Baumann,
son of the mill owner, who learns from the strike to substi-

tute the reality of working class life for the frivolity and
emptiness of the bourgeoisie. The characters are real, not
merely puppets symbolizing class strife.

1935

Adamic, Louis, Grandsons; a Story of American Lives, New
  York, Harper and Bros.
The long and complicated story of Peter Gale, his brother
Andy and their cousin Jack, all grandsons of a Slovenian
immigrant who was killed during the Haymarket Riot. Peter
is a reporter, Andy a bootlegger and Jack a union organizer
among California agricultural workers. This rather con-
trived setup enables Adamic to contrast the freebooter (read
capitalist), the petit bourgeois professional and the worker.
After arduous soul searching Peter realizes that Jack is the
only one who is "real" and the only one who finds true happiness even though Jack is murdered by the big ranchers
who oppose the union. The strike and the strikers on the
California ranches are only shadowy conceptions seen not
even at second-hand through Peter Gale's eyes but through
the words of the unnamed narrator who tells Peter's story.

Basso, Hamilton, In Their Own Image, New York, Charles
  Scribner's Sons.
Basso stacks the deck in this novel. He contrasts industrious millworkers with the idle rich who live off the mill profits, an authentic artist who has to earn a living as a mill-
worker with a mediocre painter who toadies to rich old ladies, and earnest hardworking union organizers with bored
idle society tramps. He explores the role of the artist in
capitalist society through the lives of Michael Langford, Kurt
Beach and John Pine. Langford works in the mill, participates in the strike and has to settle for odd jobs as a house
painter. Beach paints rich ladies' polo ponies. Pine remains independent, refusing to produce commercial or advertising art but he has to capitulate at last and paints
Beach's rich old ladies, if not their horses. Pine concludes
that the rich live make-believe lives, while only the workers'
lives are real. While the capitalists fritter away their lives
in loveless love affairs, the workers organize their strike.
Although the strike is lost, they will go on to future victory.

Bell, Thomas, The Second Prince, New York, G. P. Putnam's Son.
Striker Godown, a young newspaperman, becomes involved
in the Jericho Iron Works strike through his friendship with

254

the strike leader, Mike Strovenik. In spite of his sympathy
for the workers, Godown decides to marry wealthy Lee
Renault, leave Jericho and retire to the country to write a
novel. He admits shamefacedly: "I'm running away because
I haven't the guts to stay and fight, to do what my head tells
me I should do if I were true to my principles and logic."
Godown is Bell's epitome of the middle class: quitters when
faced with the real problems of the world.

Conroy, Jack, <u>A World to Win</u>, New York, Covici, Friede
   Publishers.
Robert Browning Hurley, the offspring of a misalliance between a petit bourgeois, would-be writer and a tough Irish
sawmill worker, flirts with university life, attempts at writing poetry and half-hearted volunteer work at a Communist
Party strike headquarters. He is contrasted with his half-
brother, Leo, who goes to work in a factory at fifteen.
When the Depression hits, Robert also gets a factory job
as Leo's helper. When the workers strike, Leo becomes
a scab and Robert refuses to join the picket line. As the
Depression deepens, Leo and Robert both wander the country looking for work. The brothers are reunited during a
demonstration of the unemployed. Both have learned that
their individual problems can only be solved through working
class collective action. The desperate hopelessness of the
Depression is dramatically pictured, but the moral is too
obviously drawn.

Dargan, Olive Tilford (Fielding Burke), <u>A Stone Came Roll-</u>
   <u>ing</u>, New York, Longmans, Green and Co.
A sequel to <u>Call Home the Heart</u>. This novel follows Ishma
Waycaster's growth as a full-fledged organizer in Southern
cotton and hosiery mills. By now Ishma is able to persuade
some strikers to enter the mills and turn off the switches,
a revolutionary step in the workers' developing class-con-
sciousness. The strikes in the novel are violent but incon-
clusive although they indicate a growing Socialist ideology.
The novel is didactic, poorly written and unconvincing.

Gollomb, Joseph, <u>Unquiet</u>, New York, Dodd, Mead and Co.
The story of the Leavitt family, Jewish immigrants from
Russia, and their share in the organization of sweatshops
in New York. David, the central character, becomes a
journalist. In the course of reporting the Square Deal Shirtwaist Company fire, he becomes a Socialist. He breaks
with his family and his rich fiancée and dedicates himself
to political activity on behalf of the working class. The

author is cursed with total recall and includes every dreary detail of David's life in this dull and preachy novel.

Havighurst, Walter, Pier 17, New York, Macmillan Co.
A strike of seamen on the freighter Pamona docked in Seattle spreads to include the longshoremen and tugboat crews. Seen through the eyes of eighteen-year old seaman, Adrian Scarf, the strike is a bewildering, violent, irrational and exciting event. Without really understanding it, Adrian participates in the violence and is killed in a police attack. The strike peters out without much gained except that a few workers recognize that unity among the men must replace mob action.

Rowan, Thomas, Black Earth, New York, Hillman-Curl, Inc.
The author espouses the curiously anachronistic belief (in 1935) that miners could "save their money, watch their opportunities and become American millionaires." He is obsessed with animal metaphors, referring to the miners as apes, sheep, buzzards, rats, fowl, mules, bulls and cats. Markham Crockett, one of the miners, joins the strikers reluctantly, then realizes that the callous and vicious union leaders have called the strike merely to consolidate their own power. Mark is hurt during the strike, and the unionists dynamite his home. He is killed defending the American flag from desecration. His death changes the mood of the strikers who turn on their leaders and shoot them down.

Tippett, Thomas, Horse Shoe Bottoms, New York, Harper and Bros.
A sensitive novel recounting the story of John Stafford, an Illinois coal miner, and of his long struggle to establish a national miners' union. Through a long series of strikes Stafford develops from an ignorant and brutish man into a sensitive, compassionate human being. One of the most touching of the proletarian novels of the period.

Weatherwax, Clara, Marching! Marching!, New York, John Day Co.
The Bayliss lumber mill in the Pacific Northwest is struck as the West Coast prepares for a general strike. Led by Communist organizers, the workers overcome persistent enmity among Finnish, Japanese, Filipino and Anglo workers. The novel is puerile, melodramatic and cliché-ridden.

Anderson, Sherwood, Kit Brandon; a Portrait, New York,
  Charles Scribner's Sons.
Kit is a Tennessee mountain girl who goes to work in a textile mill, then becomes a driver for a bootlegger. She is
an unusual and three-dimensional character, sensitively portrayed. Kit becomes emotionally involved with a textile
workers' strike through her friendship with Agnes, one of
the union organizers. Anderson catches some of the rhythms
of the strike--excitement at the beginning, then boredom,
fear, and finally cynicism as the strikers are deserted by
their leaders. Anderson sees the strike as a dramatic event
in which a mass of human beings learn to cooperate, to
stand together and to experience each other as brothers.
The novel misses greatness but it probes into the physical
and emotional lives of its working class characters.

Beals, Carleton, The Stones Awake, Philadelphia, J. B.
  Lippincott Co.
Esperanza Huitron begins life in a small Mexican village
dominated by feudal haciendados. When the Revolution of
1910 breaks out Esperanza is swept into turbulent action.
Slowly and painfully she struggles for education, for love
and for survival. In Mexico City she takes part in a soap
factory strike which is defeated, but Esperanza realizes
that the battlefields of the Revolution have shifted to the
struggles of the infant labor movement. Her association
with the artist, David Muñoz, brings her directly into a
bitter miners' strike in Guadalajara. Even when a tired,
jaded David becomes estranged from both Esperanza and
the labor movement, she continues her activities. At the
end of the novel she returns to her native village to teach
in the local school and to work for the implementation of
the ideals of the Revolution. Esperanza is a strong unsenti-
mentalized character and the tempestuous background of the
Mexican Revolution is well done.

Bell, Thomas, All Brides Are Beautiful, Boston, Little,
  Brown and Co.
The love story of Peter and Susan Cummings is set against
the background of the Depression of the Thirties. Peter is
a machinist who wants to be an artist and Susan works in
a bookstore. Their constant fear of unemployment, their
relationships with Susan's family and, most of all, their
tender developing love for each other are described simply
and movingly. The strike is one in which Susan's brother-

in-law, Hank Beasley, participates. From it he begins to
discard capitalist illusions and to accept Communism as the
only real solution. The Communist ideology is dragged in
by the heels and somewhat spoils an otherwise competent
and interesting novel.

Coleman, McAlister and Stephen Rauschenbush, Red Neck,
  New York, Harrison Smith and Robert Haas.
The story of Dave Houston who goes down a coal mine at
fourteen, participates in some bitter strikes and eventually
becomes a mine union organizer during the Thirties. A
militant worker, Dave fights factionalism and corruption
within the union, bigotry and despair among the miners and
exploitation and vigilante action by the mine owners. He
gradually loses hope and idealism and joins forces with corrupt district union officials. His illegitimate son, Mike
Manik, becomes the leader of a new and radical organizing
drive, opposing Dave and the other union officials who have
sold out the exploited miners. The novel is a realistic un-
sentimental picture of the pressured lives of mine union organizers.

Cuthbert, Clifton, Another Such Victory, New York, Hillman-
  Curl, Inc.
A pedestrian unsubtle account of a violent strike in a New
England textile mill. The bosses are frivolous wastrels and
callous exploiters, the workers are their serious and highly
moral victims. Under the leadership of Communist organizer Ed Hurley, the strikers learn both class consciousness
and strike tactics. The strike is lost and the union destroyed,
but Hurley has gained a few new recruits for the Communist
Party who will undoubtedly ensure that the next industrial
clash will be fought on a higher political level.

France, Royal Wilbur, Compromise, Philadelphia, Dorrance
  and Co.
A poorly written and completely unconvincing novel. The
strike, never seen directly, is merely a peg on which to
hang the hero's spiritual redemption. Emory Young becomes
a highly successful corporation lawyer and a potential Presidential candidate, but over the years he has sacrificed his
moral convictions. He proceeds with the prosecution of one
indicted prisoner even though he believes him to be innocent.
When his first love, Justine Bartlett, is killed in a West
Virginia mining strike, Emory wrecks his Presidential chances
by publicly attacking the coal mine owners.

Linn, Bettina, Flea Circus, New York, Harrison Smith and Robert Haas.
Al runs a flea circus to earn money but devotes himself to organizing workers. His efforts to organize a strike are described in painful detail--picketing, setting up a headquarters, relief efforts, a children's parade, a mass rally. The strike is defeated partly by Communist disruption and partly by the combined force of the police and court injunctions, but Al continues in his organizing efforts. The descriptions of strike activities are accurate, but the people in the novel are wooden.

Mainwaring, Daniel (Geoffrey Homes), The Doctor Died at Dusk, New York, William Morrow and Co.
A humdrum whodunit in which a fruit pickers' strike in the San Joaquin Valley is used to cover a murder. The clashes between strikers and orchard owners are well done, but the story is inconsequential and the characters unconvincing.

Steinbeck, John, In Dubious Battle, New York, Covici-Friede Co.
Probably the best of all the strike novels, In Dubious Battle shows profound insight into the lives and minds of a group of California migrant fruit pickers who strike for higher wages and a decent, dignified life. Steinbeck is an impassioned advocate of justice but wary of the admittedly successful techniques of Mac and Jim, the Communist Party organizers. Doc Burton, the humane doctor who is in charge of the strikers' tent colony, resists Mac's cold-blooded and calculated manipulation of the strikers while fully aware of the fruit growers' callous indifference to their workers. The novel is a fine example of the artistic use of factual material for a prophetic comment on the darker side of the mind of man.

Zara, Louis, Give Us This Day, Indianapolis, Bobbs-Merrill Co.
Young Charles Brabant begins to work in his father's Chicago bakery in 1900 and inherits the business when his father dies. In 1932, in the midst of the Depression, he loses the family bakery. He gets a job as a bakery foreman without realizing he is working in a struck plant. When he quits because he sympathizes with the strikers, he receives a severe beating from angered pickets. Brabant then evolves a plan for a cooperative but it is closed down by vindictive local officials. Brabant suffers a mental breakdown. A pedestrian effort.

259

Zugsmith, Leane, A Time to Remember, New York, Random House.
Two thousand workers at the Diamond Department Store strike for union recognition, a raise and improved working conditions. In the course of the strike young Doni Roberts discovers not only the class war but the love of a good man, Matt Matthews, one of the strike leaders, whose nagging wife conveniently commits suicide. Working class unity wins the strike but Matt warns the workers that they still have a long struggle ahead for their rights. Ho, hum!

1937

Cassady, Constance, This Magic Dust, Indianapolis, Bobbs-Merrill Co.
The class education of Katherine Marling, born rich, educated in snobbish schools, and working as a successful designer and book illustrator. Her friendship with social worker Ann Schuyler gradually leads Katherine into sympathy with the working class. Her final lesson comes during a steel strike in which Ann, by now a labor organizer, is killed. Katherine's conversion is shallow and hardly credible.

Duffus, Robert Luther, Night Between the Rivers, New York, Macmillan Co.
A confused novel which attempts to show the effects of a general strike in New York City on a group of intellectuals who meet at a cocktail party. The guests bicker with each other just as the workers and employers are presumably doing outside the besieged apartment house in which the party takes place. Esther Stein, the one Communist at the party, leaves to join the strikers. The others, feeling impotent and ineffectual, talk incessantly about their proper roles. Louis Flood, a former professor, offers himself as a hostage to the police and is shot. The strike is broken, but it is suggested that Flood will be the "martyred hero" who will inspire future outbreaks. An improbable plot, shadowy characters, floods of talk and extravagant metaphors make for a boring novel.

Engstrand, Stuart David, The Invaders, New York, Alfred A. Knopf.
A coalition between small vegetable growers and cannery workers leads to a violent but successful strike. The strike is led by cannery worker, Lawrence Hart, a Marxist who had been fired for his convictions from a schoolteacher's

job. He is attracted to Miriam Miller, married to one of
the striking farmers, but his love affair does not impede
Lawrence's effectiveness as an organizer. Fairly competent
writing.

Jeter, Geotze, The Strikers, New York, Frederick A.
    Stokes Co.
A novel with no redeeming qualities. Strikers speak in a
jargon straight out of the author's own head and are all
stupid, lazy, malicious, coarse, brutal, greedy and spite-
ful. The shoe company officials are crisp, decisive, disciplined, penetrating. The company men announce their goals
as "ferreting out the dissatisfaction and arranging to stifle,
distract, squash or kill it." Violent scenes are described
in loving and sickening detail.

Johnson, Josephine, Jordanstown, New York, Simon and
    Schuster.
A sensitive, poetic novel in which Allen Craig attempts to
build a farmer-consumer cooperative among onion-pickers
and striking factory workers. The factory owner, John
Chapman, is as well developed a character as the small
group of workers who support Allen's efforts and as three-
dimensional as Allen himself. The meeting hall Allen and
his friends build is burned down by a mob, but out of their
initial despair the group finds the determination to begin
again. The strike is seen only tangentially but its effects
on Chapman and on the strikers are evident and understandable.

Levin, Meyer, The Old Bunch, New York, Viking Press.
A long and extremely detailed novel about a group of Jewish
teenagers growing up in Chicago in the 1920's. A strike in
a hat factory pits two former friends against each other:
Mort Abramson, whose father owns the factory, and Sam
Eisen, the strikers' attorney. As the Depression worsens,
other strikes break out and Mort and Sam continue to be
antagonists. The endless details--popular songs, news headlines, comic strips, advertising slogans--of the time slow
the novel and obscure rather than reveal the characters.
The novel is a serious one, however, with a few flashes
of insight and some depth.

Loring, Emile, Today Is Yours, New York, Farrar and
    Rinehart, Inc.
The Romneys, owners of the struck factory in his novel,
regard themselves as a royal dynasty inherently capable of

ruling their empire. The description of the strike and its
causes is silly ("our workers have all the money they ever
asked for and more. ") The company arms the local townspeople with tear gas bombs and organizes a counter picket
line and the strike ends. Brian Romney displays his courage and intelligence during the strike and is reunited with
his wife Gay after some misunderstandings. Mrs. Loring
is much more interested in describing Gay's extensive
wardrobe for her women's magazine readers than in the
strike.

McIntyre, John T. , Ferment, New York, Farrar and Rine-
    hart, Inc.
A rather plodding account of strikebreaking techniques among
produce truckdrivers. Tom, the staunch unionist truckdriv-
er, wins out over his flashy labor-spy brother Steve and
gets the girl to boot. Realistic but dull.

Rice, Elmer, Imperial City, New York, Coward-McCann,
    Inc.
The novel deals with the complex relationships among the
members of the Coleman family, owners of the Interborough
Light and Power Co. When the Union of Electrical Workers
threatens a strike, the Colemans are all deeply affected.
Chris Coleman stubbornly refuses to arbitrate while Gaillard
Coleman cooperates with the union. The novel ends during
a complete power failure caused not by the strike but by a
fire at the central control station, an ominous warning of
trouble to come. The strikers themselves are never seen
directly. Rice gives some deft characterizations of a family
which is rapidly going to seed.

Simon, Charlie May, The Share-Cropper, New York, E. P.
    Dutton and Co.
An unpretentious account of the life of an Arkansas share-
cropper and his family. Bill Bradley, cheated and exploited
on the Nelson plantation, slowly concludes that the solution
lies in the organization of a tenant farmers' union in which
black and white sharecroppers unite as equals. Befriended
by a lawyer, Abner Young, who helps with the union organization, Bill suffers hunger, an attack by a lynch mob and
arrest but remains staunch and hopeful. The descriptions
of the sharecroppers' lives--a wedding, a shivaree, a revival
meeting--are well done.

Spadoni, Adriana, Not All Rivers, Garden City, Doubleday,
    Doran and Co.

Rhoda Townsend has her first encounter with the labor movement when she supports a group of laundry workers who are
forming a union. Later, married to labor lawyer David
Evans and working on a labor newspaper, she participates
in an agricultural workers' strike. Her activity convinces
her that all of society lives parasitically off the labor of
the working class and that her own salvation depends on her
identification with workers' causes.

Storm, Hans Otto, Pity the Tyrant, New York, Longmans,
   Green and Co.
The unnamed German-American engineer who narrates the
story works for a power company in Lima, Peru. He witnesses sympathetically a strike of Indian bus drivers and
another of "telefonistas" in Lima and notes the oppression
both native and foreign employers practice against the Peruvian workers. When he tries to defend one of the strikers
and refuses to fill in as a strikebreaker, he is fired and
leaves Lima. The Peruvian background is authentic and the
novel is well written. Better than average.

Williams, William Carlos, White Mule, Norfolk, Conn.,
   New Directions.
Joe Stecher, a German immigrant, has become foreman of
a print shop in New York. In 1893 when the shop goes on
strike, Joe remains at work. While he is contemptuous of
the idle and incompetent strikers, he also sees clearly the
chicanery and stinginess of his employers. Williams, using
the "objectivism" he had already experimented with in his
poetry, attempts with a good deal of success to portray the
events and the emotions in the Stecher family life entirely
through the use of concrete external details and unmetaphori-
cal language.

1938

Bisno, Beatrice, Tomorrow's Bread, Philadelphia, Jewish
   Publication Society of America.
The story of Sam Karenski who begins organizing sweatshop
workers in Chicago in the 1880's and continues his union organizing in spite of the failure of his three marriages and
his quarrels with the leadership of his own union. Sam's
whole life is a series of strikes out of which garment workers slowly gain recognition and a better life but which benefit Sam himself not at all. His occasional flirtations with
business investments are disastrous although many of his
union colleagues become rich and successful. He dies at

the end of the novel not really sure why he has persisted in fighting for democratic unionism but without regrets.

Breuer, Bessie, The Daughter, New York, Simon and
    Schuster.
A poetic novel depicting the love-hate relationship of Carlotta, a rootless divorcée, and her awkward teen-age daughter, Katy. Katy is sympathetic to striking fishermen in the Florida gulf town where she and her mother are living, but the fishermen have no time for this alien child. When Katy and her mother become rivals for the affections of Charlie, the nineteen-year old scion of a decayed Southern family, Katy attempts suicide. The strike points up the futility of Carlotta's life but the contrast is implicit, not preached.

Davis, Clyde Brion, "The Great American Novel--, " New
    York, Farrar and Rinehart.
Homer Zigler, a young reporter, finds work on the Denver Call and is almost immediately involved in the bitter Colorado miners' strike of 1914. In 1920 he is again closely associated with a strike, this time a violent streetcar strike. Zigler is a gentle, patient man, devoted to his family and deeply sympathetic to the strikers whose battles he reports. When the Depression begins, Homer joins the Newspaper Guild and finds himself demoted to the copy desk of the Call after more than a quarter of a century of hard work. He has been haunted all his life by two fantasies: seeing once more the first girl he loved and whom he never married, and writing the Great American Novel. At the end of the novel he knows neither fantasy will ever become a reality. A touching realistic novel.

Delany, Joseph Francis (Joel Y. Dane), The Christmas Tree
    Murders, New York, Doubleday, Doran and Co.
A detective story with a strike background. A striker and the head of a strikebreaking agency are murdered. When it is revealed that the playboy son of the industrialist is the killer, the industrialist agrees to recognize the union and the strike ends. A run-of-the-mill whodunit.

Dos Passos, John, Adventures of a Young Man, New York,
    Harcourt, Brace and Co.
The young man is Glenn Spotswood who proceeds from his courses at Columbia University to a career as a Communist labor organizer. He works with striking pecan pickers in Texas, then with striking Appalachian coal miners. As he becomes aware of the cynical double-dealing of the Com-

264

munists during both strikes, his disenchantment with the
Party grows. He escapes his expulsion from the Party by
volunteering for the Loyalist forces in the Spanish Civil War,
but the Communists coldbloodedly arrange for his death in
a suicide mission at the front. The strikes in the novel
are subordinated to Spottswood's ideological struggles with
the Communists.

Ethridge, Willie Snow, <u>Mingled Yarn</u>, New York, Macmillan
    Co.
The novel portrays a Southern journalist, Buford Battle,
whose sympathies for textile mill workers are aroused when
he reports one of their strikes. Buford continues to support
the efforts of the mill workers to organize in the face of a
flogging administered by the local Ku Klux Klan and his growing alienation from his wife, the daughter of a mill owner.
In 1930 the Gastonia strike moves Buford to decisive action.
He leaves his wife Ellen and becomes a crusading reporter
in Raleigh, North Carolina. The novel's saving grace lies
in its undidactic development of Buford's character. The
real Gastonia strike is fairly skillfully woven into the story
as the motivation for Buford's climactic decision to act upon
his convictions.

Gilligan, Edmund, <u>Boundary Against Night,</u> New York, Far-
    rar and Rinehart.
Ostensibly an account of the Boston police strike of 1922,
this is actually a Gothic novel in which murder, rape, robbery, flogging and sexual titillation run wild. By the end
of the novel all the major characters have died violently and
Armageddon seems to have arrived on the streets of Boston.
The policemen's strike releases all restraints and criminals
and respectable Bostonians alike become an uncontrolled
mob bent on pillage and murder. Nonsense.

Preston, John Hyde, <u>The Liberals,</u> New York, John Day Co.
A sit-in strike in a Connecticut factory convinces playwright
Philip Whitlock, who is a house-guest of the factory owners,
that liberals are indecisive and, therefore, superfluous men.
He recognizes that the middle class intellectual comes alive
only when he commits himself to fighting actively for the
working class. The novel consists of a long string of stilted disquisitions on sociology, labor history and Socialist
philosophy.

Sinclair, Upton, <u>Little Steel</u>, New York, Farrar and Rine-
    hart, Inc.

A detailed report of legal and extralegal methods used to destroy unions in the steel industry. Walter Quayle, head of the Valleyville Steel, allows a firm of industrial counselors to play on his fear and vanity. They organize a widespread network of spying and intimidation directed against Quayle's workers. An old friend of Quayle's persuades him to leave his mills and wander through the South. The two friends take part in a Georgia mill strike and Quayle receives a salutary lesson in labor history when he is arrested and sentenced to twenty days in a Georgia jail. The plot of the novel is ridiculous and both the steel and the cotton strikes are only dimly pictured, but Sinclair's excellent research into labor-spying techniques and his vigorous journalistic style save the novel from complete banality.

Teilhet, Darwin L. , Journey to the West, Garden City, Doubleday, Doran and Co.
A picaresque novel in which Rufus Cobb, an advertising writer, wanders in and out of adventures with Communists, Socialists and Townsendites. Rufus participates in a number of West Coast strikes among longshoremen, fruit pickers and brewery workers. From initial sympathy with the Communists Rufus becomes pro-capitalist. In the brewery strike Rufus slugs the strike leader and convinces the strikers to return to work. He is rewarded with a partnership in the brewery and the hand of his partner's lovely daughter. If Teilhet is satirical, his irony is too heavy-handed. If he is serious, his novel is a couple of generations out-of-date.

Zugsmith, Leane, The Summer Soldier, New York, Random House.
A group of intellectuals try to investigate reports of lynchings of labor organizers in Chew County during a violent textile strike. The delegation includes a social worker, a minister, a university professor and a playwright. They are intimidated, kidnapped and beaten by vigilantes with the active connivance of the local authorities and the National Guard. The experience thoroughly demoralizes several members of the delegation who scurry for shelter in their professional havens back home, but three of the delegates resolve to return to Chew County with a larger and more militant group. Based partially on the actual experiences of an investigating group which went to Harlan County coal country, the novel preaches the familiar lesson that intellectuals are weak and vacillating and that their only strength and usefulness lies in their active alliance with the working class.

Appel, Benjamin, The Power-House, New York, E. P. Dutton and Co.
A tough expose of the strikebreaking racket and its highly
sophisticated techniques for manipulating unions, strikes and
workers in order to increase profits. Bill Trent is the
Brain Guy who breaks a steel strike with the help of his
brother Joe. Bill is killed in a riot which he himself has
deliberately fomented. Appel knows his material well and
describes steel mills and strikebreaking methods in extensive
and accurate detail. The novel is full of violent action and
moves very swiftly but Bill Trent is the only fully realized
character. Appel contrasts the collective action of the strikers
with the selfish individualism of the strikebreakers and
the capitalists for whom they work.

Blake, William J., The Painter and the Lady, New York,
Simon and Schuster.
An unusual setting--the vineyards of Provence in the 1930's
--is the background for the strike in this novel. The gavaches,
nonunion mountain shepherds who work in the vineyards
during the harvest, strike against their inhuman conditions,
and Stéphane Sabatier, the hero of the novel, becomes
one of their organizers. Stéphane is a painter and
a Communist. He is convinced that his art can become a
real weapon for the working class if he combines it with
his own social action. The strike is won but Stéphane dies
on the guillotine on a trumped-up murder charge. William
Blake, obviously influenced by Joyce, has a distinctive,
rather baroque style. The novel, although diffuse, is unusual
among its proletarian contemporaries. Blake does a
good job of portraying the hot sensuous Midi and the corruption
of France during the years of the Front Populaire.

Corbett, Elizabeth Frances, Charley Manning, New York,
D. Appleton-Century Co.
A silly novel for "popular" consumption. Charley Manning,
a successful businessman, breaks an 1895 streetcar strike
singlehandedly by hiring scabs, running derisive newspaper
ads and negotiating at the same time with the Governor to
bring in the militia and with the union president to provide
the strikers with free supplies paid for by the company
treasury. Free-handed Charley rehires all the strikers
and pays them back wages for the strike period. Fun and
games and a good time for all.

Givens, Charles G., The Devil Takes a Hill Town, Indianapolis, Bobbs-Merrill Co.
God and the Devil, otherwise Mr. Peebles and Mr. Hooker,
wrestle for the souls of the residents of a Tennessee hill
town in the throes of a bitter strike at the local rayon mill.
Mr. Peebles admits at the end that the Devil has won.
Written with great charm, vigor and humor, the novel escapes the formula writing of many of the strike novels during this period. Givens uses the strike and local folklore
in this fine fantasy for some trenchant comments on human
nature.

Herbst, Josephine, Rope of Gold, New York, Harcourt,
Brace and Co.
Concluding the chronicle begun in Pity Is Not Enough and
continued in The Executioner Waits, Josephine Herbst describes the lives of Vicky Wendel, her husband Jonathan
Chance and other members of the Wendel family. Vicky
reports a Cuban sugar workers' strike. Other characters
participate in a farmers' strike and in a factory sit-down
strike. The novel oversimplifies class differentiations.
Steve Carson, a worker, leaves his beloved wife without
hesitation when he is needed in a factory strike while Vicky
and Jonathan flounder indecisively and allow their personal
troubles to derail them from effective participation in the
workers' struggles because Vicky and Jonathan are, after
all, members of the vacillating petit bourgeoisie.

Kagey, Rudolf (Kurt Steel), Judas, Incorporated, Boston,
Little, Brown and Co.
A tough detective story in the Hammett style about the brutal
tactics of professional strikebreakers. Better than average
for its genre and some accurate research into labor spying.

Klempner, John, Once Around the Block, New York, Charles
Scribner's Sons.
Workers in a Brooklyn chocolate factory confront their stupid, lazy and lecherous bosses after a ten percent wage cut
is announced. The strike is lost because the workers are
disorganized and fearful but the novel ends with the hope
that workers are learning how to unite effectively. The
scenes of working class home life are well done but the
capitalist characters never come alive.

North, Sterling, Seven Against the Years, New York, Macmillan Co.
In June 1929 seven friends graduate from the University of

268

Chicago. At a reunion ten years later Frederick Oswald
Blucher III, the most materially successful of the seven, is
struggling with marital failures and alcoholism and is devot-
ing himself to financing a Fascist gang called the Knights of
the White Gardenia. Karl Gundarson, on the other hand,
has been working in an automobile factory since graduation
and is active in the organization of the United Automobile
Workers. Blucher and Gundarson confront each other at the
reunion, while the other five alumni line up in support of
either Blucher or Gundarson, according to their own experiences during the decade of the Thirties. We are left in no
doubt that Gundarson is the real success because of his commitment and integrity. North has learned to write since
1939 but this novel is a potboiler written to formula.

Paul, Elliot, The Stars and Stripes Forever, New York,
    Random House.
Ned Bascom tells the story of a bloody strike in his brother-
in-law's Connecticut factory which produces microphones and
amplifiers. The C. I. O. has just begun to organize and
Mark Loring, the owner of the plant, is determined to keep
the union out. In the course of the strike Ned becomes
aware of the vicious and illegal methods which are being
used against the strikers--scabs, agents provocateurs,
planted stories in the newspapers, trumped-up criminal
charges, armed police and vigilante raids. From a neutral
position Ned gradually turns to active involvement with the
strikers. The strike is lost but as the book ends Ned has
decided to become a full-time labor organizer. The book is
far too long and the strikers only paper characters.

Sandoz, Mari, Capital City, Boston, Little, Brown and Co.
A chilling portrayal of the triumph of Fascism in an American State. During a long and bitter truckers' strike supported by Carl Holzer, a small independent farmer running for
the Senate, and by Rufer Hammond, a crusading labor reporter, the strikers are attacked by a combination of armed
strikebreakers, police and Gold Shirt hooligans. Holzer is
elected by popular vote but the Gold Shirts take over the
State government. The plot is too complicated but Mari
Sandoz writes well.

1940

Levin, Meyer, Citizens, New York, Viking Press.
The violent climax of the Consolidated Steel Strike in Chicago on July 4, 1937 as seen through the eyes of Dr. Mit-

chell Wilner. Wilner is an eyewitness when the armed police attack a picnic attended by strikers and their families. Wilner sets up a volunteer first-aid station to care for the injured. Levin explores in depth the lives of a group of wounded strikers whom Dr. Wilner treats. Levin has researched the strike and its aftermath meticulously and uses real events extensively in this overlong but dramatic and moving novel. Dr. Wilner becomes a very real and sympathetic human being as he is transformed from a sympathetic intellectual liberal into a deeply involved participant.

Mitchell, Ruth Comfort, Of Human Kindness, New York, D.
    Appleton-Century Co.
The story of the Banner family who own a fruit ranch in the San Joaquin Valley. Divided by personality clashes the family is reunited during a fruit pickers' strike led by the Black Widow, a beautiful but wicked Communist. When Ed Banner organizes the ranchers to drive out the Communists, his wife Mary realizes she loves him, their son Ashley realizes his flirtation with the Communists has been misguided, the strikers return to work and peace descends on the Valley.

Rothermell, Fred, The Ghostland, Philadelphia, J. B.
    Lippincott Co.
Based on an actual event, this novel describes the organization of a nonviolent sit-down strike of unemployed Oklahoma workers. Fifteen hundred strikers whose families are near starvation storm the Land Office in Littleton and demand the distribution of food and money loans. Some of the townspeople support the strikers but armed police and vigilantes attack them and the strike is broken. Rothermell's style, which sounds like a parody of Hemingway's, weakens the novel which has a few moving moments.

Wiener, Philip (Thomas Burton), And So Dedicated, New
    York, Harrison-Hilton Books.
Tom Raleigh marries an heiress of the Winthrop family which rules the town of Corinth but discovers that he really loves Fran Siddons, a militant factory worker. The strike begins in a packing plant and spreads to poor farmers and power plant workers. It is broken through a violent assault on the strikers by the National Guard. Tom decides to leave his wife and marry Fran but the two lovers are shot by Tom's wife. The action takes place during the Twenties which Wiener sees not as the Jazz Age but as a period of expectancy and preparation for the militancy of the Thirties.

Atherton, Sarah, <u>Mark's Own,</u> Indianapolis, Bobbs-Merrill
    Co.
A long sentimental family chronicle beginning in 1849 when
Mark Stone drills the first shaft coal mine in Eastern Pennsylvania and ending in 1929 when the mine is finally closed.
Strikes, always accompanied by violence and death, reoccur
throughout the novel. The Stones grudgingly grant concessions to the miners until Mark's granddaughter Sally finally
turns the mine over to the employees after a disastrous
strike in 1925. Mark's sturdy independence is diluted in
his descendants just as the rich vein of coal is gradually
sapped and destroyed. The miners themselves are shown
as quite incapable of operating a mine successfully.

Attaway, William, <u>Blood on the Forge,</u> New York, Double-
    day, Doran and Co.
A better than average novel relating with brutal realism the
struggle of Negro sharecropper Mat Moss to become a whole
man. In 1919 he heads for Chicago where he is soon recruited as a strikebreaker during the steel strike. His long
struggle against race discrimination ends in his death during
a fight between strikers and scabs but not before Mat has
realized that racism and exploitation of labor are both inherent in capitalism and will end only when capitalism is
overthrown. The author knows steel mills and Negro life
from intimate personal experiences and describes them
powerfully.

Bell, Thomas, <u>Out of This Furnace,</u> Boston, Little, Brown
    and Co.
The chronicle of an immigrant Slovak family in the steel
mills of Homestead, Pennsylvania from 1881 to the organization of the C. I. O. in 1935. There are detailed and authentic descriptions of the work in the mills and Bell has a
sensitive appreciation of the workers' pride in their creativity but like many strike novels of the period this one describes the factory and the organizing tactics of the workers
in endless boring detail. In the end the book turns out more
a sociological tract than a novel.

Kimbrough, Edward, <u>From Hell to Breakfast,</u> Philadelphia,
    J. B. Lippincott Co.
A political novel in which a corrupt Mississippi Senator is
challenged by a young crusading lawyer, Jerry Clinton.
Senator Gus Roberts cynically uses a millworkers' strike

to further his campaign. He makes a deal to defend the
union organizer charged with inciting a riot in return for
the labor vote. Roberts wins the election but at the cost
of the love and regard of his wife and daughter. The strike
is only briefly described but the details of a Southern election campaign are deftly handled.

McLeod, Norman, The Bitter Roots, New York, Smith and
    Durrell.
A fictional version of I.W.W. activities around Missoula,
Montana between 1910 and 1920. The real strikes among
lumber workers, copper miners, newsboys, etc. are woven
into the story of Crystal Craig, a university teacher, and
her two sons. Big Bill Haywood and Bill Dunne, I.W.W.
organizers, appear prominently in the novel. McLeod is
heavily indebted for his style to some of John Dos Passos'
innovations.

Meyersburg, Dorothy, Seventh Avenue, New York, E. P.
    Dutton and Co.
The trials and tribulations of Joe who runs a garment shop
in New York and Julie who is his designer and partner.
Struggling against the Depression while trying to be fair to
their employees, Joe and Julie fight against desperate odds
as the International Ladies Garment Workers Union uses
threats, sabotage and intimidation to force them to sign a
union contract. At the end Joe commits suicide. The author obviously knows New York's Seventh Avenue but writes
naively and unskillfully.

1942

Field, Rachel, And Now Tomorrow, New York, Macmillan
    Co.
The strike in the novel at the Peace-Pipe textile mills in
Blairstown, Massachusetts serves as a symbol for the end
of the era of paternalism and personal relationships between
workers and employers. It is seen through the eyes of
Emily Blair Collins, a member of the Blair family which
owns the mill. Emily is sympathetic to the strikers and
their struggle for union recognition. During the climactic
strike Emily's husband leaves her for another woman but
Emily finds happiness with Dr. Vance, who is treating her
for deafness. Bring out the handkerchiefs and have a good
happy cry.

Huie, William Bradford, Mud on the Stars, New York, L.

B. Fischer.
Peter Garth Lafavor, a graduate of the University of Alabama, becomes a reporter on the Birmingham Press in 1933.
When he reports a United Mine Workers' strike against the
Delancey mining interests, Lafavor finds himself at odds
with all the contending parties: Buck Delancey who runs
his enterprise like a feudal empire, the union which is willing to sacrifice miners' lives for the sake of building the
union, and the Communist Party which mischievously foments
violence. Lafavor would like to see a union run along truly
democratic lines but has little hope that this is possible. In
1941 to escape from a world he dislikes Lafavor enlists in
the Army. Lafavor is a rounded character but the strike
and its background never come to life in the novel.

Moore, Ward, Breathe the Air Again, New York, Harper
    and Bros.
Simon Epstein, an ardent Socialist, leads the organization of
a union and a strike at Sentry's Department Store in Los
Angeles. The police brutally attack the picket line and the
strike is broken but Simon knows that the strike is a necessary step in the political education of the workers. The corporation heads and their families are pictured as corrupt,
rapacious and incapable of love and decency in this puerile
novel while most of the working class characters are full
of the milk of human kindness. Simon is given to long,
sentimental speeches about the solidarity of the working
class.

1943

Davenport, Marcia, The Valley of Decision, New York,
    Charles Scribner's Sons.
Another weepy saga. This one begins in 1873 when young
Mary Rafferty comes to work as a housemaid for the Scotts,
owners of a Pennsylvania steel mill. During a strike in the
mill in 1883 Mary's brother, a union leader, and William
Scott, head of the company, are both killed. Paul Scott,
William's son, deplores the company policies during the
Homestead strike and deals with his own "hands" in a more
enlightened and humane way. Through the years Mary, who
is in love with Paul, remains devoted to the Scott family.
The novel is syrupy and superficial, just the kind to be
turned into a Hollywood epic, which it was.

Freeman, Joseph, Never Call Retreat, New York, Farrar
    and Rinehart.

An extremely dull and pretentious novel purporting to be the notes of a psychoanalyst's seven-month treatment of Paul Schumann. The patient, a Viennese professor, has been the victim of rising Fascism in Europe. He escapes from a Nazi concentration camp and arrives in the United States just before the outbreak of World War II. The strikes in the novel are those of Viennese workers which begin as economic protests against runaway inflation but rapidly become political strikes against the Nazi-oriented Heimwehr. They culminate in a general strike which is defeated by an armed attack on the workers' cooperative apartment houses and in which Paul's father is killed.

McKenney, Ruth, Jake Home, New York, Harcourt, Brace
    and Co.
The rise and fall of Jake Home, a Pennsylvania coal miner who becomes a full-time union organizer. Jake is a fighting strike leader who temporarily deserts the cause when he marries a superintendent's daughter and becomes a section foreman. During a violent strike he rejoins his former comrades and receives a severe beating on the picket line. As a dedicated Communist Jake organizes strikes among stevedores, lettuce pickers and unemployed workers. He becomes involved in a tempestuous affair with a rich girl, but he is an interesting and complex character, a man of great sensual drive with a powerful class conscious conviction. The strike scenes are vivid and accurately described.

1944

Norris, Charles G., Flint, Garden City, Doubleday, Doran
    and Co.
Against the background of the San Francisco general strike and waterfront union struggles between 1933 and 1938 Rory O'Brien, the leader of the longshoremen and marine workers, and Stanley Rutherford, the head of an important shipping family, carry on a stubborn bitter vendetta which ends in death for both of them. Rory is then revealed to be Stanley's long-lost cousin. The novel abounds in tedious discussions of the labor disputes of the period. It includes the extremely intricate family relationships among the Rutherford clan. The moral of this dull story is that when labor and capital disagree, everyone suffers.

Sherman, Ray W., The Other Mahoney, New York, Ives
    Washburn, Inc.
Young Pete Mahoney is active in a carpenter's strike in the

late 1880's. Fifty years later, the owner of a firm manufacturing insulators, Peter dies confronting a mob of his
striking employees. Peter cannot understand why a half
century of hard work has resulted in his failure, his business destroyed by the Depression and the strike, and his
own son Paul siding with the strikers.

INDEX

This is essentially a name index, excluding fictional names and, generally, locations of fictional events.

Not covered are the notes at the end of chapters and the bibliography, pages 185-206. The annotated bibliography beginning on page 207 <u>is</u> indexed by author and title.

One subject entry is included in the index--"strikes." Under this heading real strikes mentioned in the text are listed; fictional strikes are omitted.

279

287

San Francisco 19, 129
  Race riot 19
Sandoz, Mari 136, 269
Saturday Evening Post (periodical) 97
The Scarlet Shadow (Hurt) 231
Schuylkill County, New York 37, 38
Scott, Leroy 65, 73, 82, 229-30
Scott, Milton R. 221-22
Scott, Sir Walter 109
Scranton, Pennsylvania 39
Scudder, Vida D. 60, 227-28
Seaver, Edwin 153
The Second Prince (Bell) 124, 125, 134, 254-55
Seven Against the Years (North) 164, 165, 169, 171, 268-69
Seventh Avenue (Meyersburg) 128, 139, 272
The Shadow Before (Rollins) 165, 170, 172, 253-54
The Share-Cropper (Simon) 162, 173, 262
Sheldon, Charles 24, 221
Sherman, Ray W. 127, 274-75
The Silent Conflict (Swafford) 98, 237
The Silent Partner (Ward) 32, 35, 72, 210
The Silent Workman (Ross) 35, 214
Silver Shirts 136
Simon, Charlie May 162, 173, 262
Sinclair, Upton 66, 76, 81, 82, 89, 90, 91, 92, 175, 230-31,
  238-29, 244, 245, 265-66
Sister Carrie (Dreiser) 81, 83, 224
Slag, a Story of Steel and Stocks (McGibeny) 97, 241-42
Sloan, John 90
Smedley, Agnes 89, 246
Smith, Elizabeth 5, 209
Smith, Francis Hopkinson 58, 222
Socialist Party 91
South Carolina 59, 82
South of Joplin (Davidson) 159
Spadoni, Adriana 139, 262-63
Spanish-American War 55, 88
Spanish Civil War 117
The Spider's Web (Kauffman) 103, 236
Spies, August 29, 78
The Stars and Stripes Forever (Paul) 172, 176, 269
Steel Chips (Jones) 89, 99, 103, 104, 246
Steele, Kurt, pseud. 268
Steele, Wilbur Daniel 90
Steffens, Lincoln 90
Steinbeck, John 160, 162, 167, 168, 169, 178, 179, 180,
  181, 259
The Stillwater Tragedy (Aldrich) 22, 25, 28, 35, 42, 49,
  212

Tourgée, Albion W. 27, 216
The Trail of the Axe (Cullum) 234
Train, Arthur 97, 243
A Traveller in Altruria (Howells) 28
Triangle Fire 105
Trollope, (Mrs.) Frances 14
Trotsky, Leon 154
Tyler, Martha W. 9, 11, 12, 209

U.S.S.R. 90
United Mineworkers 130
U.S. Attorney General 91
U.S. Commissioner of Immigration 62
U.S. Commissioner of Labor 18, 40, 45
  Annual Report (1888) 45
U.S. War Department 6
Unquiet (Gollomb) 124, 255-56
Untermeyer, Louis 90

The Valley of Decision (Davenport) 123, 130, 273
Valley of the Moon (London) 99, 103, 104, 236
Van Vechten, Carl 89
Van Vorst, Marie 59, 71, 74, 81, 82, 230
Vanzetti, Bartolomeo 91
Venture (Eastman) 89, 99, 244-45
Vorse, Mary Heaton 162, 165, 247

The Wage Slaves of New York (McCardell) 68, 223
Waiting for the Signal (Morris) 223
Walker, Charles Rumford 89, 245
The Walking Delegate (Scott) 65, 71, 73, 229-30
Walter, Eugene 68, 233
Ward, Elizabeth Stuart Phelps, 32, 35, 72, 210
Warner, Charles Dudley 21, 23, 216
The Warners (Daniels) 62, 73, 225
The Wars of Peace (Wilson) 228
Weatherwax, Clara 161, 171, 174, 256
The Web of Life (Herrick) 55, 56, 82, 224-25
Webster, Henry Kitchell 73, 98, 226, 239
Western Miners' Federation 88
Where Copper Was King (Wright) 70, 75, 230
White, William Allen 90, 94, 99, 240
White Mule (Williams) 143, 145, 263
Wiener, Philip 143, 270
Wiggins, Ella May 165, 166
Wilkes-Barre, Pennsylvania 39
Williams, William Carlos 143, 145, 263
Williamson, Thames 109, 246-47

291